Literary Couples and 20th-Century Life Writing

Literary Couples and 20th-Century Life Writing

Narrative and Intimacy

Janine Utell

BLOOMSBURY ACADEMIC
LONDON • NEW YORK • OXFORD • NEW DELHI • SYDNEY

BLOOMSBURY ACADEMIC
Bloomsbury Publishing Plc
50 Bedford Square, London, WC1B 3DP, UK
1385 Broadway, New York, NY 10018, USA
29 Earlsfort Terrace, Dublin 2, Ireland

BLOOMSBURY, BLOOMSBURY ACADEMIC and the Diana logo are trademarks of Bloomsbury Publishing Plc

First published in Great Britain 2020
This paperback edition published in 2021

Cover design: Eleanor Rose
Cover background image © Getty Images

A catalogue record for this book is available from the British Library.

A catalog record for this book is available from the Library of Congress.

ISBN: HB: 978-1-3500-0345-3
PB: 978-1-3502-3441-3
ePDF: 978-1-3500-0347-7
eBook: 978-1-3500-0346-0

Typeset by Deanta Global Publishing Services, Chennai, India

Must you tell me all your secrets when it's hard enough to love you knowing nothing?

—Lloyd Cole

Contents

Figures

Acknowledgments

This book has been part of my life for a long time, and I have benefited immeasurably from many wonderful people in all parts of my life as I have worked on it. Thanks are due first to the editorial team at Bloomsbury Academic: David Avital, who has not only been a pleasure to work with but brought his creativity and critical insight to bear on many rich conversations about the study of and research in twentieth-century literature; and Clara Herberg, Mark Richardson, Lucy Brown, and Angelique Neumann, who supported and expertly shepherded this project. Thanks also to my anonymous peer reviewers at the proposal and manuscript stages. Their generous and genuinely helpful feedback dramatically enhanced this project. I would also like to acknowledge those with whom I have worked on my previous books; this project builds on those endeavors.

Much of the work here was conceptualized at the 2011 Project Narrative Summer Institute at Ohio State University, under the direction of James Phelan and Frederick Luis Aldama. I cannot thank them enough for guiding this project toward a shape and direction, and for facilitating my processes of analysis and problem-solving. My gratitude also goes to my PNSI cohort; parts of Chapter 4 were written and shared over the course of the institute, and I benefited greatly from their feedback and in general from their conversation and enthusiasm. I owe a debt of gratitude to Robyn Warhol for providing a quiet and lovely space to live and write. Special thanks go to Emily Anderson and Todd Cesaratto, and especially to Leah Anderst, James Donahue, Jennifer Ho, and Shaun Morgan for interest and support during and after those weeks in Columbus.

Like others who have lived with book projects for an extended period of time, I have taken advantage of the generosity (and patience) of mentors and colleagues. Friends and colleagues online as well as at gatherings of the Modern Language Association, the Northeast Modern Language Association, the International Society for the Study of Narrative, the Modernist Studies Association, and The Space Between Society have all contributed to this project with their enthusiasm, interest, and intellectual companionship. Particular thanks go (in no particular order) to Emily Kopley, Claire Battershill, Stephen Ross, Elizabeth Alsop, Anne Langendorfer, Erin Templeton, Beth Wightman, Greg Erickson, Kevin Dettmar, Geneviève Brassard, Jeffrey Drouin, Melissa Bradshaw, Allison Pease, Celia Marshik, Anne Fernald, Polly Atkin, Kathryn Holland, Amanda Golden, Jim Berg, Elizabeth Blake, Susan Van Dyne, Melanie Micir, Nicholas Roe, Marie-Laure Ryan, Siobhan Phillips, Rachel Hollander, Ella Ophir, Lara Vetter, Sean Weidman, and Aimee Armande Wilson. (I have also tried to acknowledge specific interlocutors in the notes, and this book owes everything to those scholars cited throughout.) Very early on in the work on this book I had the pleasure of attending Writings of Intimacy in the 20th and 21st Centuries at Loughborough University, organized by Jennifer Cooke; this conference provided a collegial and invigorating space within which to begin formulating my arguments, and I would like to acknowledge particularly Rosamund Davies. I would like to also especially acknowledge four people who at various points were invaluable. Tim Carmody shared a number of resources with me early on that proved most helpful. Melissa Dinsman has been a friend, a collaborator, and my accountability partner. Theodora Dryer helped turn our Queen Village apartment building into the best little writers' colony in Philadelphia. Sadly, the last must be acknowledged *in memoriam*: Georgia Johnston, who was a great advocate for this project and who is missed. As one of my anonymous readers said, it is a sadness that Georgia is not here to see this in the world, and it stands as a tribute to her influence and generosity.

This endeavor received support from several sources. I am happy to acknowledge assistance from staff and faculty members at: Wolfgram Memorial Library at Widener University, especially interlibrary loan services and especially Susan Tsiouris; Morris Library at the University of Delaware; Van Pelt Library at the University of Pennsylvania; and the Billy Rose Theatre Division of the New York Public Library for the Performing Arts. Profound thanks go to Susan Purcell, senior services coordinator of the Delaware County Public Library System, and to the Pennsylvania Humanities Council; the PHC awarded us several grants to create public reading groups on the topics of intimate life writing and biography, which I had the privilege of facilitating from 2009 to 2011 at several libraries around Delaware County. Those conversations very much informed the writing here, and my gratitude goes to the reading group participants and sponsoring libraries. My home institution,

Widener University, provided much-needed support in the forms of travel funds, Provost Grants, Faculty Development Grants, and two sabbatical leaves. I am grateful to the administrators, staff, and faculty colleagues who made this support possible: Stephen Wilhite, Matthew Poslusny, Scott Van Bramer, Mara Parker, Beth Homan, and the Faculty Council Grants and Awards and Faculty Council Faculty Affairs Committees.

My Widener colleagues, in English and Creative Writing and beyond, deserve my most heartfelt thanks for their support of and interest in this project: friends, colleagues, and fellow writers Chris Murphy, Diana Vecchio, James Esch, Annalisa Castaldo, Michael Cocchiarale, Ken Pobo, Mark Graybill, and Kate Goodrich; and the members of the Widener University Faculty Writing Group. Thanks, too, to my students past and present, who have been engaged in these conversations with me all along.

Finally, as always, my deepest gratitude goes to my family. Thank you to my parents, John and Linda Utell, without whom this would not be possible. Many, many thanks to my sister and brother-in-law, Tracy and Glen Farber, for more than I could begin to put into words but which includes overwhelming love, support, patience, and humor. John-Paul Spiro has been my steadfast support and my best interlocutor—he makes our world of two a wonderful place to be.

This book is dedicated, with all my love, to my niece Abigail Lindh Farber. I started working on it in earnest the year she was born, and while this book has not always given me joy, she has, from the day she came into my life.

Permission granted by Lloyd Cole and Maine Road Management to use the line from “Four Flights Up” (from the 1984 album *Rattlesnakes* by Lloyd Cole and The Commotions) as an epigraph is gratefully acknowledged.

Parts of Chapter 1 appeared in slightly different form in the *Virginia Woolf Miscellany* (89/90, 2016; 79, 2011). Acknowledgment is due to the journal and to Vara Neverow for permission to include this material herein.

Permission granted by Jenny Olivia Johnson to use the image of *Glass Heart (Bells for Sylvia Plath)* featured in Chapter 5 is gratefully acknowledged.

Introduction: Reading Intimate Life Writing: Act, Practice, Process

In *The Textual Condition*, Jerome McGann writes, "We make love and we make texts, and we make both in a seemingly endless series of imaginative variations" (4). The purpose of *Literary Couples and 20th-Century Life Writing: Narrative and Intimacy* is to identify and theorize some of these variations. This book conceptualizes modernist and late modernist intimate life writing between partners in a couple as a particular, and particularly performative, practice of relational life narrative. I argue that the literary couples under consideration here engage in the act and practices of intimate life writing such that individually and together they undertake and narrativize a process of becoming as subjects in relation to and with, and in recognition of, a significant other—acts, practices, and processes with radical ethical implications. I analyze intimate life narratives in some of their various configurations and assemblages, with particular worldmaking features, through a series of case studies. I look to see where we find patterns of affects and discourse and how they coalesce into narrativity; how this constitutes subjects relational in intimacy; and how we perform an ethics of reading that relies on recognizing such subjects even as we bear witness to their recognition of each other.

The early to mid-twentieth-century couples under study here produced a great deal of such writing, in a plenitude of forms, as part of making their togetherness. And they did so at a cultural and historical moment where new genres and forms of auto/biographical writing were emerging, as were new ways of talking about gender and sexuality. Virginia and Leonard Woolf and the writers associated with their Hogarth Press and Bloomsbury were experimenting with what would come to be known as "the new biography," as well as with novel thinking about intimacy. Gertrude Stein and Alice B. Toklas created a kind of modernist intimacy integrally connected with both their lesbian love and their radical forms of narrative. Sylvia Townsend Warner and Valentine Ackland took advantage of a variety of genres and modes of self-consciously performative life writing to capture the domestic and erotic bliss, and manage the personal upheavals, they experienced throughout the 1930s and 1940s. Christopher Isherwood and Don Bachardy conceived of their relationship as multiple versions of the processural subject, while also emerging as key figures shaping shifting perceptions of gay male intimacy during the midcentury into the 1970s. Finally, Sylvia Plath and Ted Hughes grappled with a heterosexual ideal of marriage as fusion, only to run up against norms that made their individual and autonomous artistic pursuits, and the fulfillment of their processural selves within that union, deeply fraught.

The intimate lives of these couples have *afterlives*, have prompted literary biographies emerging from and seeking to narrativize in turn the rich archives created over the processes of fabricating these intimacies. My work draws upon affect theory, feminist and queer theory, contemporary thinking on ethics, conceptualizations of intertextuality and intersubjectivity, and narrative studies to probe the functioning of literary couples writing couplehood and processes of becoming more broadly. My reading practice is somewhat capacious, while also being constrained by my expertise in modernist studies. I see this constraint as, in fact, a kind of affordance, allowing me to focus on couples working in a moment of reconfiguration of form as well as of identities and categories related to gender and sexuality. I see myself in conversation with those who have prioritized relationality in life narrative studies and who seek ways of reading forms and apprehending practices of relational life writing. I seek to engage those who have expanded the field of life writing studies through queer and feminist theory and reading acts. I consider the possibility I might add to narrative studies, and the study of narrativity in life writing, especially narrative ethics. Finally, I work to reach those who have intervened in modernist and twentieth-century studies via the analysis of autobiography, biography, and life narrative, as well as via the conceptualization of intimacy and forms of feeling.

Life writing is multitudinous, encompassing a plethora of textualities, discursive moves, and forms of multimodal narrative. Sidonie Smith and Julia Watson argue for "life writing" and "life narrative" as "more inclusive of the heterogeneity of self-referential practices" in "all kinds and in diverse media" (*Reading* 4), and I follow suit.[1] This book will consider letters and diaries; auto/biographical writing taking a variety of forms such as confessions, memorials, and portraits; tales from life taken for fiction, or "autobiografiction," to use Max Saunders's terminology; comics and documentary film; and dual biographies, what I call couple biographies. I am not claiming that intimate life writing is a specific genre or form, but rather a set of practices, acts, and utterances, emerging from relational life narratives and the ways those narratives enact a subject becoming with and through an other.

The question of "genre" has been a perennial preoccupation of theorists of auto/biographical writing.[2] Laura Marcus, in her study of the discursive fields of auto/biography, shows that theorists have sought "coherence" either in "generic properties" or in "the unity of the writing subject," all toward "stabiliz[ing]" the form (*Auto/Biographical* 179). Salient critiques of such an endeavor, critiques which have dramatically reshaped the field, rest on two important points. First, by seeking to identify "generic properties," one risks excluding forms of life writing that do not conform, a move which, in the past, has meant the erasure of multiple varieties of narratives from a plurality of subject positions. Second, such "coherence" presumes the "unity of the writing subject," which theories of performativity, positionality, and relationality have "decentered" (Smith and Watson, *Reading* 218; "Trouble" 357).[3] Echoing an early point made by Paul de Man on autobiography, wherein he claims that autobiography "is not a genre or a mode, but a figure of reading or of understanding" (921), theorists including Smith and Watson, Marcus, Paul John Eakin, and Liz Stanley see the auto/biographical subject as one written into becoming, always in process, always contingent, always relational. Eakin sees life writing as a process of constructing a "narratively constituted identity," while Smith and Watson see it as an instantiation of an autobiographical subject (*Reading* 214; see Eakin, *How* and *Living*). I think it might be a little of both (if I can indeed have it both ways). Life writing is thus a discursive and narrative act toward becoming. It is both practice and process, its utterances instances of that practice and process (Eakin, "Foreword" x).

Intimate life writing can be analyzed for those specific worldmaking functions which engender narrativity as part of that practice and process. By "worldmaking," I mean not only the story world, the world of the narrative, as theorized by David Herman, Marie-Laure Ryan, and Claudia Breger, but also the world of the couple, the "interworld," to use Merleau-Ponty's term (356–57), or the world of the "we," to use Robert Nozick's term. This "we" is not "prediscursive" (Smith and Watson, *Reading* 218); rather, it is narrativized and thereby performed through many different forms of relational discursivity.[4]

This book will analyze the narrativity of intimate life writing and its discourses from the inside and the outside. It will consider the life narratives produced by the subjects and their intimate others whom I have chosen as my case studies with an eye toward discerning signature worldmaking features of narrativity. And it will consider couple biographies as intertextual and intersubjective versionings of those stories (see Stanley 9, 15), wherein those outside the couples—biographers—construct narratives of intimate life to which they always have incomplete access; and wherein we as readers come to see the constructed and contingent status of biography and biographical selves. I would like to note here that Smith and Watson suggest those who would bring a narratological lens to life writing should proceed with caution, as there are concerns central to autobiography studies which have yet to inform narrative theory ("Trouble" 356). Coming to the study of life writing from a narrative studies perspective means I am probably not intervening meaningfully in this work. I am a narrative critic, not a narrative theorist (though my readings are routed through and apply narrative theory as well as feminist and queer theory; cf. Warhol and Lanser 3). However, I offer that my interest in the work of patterns of discourse that might be found in studying narrative may have some modest impact on reading relational life writing, specifically relational life writing of literary couples.

My corpus is drawn from the writings of early and mid-twentieth-century literary couples—Gertrude Stein and Alice B. Toklas, Sylvia Townsend Warner and Valentine Ackland, Christopher Isherwood and Don Bachardy, Sylvia Plath and Ted Hughes, along with an early, more conceptual, foray into some of the writers associated with Bloomsbury, Virginia and Leonard Woolf, and their Hogarth Press—and is in no way meant to be exhaustive. Indeed, it should be acknowledged as limited and idiosyncratic.[5] The problem with using literary lives to talk about life writing is one ends up with a very particular, even exclusionary, understanding of the concept (Marcus, *Auto/Biographical* 6). This work winds up being shaped by the priorities of literary criticism, not only or necessarily biography, and those priorities tend toward attempts to "discov[er] recurrent images and recurrent modes of thought; patterns which have a way of repeating themselves" (Edel 49, 52–53). These figures made creative work their vocation, and that work shaped much of their lives together. This makes them highly interesting to *me*, but potentially problematic subjects for a study of life writing. In many ways they are extraordinary, exemplary, and as writers themselves require a particular way of reading; and thus I am at risk of perpetuating conceptualizations of auto/biography that depend, as they have historically and conventionally, on extraordinary and exemplary lives.

Still, perhaps I can attempt to further account for my choices. To do so, I will take as one recourse the emphasis in life writing studies on such texts and discourses as performing subjectivity and instantiating and telling ways of becoming. Essential to my analysis is the selection of couples wherein both members were active participants in the creation of texts and discourses of intimate life, with the purpose of collaborating on the shared project of making a couplehood through narrative.[6] I also want to draw attention to the ways in which the discursive production under study is deployed in service of creating something purposefully: a "coupled world," in Diane Enns's apt phrase (60). This work of creation is processural; it is embedded, embodied, and situated, and in the creativity evinced by the couples involved—themselves involved in the modernist and late modernist twinned projects of reenvisioning auto/biography along with the subject/other relationship—we find something made from nothing, something where before there was nothing. In most of my cases, it might be perceived that one member of the couple is less well known, "minor" in both the literary-canonical sense and the Deleuzean sense.[7] However, in *all* of my cases, that less well-known member is more than integral to the cocreation of the couple narrative; the performance of couplehood and the creation of the "coupled world"; and the concomitant processes of becoming through discursive and textual production. In all my cases, both members of every couple share the work of authoring and narrativizing the "we," across a multiplicity of forms and assemblages of life writing texts, which I believe raises an important point about the ways we can destabilize the hierarchies of "major" or "great" and their shaping effect on genre (Marcus, *Auto/Biographical* 231; Stanley 8). It is the narrative products of that authoring in which I am interested—for which I see *shared* authority—and the textual creation of couplehood and how those texts not only tell a story about intimate life but *make intimacy itself*. In other words, the narrative made together constitutes the very togetherness of the couple, and that togetherness is then reinscribed throughout biographical writing *about* the couple. I focus on the affective work enacted through narrativity, on the work done by these couples in creating a "palimpsestuous" (to use Sarah Dillon's term) archive, intertextualizing each other through these shared narratives as a way to create an intersubjective space wherein the ethical implications of grappling with the other in all their becoming are made visible.

This book is not a study of early to mid-twentieth-century ideas about intimacy, couplehood, marriage, sex, and desire, although, again, it is informed by such investigations, and it was written with Smith and Watson's imperative to consider subjects as historically positioned in mind (*Reading* 215). The figures selected for this study were shaped by tectonic shifts in thinking about gender, sexuality, and marriage, and have themselves been taken as the subjects for scholarship on these topics. Scholars of sexuality and modernist cultures such as Allison Pease, Celia Marshik, Aimee Armande Wilson, Heike Bauer (to name just a few whom I have found particularly helpful) analyze transformations in desire and private life wrought by the emerging field of sexology, the demand for safe and widely available birth control, the visibility of a lesbian modernity, debates surrounding free love, and the preoccupation with the state of (companionate) marriage overall. The couples under examination here are exemplars of, and were affected by, ways of thinking about sex, love, desire, and couplehood in the modernist and late modernist period. They evince a self-consciousness in thinking about these aspects of their identity; and, as we shall see, what it meant to be in a couple, to desire and be desired, to experience the passion and loss that comes with love, inflected much of their everyday lives. Indeed, the intimate life writing produced by these subjects in order to narrativize couplehood suggests that the place of love and desire in everyday life can be theorized by means of just such writing, a claim I believe is substantiated by Paul John Eakin's observation (via Michel de Certeau) that "the activity of making . . . life stories is . . . [an] everyday practice" (*Living* 106). They *perform* love and desire in everyday life, and *work through* its place in everyday life, through the generation of autobiographical discourse toward a shared narrative of lived intimacy.

The subjects here are invested in understanding their own processes of becoming, and in becoming in relationality with and recognition of another such that they seek to fulfill what Rosi Braidotti calls *potentia*, a powerful force of potential, both for themselves as individuals and for others. Love effects radical ontological change in a person, as a person becomes part of a "we," and it plays a significant role in the becoming of everyone involved—even as a new entity, the "we," is brought into being and itself is subject to becoming. Braidotti sees individuals open to the creativity and affirmation of intense relationships and the role they play in such becoming as available to a transformative ethics (162, 169–70); this is what she refers to as "the art of living intensely" (190). It is this formulation, and its implications for the processural subject and an ethics of recognition, that I find most valuable for the work here. Another way to put this might be to recall Julia Watson's comment that we should see relational life writing as "intimate and radical practice" ("Is"); it is a reading and writing act that recognizes the other. I do not read the texts created by these subjects as symptomatic of a historical moment or ideological position. Attentive to the textual, discursive, and narrative moves being made, allowing for an extensive thick critical description which in turn makes an ethics of reading love possible, I read these texts and subjects more reparatively than symptomatically, generous to the richness of the lives lived (cf. Sedgwick 149; also Best and Marcus 10–13).

Relationality, couplehood, and intimacy

In *A Lover's Discourse*, Roland Barthes offers tesserae that when brought together approximate the experience of falling in love; the "fragments" in the book's subtitle refer to the incompleteness of becoming sparked by the ontological shift generated by falling in love, as well as the impossibility of constructing a coherent vision or version of what love is. Of great significance to that process, to catalyzing that process in all its affective and ethical power, is the encounter, *rencontre*, which Barthes defines as "refer[ring] to the happy interval immediately following the first ravishment, before the difficulties of the amorous relationship begin" (*Lover's* 197). The word "ravishment" is a clue to the way Barthes casts this initial moment of erotic origination, the opening scene of the story. His language is that of transformation, perhaps itself transformational: "dazzlement" (three times in two and a half pages), "radiant," "marvel," "bliss." The encounter is ecstatic, and the rapture alters time and the telling of the story of the encounter. Braidotti offers a similarly "vital" apprehension of the "encounter": seeing it as "interrelational" and enchained by "multiple becomings" (198).

Further Barthes writes, "The encounter is radiant; later on, in memory, the subject will telescope into . . . moments of the amorous trajectory. . . . Neither knows the other yet. . . . This is narrative bliss, the kind which both fulfills and delays knowledge" (*Lover's* 198–99). The initial encounter, *rencontre*, is commemorated and replicated throughout the writing the couples under study do with and for each other. The work of intimate life writing calls upon its actors to reinscribe the originary moment, particularly when confronted with crisis, as we shall see. Significantly, these moments of crisis pivot precisely on the question of recognition and of knowledge. The "narrative bliss" of fulfillment that simultaneously recognizes the mystery of the other and the joyful affirmation of acknowledging the alterity of the other—one desires to know the other, and the infinite receding of complete knowledge prompts the desire for further worldbuilding and thus greater ontological and epistemic fulfillment—gives way to the unhappiness, even the agonizing despair, of *not-knowing* which must be part of couplehood but is often only made visible in the event of betrayal and loss.

In a discussion of Simone de Beauvoir and Jean-Paul Sartre, Alice Jardine writes, "Couples. We tend to think in couples even when we try very hard not to; we revise the concept of the couple, we re-write it, we mediate it in new ways, but couples are very hard to get away from" (121). It is not my purpose here to suggest that romantic or erotic couplehood is the most important relationship in everyone's—or even most people's—lives. Nor is it my intention to suggest that such relationships should take precedence over other forms of connection. Certainly the category of relational life writing encompasses the infinite variety of relationships, and there are many types of intimacy. I have also come to interrogate the idea that couplehood should be conceived of as fusion or union, with the "goal," to draw on Robert Solomon's thinking, of "shared selfhood" (250–51). The creation of a "we," as Robert Nozick understands it, is an ontological transformation of two people into an entirely new entity, not necessarily a "one." In her study of modernist and contemporary novels about love, Ashley T. Shelden offers a strong critique of those who would posit "1 + 1 = 1," writing that "this coherence-producing love universalizes the fusion of two into one as the index of absolute amorous value" (7). Drawing on queer theory which permits an accounting for negativity in discussions of love and the erotic, rather than a utopian fantasy of unity, Shelden claims, rightly, that "unmaking" love requires a valuing of multiplicity as a way out of the totalizing hegemony of "oneness" (9; see Edelman, Berlant, Love). Shelden also further subjects queer theorists and critics, including José Esteban Muñoz and Michael Snediker to critique for their embracing of the positive affective potential of

Sedgwick's reparative reading (4). We will return to the complexities of such reading, and of the "happiness" promised by "oneness," in Chapter 5.

What a consideration of couplehood in life writing does permit is the positing of a particular type of intimate life writing as a specific practice of relational life writing. Relationality as a key concept in auto/biography and life writing studies has its roots in interventions by feminist theorists and critics, including Mary Mason and Susan Stanford Friedman, and drawing on the work of Jessica Benjamin. Laura Marcus explains thusly: "Many of the debates in feminist autobiographical criticism constitute an ethics of (gender) difference, arguing for a new valuation of self in relationship, embodied and empathetic consciousness, identity as likeness to an other rather than as the self-same" (*Auto/Biographical* 220). In large measure due to the arguments of Nancy K. Miller, as well as Smith and Watson and Eakin, relationality is regarded at this point in the field to "characteriz[e] all autobiographical writing" (Smith and Watson, *Reading* 279), and to have been decoupled from its original context of gender difference. This has both narratological and ethical implications. As James Phelan has pointed out, situating the subject in relation to the other in life writing and narrative more generally requires attentiveness to the rhetorical strategies deployed, the perspectives of narrator and narratee, and the significance of voice (Smith and Watson 86; see also Phelan 23). Liz Stanley comments that a focus on the other in auto/biography means "an insistence on intertextuality . . . [on] discourses as sets of 'voices'" (15). Then, further, as Judith Butler argues, the central role of relationality in life narratives makes ethical demands regarding the subject's recognition of the other, and how the subject accounts for oneself in relation to alterity (Smith and Watson 217; see also Butler 64).

So then, relational life writing bears an ethics all its own, emerging from its theoretical and practical prioritization of processes of recognition and of becoming, through narrative, for the subject in and through relationality with an other. My thinking on narrative ethics is influenced by Emmanuel Levinas, Sara Ahmed, and Rosi Braidotti. Braidotti's thinking on ethics and affects specifically resonates with this aspect of conceptualizing relational life writing, emphasizing as it does becoming in intersubjectivity. For Braidotti, the self as affectual means decentering the *cogito*, and thus undoing the focus on the unified, unitary self, the autonomous "one." I find Braidotti's call to think of the self not as *monadic* but as *nomadic*, to dissolve "firm boundaries between self and other, in the love encounter, in intense friendship, in the spiritual experience as in more everyday interpersonal connections," as salient here, insofar as to do so is essential for "the enlargement of one's fields of perception and capacity to experience" (197). We can read these writers' attempts to do just this through such a theoretical lens. The nomadic is a necessary precondition for becoming, an affirmative, creative, and profound process of transformation (169–70). In Braidotti's formulation, the self comprises multiplicities, and is in interrelationality with multiplicities. What this means for couplehood, then, would have to be: a person comprising many comes together with a person comprising many, and together they are multiplicities embarked on a continual process of becoming. As Braidotti writes,

> Sets of interconnections or encounters constitute a project, which requires active involvement and work. . . . Between the no longer and the not yet, desire traces the possible patterns of becoming. These intersect with and mobilize sexuality, but never stop there as they construct space and time and thus design possible worlds by allowing the unfolding of ever intensified affects. (197)

This transformation is "the ethical moment," the "cultivation" of "productive" "interaction [wherein] one has to think the unthinkable and imagine the unimaginable" (201). Braidotti's ethics depend upon an "open-ended, interrelational self" (202).

Returning to Jardine's comment, perhaps we find it "hard to get away from" couples because they concentrate our attention on something that is fundamental: we are relational subjects. Our positioning within relationships, some of them intimate, facilitates our becoming, fosters our always-in-processness. My definition of intimacy, and the affective and ethical implications derived therefrom, circulates through these ideas. Intimacy is the mutual understanding—shared by persons in relationship through thinking and feeling who recognize each other's alterity—that the collaborative process of cocreating a world, wherein the persons involved have the potential to fulfill the process of becoming, might be undertaken (even flourished). Accounting for affects in this formulation is essential, because the awareness of thinking and feeling, of the ways the body is "networked" to experience process, perception, corporeality, desire, emotions, everyday embeddedness—all contribute to what Seigworth and Gregg call "worldings" (8). Through the affects, we make the world and we are in the world, and we are in that world with others whom are likewise subject to and shaped by our affective experience. In thinking and feeling, we encounter the other affectually. Via that encounter, we activate the process of shared worldmaking, which I, following Claudia Breger, see aligned with the work of worldmaking we find in narrative. The course of shared worldmaking provides a space wherein *potentia* may be found and fulfilled, wherein becoming may be enacted. In engaging Braidotti's work, as well as the thinking of Levinas, I am able to see the requirements of creativity and imagination in intimacy and ethical recognition, which may be why I am drawn to thinking this through via narrative. The individual, in relationship with the other, needs to be able to imagine that other, the situatedness and affective life of the other, in order to undertake the process of cocreating a world. From this, I derive an ethics of intimacy, one that requires the recognition of the other as other, in all their unknowability and distance, in all of the ways they experience the world that can never be truly understood; upon that recognition, an ethics of intimacy demands the creative and imaginative intervention of shared worldmaking, wherein that mysterious, unknowable other can *become*, and ideally flourish.[8]

Throughout the tellings that follow we will find disruptions, vulnerabilities, incoherences, failures. The writings of these subjects, and the writings about these subjects, evince a high degree of narrativity. This does not mean their life writings have coherence. The couples involved sought to make a unit. This does not mean they, or their selves, are unified. What we find in their intimate life writing is *process*. Hannah Sullivan, in her observing the incompleteness of autobiographical texts, makes the helpful point that these texts by their very nature are unfinished because they are part of the process of making something always in process: the becoming subject. Intimate life writing, therefore, like other forms of relational life writing, is processural, because its work is to create a space where people in relationship can each be becoming, and be becoming together.

The couple biography

What I am attempting to describe—including biographical narratives written about our subjects—can be understood better if we once again return to the importance of thinking not only about writing, about composition, but also about narrativity in light of the affects. For Claudia Breger, drawing on Deleuzean formulations of assemblage and the affects, narrative worldmaking is "a performative process of configuring affects" through a mutual "rhetorical loop[ing]" among authors, narrators, and readers that generate "narrative worlds as multidimensional, 'multivectoral' assemblages" ("Affects" 231). These "assemblages," comprising "affect and sensation . . . association and memory . . . intertextuality and trope," generate a narrative world that might be seen productively and experienced affectively as complex, "fluid" and "unstable" ("Affects" 231; cf. "Critically"). Thus Breger brings together the concept of "worldmaking" from narrative theory and the concept of "worlding" from affect studies ("Affects" 230), showing how these processes align in a way I find especially fruitful for studying intimate life writing. The processes bear family resemblances, and joining them makes even more visible the necessary implications for affective and ethical work inherent in narrative studies.

Rachel Morley issues a call to rethink biographical praxis through the theory of affects and a deeper awareness of the importance of intimacy, and I think her words can be extended to apply to all intimate life writing. She says,

> The thinking-feeling body of experience offers the biographer the opportunity to transform and imagine the life of someone else. . . . Not simply a text then of "who did what where when," biography is the story of the body at its most mundane and at its most extraordinary, lived out through passion, experienced through pathos. . . . Biography is not solely a quest to imagine and transform the other. No. It is also a quest to understand and transform the self through a journey mediated by feeling and self-discovery. (79)

Morley's understanding of biography is as of a space of intimacies, made by a praxis that values those intimacies and the role they play in becoming. Intimacy, and narratives thereof, permit a deeper awareness of that "thinking-feeling body of experience," or, in other words, the affects and our affective life. Such awareness is part of becoming, and part of ethical relationship with the other. As we shall see throughout this study, couples creating an interworld through shared discourse and narrative find a means of achieving this very thing, in all its joy and pain.

Couple biographies insist, up to a point, on a couplehood as a fixed, finished object with a *telos*, but the examination of the assemblages produced by these couples shows that there are states playing out over time, "contingent manifestations" of becoming (Jed Deppman qtd. in Fordham 22). These contingencies exist within and help shape the narrative structure of the couple biography, and suggest that, in the case of intimate life writing, we may be able to have structure and contingency simultaneously. Finn Fordham picks up on a term used by Roland Barthes, the "ergography," to suggest that works have a life story in the same way the subject who created the work might have a biography. For Barthes, this is a "playful succession of texts," as he posits to Stephen Heath in a 1971 interview ("Interview" 145). In some respects, considering such a "playful succession of texts" makes this just as much a study of intimate *ergography* as it is of *auto/biography*.

This work itself has an ergography, and its originary moment is the discovery of a narrative text of intimate life. While traveling, browsing a local used bookstore, I came across Diana Trilling's memoir of her marriage to Lionel Trilling, *The Beginning of the Journey*. The title takes its inspiration from a novel by Lionel Trilling, *The Middle of the Journey*, and so might be thought of as the wife speaking back to the husband in a form other than those he had chosen to work in over his career, namely in the form of life writing. Diana Trilling states at the outset, in her preface (that most important paratextual articulation of purpose crafted by biographers and memoirists alike), "This book is in part an autobiography, in part a biography of my husband, Lionel Trilling, and in largest part a memoir of our marriage" (ix). Diana Trilling, occupying the position of memoirist, describes her managing of temporality—when the events of the narrative take place in terms of the duration of the marriage, when she chooses to activate prolepsis within the temporal confines she has established—but she also suggests that the narrative of a marriage might have particularly unique interest. She writes, "Someone going through the documents of our marriage might even perceive that the two of us together made a more interesting subject than either of us alone" (x). Diana Trilling anticipates the drawing in of readers through the telling of intimate life, but she gives particular consideration to what it means to narrate a relational life, a life of two brought together into one, a "we." She suggests that it is the "documents" of this "we," the texts of that marriage that make the couplehood and thus generate the site for readerly interest, that are key. The self-conscious articulation of the project of narrativizing a couple, and the ways such a project might deploy forms of narrativity not available to or regularized through conventional biography or memoir, piqued my interest. How might such intimate narratives work, and what questions might they raise?

Couple biographies are structured by two lives coming together as one. They depend on parallel lives intersecting, an originary moment of encounter and union, and the inevitable end of one member of the couple dying and the other living on. They are crafted to be teleological narratives of fulfillment, inherently proleptic as the parallel lines of two bodies moving forward are "twirl[ed] into one," to pick up on a line from the Paul Simon song "Hearts and Bones." Couple biographies take as necessary the premise that lives are relational, and that one becomes in relationship with another. In this way I perceive them as diverging from conventional biographies of exemplary, solitary, autonomous selves. The couple biography does not necessarily accommodate all varieties of intimacy, even as intimate life writing—and versions of couplehood itself—might be infinitely varied. I recognize that this is one of the interesting—and troubling—things about the form.

The couple biographer inserts themselves into the common project of making a couplehood, appropriating the discourse of the "we"; polyvocalizing the numerous voices in assemblages of intimate life writing; and bringing the perspective of an outsider, an "arranger," to bear on intimate life. Intimate life writing and the nature of intimacy are dilemmas for any biographer, a problem of epistemology as well as a problem of ethics, one that bears a family resemblance, and reenacts in revised form, the epistemic problem confronting the individuals in a couple relationship. How does an outsider, subject to the interlinked distances of time, space, alterity, enter into the most intimate realms, the interiority, of a subject? The problem is compounded for the writer of a couple biography. In her analysis of biography, its style and rhetorical devices, Paula Backscheider proposes six concentric circles of concern for writers in the form; this formulation, explicitly feminist-inflected, is of special relevance to those preoccupied with the epistemological problem of intimacy in biographical discourse. The last three—"social privacy," where "intimate thoughts . . . are shared"; "personal space"; and "inner life"—constitute for Backscheider "layers of interiority" (136). She notes that these "circles" are not meant to delineate clear boundaries among aspects of a life, but rather to demonstrate that the borders among private and public selves are semi-permeable; couplehood occupies such a space, negotiating both public and private identities. Her model further recognizes, of course, that lives are relational. While biographies devoted to the life of the supposedly autonomous individual might start from the outermost circle and move in, biographies focused on the "we," on the couple, assume relationality and take as their starting point that innermost point in the circles, the core of the interior, and the thing that is most difficult to know. This is how they address the "elemental" issue of "coherence" and "order," to frame the point as Nadel might: "Either a factual pattern arranged along a chronological axis or an interpretive pattern based upon a sense of the inner life of the subject" (155). Furthermore, the couple biography, and intimate life writing more broadly, must negotiate the innermost experiences and affects of not just one person but two people; not just two people, but the unit those two make, their "coupled world." We should think, then, of the couple biography not so much in terms of one set of concentric circles ascribed to an individual, but perhaps two sets, one for each individual, aligned in a Venn diagram. Our epistemological problem—writing and reading intimacy—resides at the locus of the intersection of these circles.

Chapter 1 of this book will consider, briefly, the development of "the new biography" in the early twentieth century, especially its origins in new ways of thinking about and writing private life. Here, it might be worth mentioning, before moving on to the final section of this introduction, the factors that have led to the couple biography in its distinctiveness. We can return to the influence of feminist and queer theory and practice. Backscheider attends to a rise in the importance of private lives and private selves in biography, the concentration on which she attributes to "pressures" exerted by feminist scholars, authors, and readers and their changed "expectations for the treatment of biographical subjects' sexuality . . . [and] private life" (153). At the conclusion of her reflections on feminist biography, Backscheider suggests that such shifts mean the possibility for greater experimentation in writing lives. While we find that couple biographies often follow very similar patterns, we also find that such texts are seeking to accommodate narratives of lives beyond the single, autonomous self. Nigel Hamilton makes a point along these lines as well, seeing in biographers from the mid-1990s and on an interest in "intensely moving sexual revelation . . . [as] a way of enticing readers towards greater empathy and knowledge" (254–55). The study of the couple biography raises important questions about the tension between public and private, the nature of intimacy, and the role of the biographer themselves as they write the intimate lives of others. It also enacts the signal claim that all lives, and life writing, are relational; and performs the attempt to undo the hierarchies which have shaped writing and thinking about biography in its "canonical" forms and "exemplary" "autonomous" subjects.

We will conclude our attempts to account for the couple biography in the twentieth and twenty-first centuries with Hamilton's emphasis on reader expectations and interest in sexuality, along with comments on what it means to read and write such texts. Hamilton traces this development to the publication of Michael Holroyd's groundbreaking biography of Lytton Strachey in 1967–1968. Incidentally, the event of the publication of the Strachey biography, eminently noteworthy for its frankness regarding Strachey's sexuality and private life (something Sylvia Townsend Warner, a biographer herself, found distasteful), occurred contemporaneously with the Sexual Offences Act of 1967. This effectively decriminalized homosexuality in England and Wales. Hamilton writes, "It would eventually be the highly combustible chemical of suppressed human sexuality that, liberated at last, would refuel biographical curiosity and output in the final decades of the twentieth century" (155). Hamilton points to an embracing of the potential multiplicities inherent in a life and its telling. But we can in fact trace this embracing to life writing and "the new biography" of the early twentieth century, itself made possible, in large measure, by none other than Lytton Strachey. Thus the life of the individual and the life of the couple—who that individual is in their most intimate space, not just as a single autonomous self but as part of a "we"—become the same but different story, each worth telling. Yet telling multiple versions of these stories brings its own complications. The deeper into our concentric circles we go, and the more intimately they overlap with another's, the more limited our access and the more imaginative, and thus affective and ethical, work is required.

In her theorization of reparative reading, Eve Kosofsky Sedgwick suggests that its practices and ways of knowing may be found within "gay, lesbian, and queer intertextuality" (149). Such reading seeks to "nurture," to "confer plenitude," in order that an "inchoate self" might have the "resources" of love and hope (149).[9] Applying such practices and ways of knowing drawn from gay and lesbian and women's writing more expansively, I see the subjects under study here as enacting such plenitude on, in, and through their intimate others, and I see that reading and writing provide such resources to beloved persons in joy and pain. Such stories need to be told, and they need to be analyzed for us to learn how and why they are told. This assertion echoes the thinking of Wendy Moffat, who, after publishing her "queer biography" of E. M. Forster, called for similar such lives to be written. Queer biography, for Moffat, is reparative, "because it is so full of surprises" (225). One of those surprises is that these narratives can and will continue to suggest that there are more ways to tell intimate life stories than can be dreamt of in our philosophy—affirming and capacious though that philosophy may be.

Chapter outline

This introduction has sought to consider intimate life writing as a practice of relational life narrative, and to situate the couple biography within that context. Foundational to my efforts at the start have been the definition of intimacy; an articulation of an ethics informed by relationality, affects, and becoming (via Levinas, Ahmed, and Braidotti); and an anticipation of significant elements of narrativity to be analyzed from here on out.

It remains to outline what is to come. Chapter 1, "Early Twentieth-Century Life Writing and the Making of Intimacy," provides an overview of scholarship on "the new biography" with an emphasis on its interest in intimate life, followed by analysis of Leslie Stephen's *Mausoleum Book*, Vita Sackville-West's *Portrait of a Marriage* (edited and published with commentary by her son Nigel Nicolson), and Virginia Woolf's *Flush* as instances of intimate life writing and auto/biographical writing on couplehood. Chapter 2, "Worlding: Gertrude Stein and Alice B. Toklas," shows how Stein and Toklas created their coupled world through shared discursive moves and a reenvisioning of forms of autobiography in the context of Stein's thinking about narrative. Texts to be considered include Stein's "Ada," *The Autobiography of Alice B. Toklas*, and *A Book Concluding With As a Wife Has A Cow: A Love Story*, along with Toklas's *The Alice B. Toklas Cook Book* and Tom Hachtman's comic *Gertrude's Follies*. These last two suggest the possibilities for investigations into multimodal narrativity in intimate life writing, and exemplify the ways the (story)worlds of a couple narrative might evolve their own afterlives.

The next two chapters focus more on specific aspects of narrativity: emplotment, gaps, time and temporality, narrative layers including metalepsis, intermentality, perspective, voice, and the relationships among narrator and narratee, teller, tellee, and told. Informing much of my analysis here is the work of Seymour Chatman (on types of narrators and plots), Ellen Spolsky (on gaps and gap-filling), Gérard Genette (on focalization, perspective, and narrative levels), Alan Palmer (on intermentality), and James Phelan (on the relationship between teller and tellee). Chapter 3, "Encounter and Loss: Sylvia Townsend Warner and Valentine Ackland," reads the multiple intimate life writing plots created and cocreated by Warner and Ackland, from the kernel of their originary encounter to the catastrophe of loss. Of particular interest in this chapter is other forms of life writing including diaries and letters. Texts discussed include Warner's diaries, letters among Warner, Ackland, and lovers and friends, Ackland's memoir *For Sylvia*, Warner's commemorative text for Ackland *I'll Stand By You*, and biographies by both Claire Harman and Wendy Mulford. Given that Warner and Ackland may be somewhat less well known, this chapter does the important work of situating their writing among other modernist and late modernist authors, as well as raising key questions regarding "minor" figures and canon.

Chapter 4, "Time and the Other: Christopher Isherwood and Don Bachardy," looks more closely at time and temporality as an aspect of narrativity, and the ways in which the relationships among teller, tellee, and told change over time. This is a particularly salient intervention into the critical discourse surrounding time, narrative, and queerness. I undertake analyses of the collaborative text *October*, Isherwood's diaries, and letters between Isherwood and Bachardy. In furtherance of an interest in multimodal narrativity across intimate life writing, I also consider the long-form serialized podcast adapted from the couple's letters by Katherine Bucknell, the documentary film *Chris & Don: A Love Story*, and Bachardy's *Last Drawings*, created of Isherwood while he was on his deathbed. As will be seen, multimodal intimate life narratives bear many of the same regularities as intimate life writing, but allow for different ways of creating relationships between narrator and narratee, particularly over the course of narrative time.

The final chapter, "Gaps and Closure: Sylvia Plath and Ted Hughes," takes up the ethical implications of intimate life writing as an act and utterance of becoming, for which intermentality is a signature feature of narrativity, when positioned within the priorities, practices, and challenges of couple biographers. The texts for analysis in this chapter include the letters and journals of Plath and Hughes, as well as biographies written of the couple, and recent gallery exhibitions and multimedia installations the curatorial work of which draws on auto/biographical writing. The chapter concludes with a brief coda interrogating "happiness" in intimate life narratives and the problems of resolution, of narrative and emotional closure.

In *Phenomenology of Perception*, Merleau-Ponty writes, "Let us try to see how a thing or being begins to exist for us through desire or love and we shall thereby come to understand better how things and beings can exist in general" (154). This may be an extravagant claim to make for this study, but I do think that Julia Watson is right when she calls relational life writing a form of storytelling that is radical in its practice of intimacy and recognition of the other. She is right because such narratives, emerging as they do here from desire and love, do say something about how beings can and do exist in general, and can and do exist in ethical relationship, in becoming alone and together.

1

Early 20th-Century Life Writing and the Making of Intimacy

In 1890, T. F. Thiselton-Dyer published *The Loves and Marriages of Some Eminent Persons*, a prosopography focusing on the courtships, romances, marriages, and family lives of notable men from Boswell and Smollett to Dickens and Livingstone. The table of contents is organized according to "Married Happiness," "Marriage Influence," "Marriage Romance," "Eccentric Marriages" (the chapter dedicated to this begins with the delightfully understated opening line, "Courtship and marriage have often been conducted in a somewhat unconventional manner" [242]), "Early Flirtations," and "Irregular Marriages" (or elopements). Despite the book being about "loves and marriages" of "persons," the focus is almost exclusively on the experiences of *men* as lovers and husbands, and exemplary, noteworthy men at that. The table of contents lists the names of all the men taken as subjects, and their names appear singly, not in tandem with the other person ostensibly also involved in the love and marriage being told. The wives of these "eminent persons" are subsumed via the book's paratext.

In his writing, Thiselton-Dyer relies heavily on letters and reminiscences available from previously published (and thus authorized and therefore also possibly appropriately sanitized) sources. He follows a model of writing on "great lives," with men as his subjects, even if his attention *is* paid to the achievements of love and marriage rather than noble acts of public life. Further, he follows the decorous conventions which constrain Victorian biographical writing on intimacy and private life. In his piece on Dickens, for instance, who had died two decades before the publication of *Loves and Marriages* at the height of his popularity, Thiselton-Dyer describes an early romance that prompted a spell of picturesque melancholy in the author as a young man, rather than the unsettled marriage to and separation from Catherine Dickens and the affair with Ellen

Ternan.[1] Thiselton-Dyer's rather lively compendium does provide some indication of Victorian reading interest in the field of biographical writing, as it does some indication of Victorian practice, publishing realities to which as a popular writer he might have been attuned—namely, that there was a market for stories about couplehood, marriage, and intimate life, told with an element of humanity, humor, and (at least here) surprisingly little moral judgment. This text suggests that a desire existed among late Victorian readers to engage intimate worlds, that conventions constricting the telling of intimate life did not mean that readers resisted engaging with these narratives. As Trev Broughton and Sarah J. Heidt have shown in their studies of the "embroilment" surrounding James Anthony Froude's biographical work on Thomas Carlyle and Carlyle's marriage to Jane Welsh Carlyle, breaching the boundaries of intimate life via auto/biographical narrative created considerable anxiety, particularly around gender and the nature of marriage in relation to public life. Nevertheless, we find that interest in intimate life writing is not limited to writers, readers, and theorists of "the new biography" as it later emerged in the 1920s and 1930s.

Indeed, the continuities among Victorian and modernist theory and practice of auto/biography, among other factors, shaped what I see as a relationship between and interest in life writing and intimacy, while also shaping the discursive and affective patterns of early and mid-twentieth-century relational life writing more broadly. This chapter will take up, in turn, an overview of the scholarship which has been essential to defining both those continuities and early twentieth-century life writing, including "the new biography," as well as instances of intimate life writing from authors identified as integral to these continuities and developments. I examine Leslie Stephen's *Mausoleum Book*, an intimate life writing text created in response to the loss of his second wife (and Virginia Woolf's mother) Julia Duckworth Stephen; Vita Sackville-West's writing on and through her marriage to Harold Nicolson in *Portrait of a Marriage*; and Virginia Woolf's *Flush*, a text I argue functions as a couple biography.[2]

Rather than traverse the vast landscape that is scholarship on modernist life writing and "the new biography," I will identify several themes and threads in that scholarship that are especially salient to the texts I have chosen to analyze. First, we will take a look at what constitutes "the new biography," the ways its modernist theorists and practitioners sought to distinguish it from its Victorian forebears, and the suggestion that we attend to continuities rather than reify schema of rupture. Second, we will note the aesthetic, social, and cultural factors that contributed to the development of "the new biography," what made the mode and its readers possible. Finally, we will emphasize the importance of the idea of relationality, particularly as it emerged via the thinkers and writers of Bloomsbury, and particularly as a function of performing and narrativizing becoming.

Modernist formulations of "the new biography," and of early twentieth-century life writing generally, privilege the instability, the fragmentary nature, of the subject. In her groundbreaking work on modernist women writers and autobiography (and in her own prosopography *Women of the Left Bank*), Shari Benstock argues that modernist women's life writing, especially that of Virginia Woolf, reveals the fissures in the notion of a unified subject, decentering the autonomous, individual, coherent self ("Authorizing" 21, 22–29). Woolf remains central to discussions of "the new biography," with many scholars taking her 1927 essay "The New Biography" (a review of Harold Nicolson's *Some People*) and her 1939 essay "The Art of Biography" as germinal texts. "The New Biography," along with Harold Nicolson's 1927 *The Development of English Biography* (published by Virginia and Leonard Woolf's Hogarth Press, in their *Lectures on Literature* series) positioned radical shifts in life writing, coinciding with similar shifts in fiction, against the work of the Victorians. Max Saunders has detailed the conversation between Nicolson and Woolf, specifically around "The New Biography" and *Some People* (458–70). Harold Nicolson pronounces that "Victorianism only died in 1921," when biographers finally did away with the "essentially commemorative" impulse governing their writing (145). Meanwhile, in her oft-cited dichotomy of "granite" and "rainbow" from "The New Biography," Woolf notoriously juxtaposes the "granite" of the Victorian biography as monument with the "rainbow" of life writing dedicated to the fluidity of character and personality.[3] The emphasis on subjectivity, on "identity rather than event or action," on "self-consciousness about form" and "psychological and experiential complexity" (Marcus, "Newness" 205), was meant to do away with what was perceived to be the Victorian monumentalizing of heroic deeds by great and noble men. As Alison Booth puts it, according to the modernists, the Victorians "were a nation of undertakers, indulging in mortuary pomp" (237). Booth does also suggest that the primacy of Woolf in the study of twentieth-century life writing displaces other possible conceptualizations of the forms of auto/biography, particularly those not embedded in privileged modernist cultural discourses (239–40). She writes, "Feminist researchers seeking critical ways to think back through foremothers need to rethink the history of life writing as well" (226).

While modernist life writers may have required resistance to Victorian ways of doing things in order to position their own work and thinking, the cultural and historical position of such writers did shape what we continue to call "the new biography." As Laura Marcus and Max Saunders have shown in their essential and helpful work on the subject, two factors contributed to the development of emphases on interior life and the unconscious, subjectivity and consciousness, and relationships and intimate life in early twentieth-century life writing. The first is an openness to focusing on sex and sexuality. As noted in the introduction, Paula Backscheider and Nigel Hamilton point to this shift as integral to the development of relationality and private life as priorities in biographical writing later in the twentieth century; we might discern the roots of this preoccupation here. The biographical interest in sex is traced by Marcus to Woolf's "The Art of Biography" ("Newness" 214–16), in which Woolf writes on Lytton Strachey's *Elizabeth and Essex*, and to a wider cultural interest in engaging with sexuality. We might look as well to the rise of sexology as a field and the emerging discourse of *scientia sexualis*.[4] Relatedly, and secondly, life writing ideas and practices were affected by growing interest in Freud, brought to English-speaking audiences through the translations of Alix and James Strachey published by the Hogarth Press; Lytton Strachey's biographical writing, especially *Elizabeth and Essex*, furthered Freud's reach with readers. Marcus makes the point that "Strachey and Freud were, it could be argued, the two primary influences on biography in the 1920s" ("Newness" 216). Saunders notes that sexologist Havelock Ellis was an important influence on Strachey, too, and suggests that while biographers did not fully grapple with the implications of Freud's theories until after the Second World War, "the new biography" laid much groundwork for ways of writing and reading intimate life (454–55).

In a consideration of Bloomsbury—"queer Bloomsbury"—Madelyn Detloff and Brenda Helt point to the importance of "personal life" and "*being together*" for Bloomsbury figures:

> While identity is important, especially as a strategic way of understanding one's position within social hierarchies, as an analytic tool it has the unfortunate

> side-effect of fixing one's objects of study into relatively static categories or characteristics of *being* at the expense of *becoming*, of co-evolving, or (a phenomenon that has special resonance for the Bloomsbury Group) of *becoming together*. (1–2; emphasis in original)

My introduction has made clear the necessity of theorizing "becoming" ontologically and ethically, as well as narratively and discursively, in the study of relational life writing.[5] We can hone in here on Detloff's and Helt's emphasis on "co-evolving" and "becoming together," beyond identity, a point echoed by Rosi Braidotti (Ryan 104–5). Writers associated with Bloomsbury, Virginia and Leonard Woolf, their Hogarth Press—the writers under consideration in this chapter—evince a preoccupation with relationality, its ethics, and the transformative effects of relationships on the singular person, along with a heightened interest in the writing of the interior and the personal.[6]

The aesthetics of representing subjectivity as it emerges in the modernist "new biography" reverberates throughout the critical writing on the subject. Maria DiBattista and Emily O. Wittman, for instance, describe twentieth-century life writing as seeking "to accommodate the fluidity and variousness of life and how it feels to be living it" (xiii). The attention to the processural subject, to becoming, and the ways the practice of life writing enacts, performs, even prioritizes, that process, renders intimacy more visible. It should be noted again, though, that Booth, along with Laura Marcus and Ruth Hoberman in their writing on "the new biography," have all suggested that continuities among Victorian and modernist life writers should not be discounted. I believe we find such continuities in an interest in relational and intimate life, both the reading and the writing of it.

Leslie Stephen, notable literary critic and mountaineer, editor of the *Dictionary of National Biography*, and Virginia Woolf's father, is often set as the "granite" to Woolf's "rainbow," an eminent Victorian against whom the polemics of "the new biography" is directed. Stephen was himself a reader of intimate lives, even as the practice came in for some of his criticism, as Trev Broughton has shown in the Froude/Carlyle "embroilment" ("Froude-Carlyle" 558–61). And he was a writer of intimate lives, as well. His *Mausoleum Book*, composed privately, unlike his literary criticism, biography, or alpine writing, is an elaborated instance of writing through death, and an exemplar of the late Victorian memoir of widowerhood. Stephen enacts the impulse to narrativize the life of a dead spouse, and the life shared as a couple, and through that process to narrativize a major ontological shift.[7] As much as Stephen claims to *not* be doing this, at one point apologizing for "dropping into narrative" (66), the process of fitting his narrative alongside his wife's, and thus within an emplotment of couplehood as a way of managing grief, is made visible in spite of his protestations. The writing of a memoir of widow(er)hood is an attempt to claim the life story of the deceased, and by extension the story of the couple itself once it no longer exists. By writing the memoir of the deceased, the surviving spouse appropriates the life, claiming a place of centrality for themselves, and making the shared world available to others. Such writing becomes a means of managing the alteration of ontological status experienced by the one left behind, allowing for the generation of possible worlds wherein the experience of the now-distant and unknowable other can be realized and shared. The writing becomes a way to assert the intimate knowledge of both body and mind.

Meant as a testament about his second marriage to Julia Duckworth Stephen after her death in May 1895, the *Mausoleum Book* was conceived as a letter for their children as well as a family album, not to be published: "I mean further to write in such a way as to put out of the question any larger use of it than I have indicated, even after my death" (4). Stephen began his labors in 1895 and ended with a chronology and summary of events going from 1895 to 1904; the compilation was first published in an edition by Alan Bell in 1977. The text covers most of Stephen's life, beginning with his childhood and including his first marriage and his work, with the ostensible purpose of commemorating Julia Stephen. Stephen asserts continually that he will resist any impulse toward autobiography: "Now I have no intention of writing autobiography except in this incidental way" (4). Stephen's insistence that he does not consider what he is doing in the *Mausoleum Book* as autobiography at all is striking. It is true that the work is an assemblage of commentary, letters, and chronology—not unlike Sylvia Townsend Warner's own assemblage of memoir, annotations, letters, and poetry created after Valentine Ackland's death, as we shall see in Chapter 3. It is also true that as the text was never meant to be made public (unlike in the case of Warner, who at least considered making it available to scholars; see Micir), perhaps, in Stephen's mind, it escapes the generic or formal signifier of "autobiography." Perhaps he seeks to mitigate (self-)accusations of exhibiting his personal life, something regarded as problematic for the Victorian life writer, as emerged in the instance of Froude and Carlyle. Here, according to Stephen, he functions merely as an "arranger," laying out material in order to "come nearer to my darling's story" (30), including her love letters to her first husband; and gesturing toward distancing and concealing even as he seems to lay bare his intimate life (Broughton, *Men* 7). We will consider the distinction between arranger and narrator in our discussion of *Portrait of a Marriage* later in this chapter, as well as in Christopher Isherwood's *Kathleen and Frank*. Whether he admits it or not, the telling of his own life is essential to Stephen's construction of his couplehood with Julia Stephen, as is his appropriation, as husband and ideal reader, of her private papers. The *Mausoleum Book* is a phenomenological documentation of his perceptions of what their couplehood comprised, and the ways their two stories came together as "one" in what he understands as a process of shared worlding. As far as he is concerned, his own story is significant only insofar as it is "involved in hers": "I have put all this down to make our story clear" (85, 88). "This" includes his years at Cambridge, his renunciation of his faith, his first marriage, and—importantly—his literary labors.

The scholarship on Virginia Woolf's relationship to Leslie Stephen is copious, including work delving into their respective positions on biography and life writing; some readers see the assertions of "the new biography" previously detailed here not only as responses to Victorian biographers but also as Woolf writing back to her father.[8] In relation to Stephen's *Mausoleum Book* and Woolf's own life writing, including her fragmentary memoirs (published posthumously), Alex Zwerdling writes, "Virginia Woolf learned about the danger of reverence from her father's memoir, with its tendency to turn flesh and blood into a marmoreal object. What concerned her was not the proper attitude to the dead but their individual identities. . . . She focused not on essence but on particulars" (63). Zwerdling's point is well taken, especially considering what we know about the difficulties Woolf had in her relationship with her father after her mother's death. Yet to narrativize love is to rely on particulars, even as love stories are shaped by a common emplotment, consisting of narrative regularities. In other words, love stories might look similar, as this study will show—but any love story depends on the particularity, and the singularity, of the loved person in order to be told in the first place. Stephen's attempts to fix Julia Stephen in death, in his "mausoleum," require him to attend to her lovable particularity, her irrevocable singularity:

granite *and* rainbow. To gesture toward a reading that accounts for the affects of love and loss, one could argue that by fixing Julia Stephen in her mausoleum, her husband seeks to hold on to her, to possess her eternally, to maintain an intimate connection with her, what he called "the romance of my life" (25); all of the work of the book is to "come nearer to my darling's story" (30). In a word, he seeks not simply to entomb her in "granite" but to contemplate the "rainbow" of who she was and what it was they shared. The creation of the book makes something that stands in for the woman herself, and provides a means to reflect on who she was and what she meant in the context of the marriage.

When Stephen comes to "my darling's story," he begins by discussing a series of portraits made of Julia over the course of her young womanhood and adult life. Portraits can serve to capture the "rainbow," the dynamism of the subject, their character and their becoming, not necessarily always a fixed or static figure, a process of seeing, perceiving, contingent upon the position of the beholder. Stephen's ostensible purpose for this move is to "dwell a little more upon her beauty: for beauty, as it seems to me, was of the very essence of her nature" (31). He describes pictures by George Frederic Watts, Burne-Jones, and the famous photographs by Julia Margaret Cameron, commenting on the extent to which they are "like," and particularly the extent to which they successfully capture her delicacy, tenderness, and "nobility of character" (32). The significance of the evaluation of portraits of Julia Stephen lies in Leslie Stephen's attempt to capture the ineffable, what it was that made his dead wife lovable and exceptional. At the same time, she remains distant, lovely but unreachable not only in death but in life, particularly in her own grief over the death of her first husband, Herbert Duckworth—something Stephen can *tell* but not completely *see*—narrativized not by her but by Stephen, save glancingly, through his voice.

Additionally, the discussion of the portraits represents Stephen's desire to hold on to some physical aspect of her, and becomes a way to narrativize embodiment; as Carol Christ has claimed in her own discussion of Victorian mourning (specifically the use of death masks), a portrait serves to "record an ambivalent desire both to look at a forbidden sexual object and to appropriate the life of the dead, the feminine body" (qtd. in Goodwin and Bronfen 14). The passion felt by Stephen toward his dead wife is clear in his words which suggest a physical force (the last quotation even seeming to evoke the possible reparative magic of Shakespeare's *The Winter's Tale*): "Her loveliness thrills me to the core," "we had become one in spirit: nothing could be sweeter," "my darling came to life. After our marriage she ceased to be numbed or 'deadened'" (33, 50, 60). But words alone cannot fully replace the erotic body lost to death, while evoking the portraits of a wife of famed beauty through the discourse of passion allows him to speak what cannot be spoken.

Stephen contains elements of his wife's embodiment in his mausoleum, first by attempting to work through her death, then by seeking to integrate the story of her first marriage into their experience of couplehood. Yet these unruly parts of the dead wife and the life she lived cannot be entirely contained. He can bear witness to her becoming, but cannot fully grasp her. One wonders which aspect of this process is more troublesome, and one comes to see that the two are linked. It is as though the trauma of her death catalyzes an analeptic gesture to an earlier affective struggle. Stephen has to work to accommodate his wife's past, as he must now work to accommodate her death. His apprehension of her is shaken by the transmogrification of the erotic body into the dead body; and then again by the return to the revelation of an erotic life separate from the one they shared. There are other ways that Stephen might be seen to transgress propriety, and privacy, in the eyes of readers throughout his memoir of his wife—for one, his inclusion of details from Julia's letters to her first husband, as well as his own feelings on reading them. He writes of her letters, "She made a complete surrender of herself in the fullest sense. . . . The two lives were to become one; there was to be no shadow of difference or discord, and she speaks in a way, the more touching from its quiet simplicity, of her entire unity with him" (37). First, Stephen uses his wife's letters as an opportunity to idealize a certain vision of marriage, one of "entire unity," but he also participates in a signature and related trope of couple writing: to narrativize the making of one from two, the creation of the "we." This is not the "we" of himself and Julia Duckworth Stephen, but he sees the appreciation of that first union as essential for the formation of his own, and he seeks to transform, to reconfigure, himself from outsider to participant in his wife's first marriage.

Then, one of the problems of auto/biographical writing on couplehood, both narratological and epistemological, is how to capture the lives of each member of the couple before the moment of intersection. When does knowledge of each member's intimate past become shared, and when does the moving forward in a new life, a "we," collaboratively building a story together, begin to happen?

Here, Stephen becomes privy to a life prior to the life of the couple he helped to build; he appropriates the erotic texts of his wife and makes them his own:

> Of all this, however, I know nothing or next to nothing. In these dark days, I have looked through a number of letters and papers referring to him. . . . I felt—you will understand why I felt—that it was hardly right for me to examine too closely records—so tender and intimate as some of them were—of my Julia's first love. Yet I could not quite refrain. I looked into them: I was deeply moved by what I read. (36)

The record of his wife's past, her own writing, and her own erotic life, is enfolded into Stephen's telling as a way for him to possess something disruptive, possibly as disruptive as death. Furthermore, by co-opting these letters in such a way, he is able to position himself as his wife's ideal reader: "To me who am able to read between the lines, it was impossible not to perceive the deep underlying tenderness which strengthened as the days went on" (38). The phenomenological work of reading the letters facilitates Stephen's development of a perception of their love, a perception that allows him to imagine himself as tender, and sympathetic in every sense of the word. It also foregrounds the significance, the necessity, of interpretation in the affective and imaginative work of couple-worlding. Stephen must be able to read the texts of his wife in order to make, and then to commemorate, their couplehood.

The memoir thus becomes a means by which the disruptive dead wife is contained so that narrative perceived as coherent, shaped by the management of affects, might proceed. This "coherent" narrative includes the crafting of Stephen's perception of their marriage and his role within it. He writes, "*I believe* at the very bottom of my heart, [she] had after our marriage a life **which**, though it had many troubles, was a life of deep inward peace and happiness and of many hours and seasons **which**, *if I may venture to judge* from my own participation in them, were of such rare and delightful happiness as her most lovely nature deserved and could appreciate" (61–62; typographical cues mine). First, indicated in bold, are the enfolding of qualifiers within dependent clauses and appositives. The slightly knotty syntax deployed by Stephen here could arise from one or several factors. We may be witnesses to a kind of self-effacement here, a kind of modesty. Or, we could be witnessing a kind of self-deprecation, a hesitating acknowledgment that the "many troubles" were perhaps brought on by marriage to a cantankerous "Man of Letters," as Broughton might suggest and as Stephen himself witnessed in Carlyle's memorials as compiled by Froude ("Froude-Carlyle" 564, 566). Second, indicated by italics, are Stephen's own attempts to convey his perception of the couplehood he shared with Julia Stephen; these perceptions are themselves qualified with "believe" and "venture." It is the case that he can only speak from experience, and it is also the case that the *Mausoleum Book* throughout reminds us over and again that he—and we—can never be fully cognizant of the experience of Julia Stephen. Stephen reports his own mental activity here, in service of suggesting what Alan Palmer might see as the narrativization of intermentality, a connection believed by Stephen to perpetuate an intersubjective worldmaking with Julia Stephen. Likewise, he reports his perceptions, suggestive of his own processes of worlding—which may in fact diverge from those of his wife.

At this point, Emmanuel Levinas's thinking about knowledge and violation, alongside a phenomenologically informed reading of Stephen's narrative of affects, might assist in working through this project, and the turning toward a different way of thinking about intimate life. The narrative of Stephen's life as put forth in the *Mausoleum Book* is what Adam Zachary Newton calls "a constant interplay across the borders of self and other" emerging from "the very fact of alterity" (48). Stephen's desire to possess his wife in life and after death can never be fulfilled, and it is the pain of that inevitability that drives the memoir. Levinas writes that "desire without satisfaction . . . understands the remoteness, the alterity, and the exteriority of the other" (*Totality* 34); this lack of understanding, the inability to recognize the other as infinitely separate not only in death but in love, is the anxiety behind the memoir of widow(er)hood. Such an inability to recognize is always there. Betrayal, loss, and death just makes it more visible, and mourning provides the narrative opportunity required to right/write the relationship with the other.

At the same time, the contemplation of intimate life as effected by Stephen in the *Mausoleum Book* performs affective and ethical work; and even as he shares the fruits of that contemplation with his children, the intended audience, he indicates that they themselves can never truly know the world made by their parents. The overspill of feeling does not necessarily lead to greater knowledge on the part of the tellees. For all of the impulse to reveal demonstrated by the text, Stephen maintains something like a resistance to access of his intimate life with his wife. He writes, toward the end of the commentary that precedes the final chronology, "In truth, husband and wife, living together as we did in the most unreserved intimacy . . . do not require the language of words. . . . Proofs of her love are not wanted by you. Abundant proofs are indelibly fixed in my memory, many of them too sacred to be revealed to any human being" (90). True intimacy is beyond language, even as copious and varied forms of discourse are deployed to inscribe intimate life. From a Levinasian perspective, intimacy is inherently an epistemological and ontological problem: we can never know the other, yet the very nature of their otherness demands acknowledgment, recognition, a reaching toward.

Such reaching toward knowledge of subject and other, especially in response to disruptions that threaten the worlding of a couple—such as betrayal—forms the substance of Vita Sackville-West's writing about her own intimate life, through *Portrait of a Marriage*. Sackville-West's telling of what she perceives to be unspeakable sins fosters her recognition through narrative of the alterity of the source of marital affection, namely, her husband Harold Nicolson. Her ability to love through that recognition and to desire his happiness, even in the face of what Sara Ahmed calls "hap," is a deeply ethical move, one achievable through the act and practice of intimate life writing. Ahmed's "hap" is what happens, those contingencies that disrupt what we believe to be "happiness," allowing us to "live in the gaps between its lines" (222–23). Writing through the "hap"—here, a torrid and scandalous affair by Sackville-West with another woman, Violet Trefusis—facilitates Sackville-West's becoming, allowing her to once again participate in the creative and affective project of worlding with Harold Nicolson. The work of much of *Portrait of a Marriage* was performed singly by Sackville-West; she wrote it for Nicolson, and for future readers who might be grappling similarly with transgressive desire, but by all accounts he never read it. Nevertheless, the work of that text is informed by and did the work of shaping who they were in relationship.

Sackville-West's *Portrait of a Marriage* comprises five sections. Two are her own writing and the remaining three consist of commentary by her son Nigel Nicolson, who describes finding the manuscript in his mother's study after her death and deciding to publish first because he believed it was Sackville-West's wish to have an audience for the narrative, and second because he felt it would "help and encourage those" with queer sexualities struggling against society (x). Thus the book is framed—and Sackville-West's writing interrupted—by her son's complementary narrativization of the parents' relationship and his sense of the text as "autobiography," "confession" (vii), "the story of two people who married for love," and "a panegyric of marriage" (ix). In addition, interpolated between each section is a chronology of events covered by the narrative. In this way, a sense of order and coherence is imposed on a story Sackville-West can barely bring herself to tell, let alone tell in an orderly fashion. Narrating the effort of doing so is as much a part of the telling as the events themselves. I will attend first to the sections composed and narrated by Sackville-West herself, and then to those by Nigel Nicolson, whom I deem here to be a "narrator-arranger," with some special emphasis on Part V, the final section, in which the narrative efforts of gap-filling become paramount.

Sackville-West, in her two sections of the book, generates a burst of private, erotically and affectively charged writing in quasi-diary form produced from July to October 1920, with a short coda written on March 28, 1921. The book itself was published in 1973, roughly contemporaneous with Holroyd's 1697–1968 biography of Strachey (and with the 1971 condensed edition) and Isherwood's 1976 *Christopher and His Kind*, leading one to believe that Nigel Nicolson showed some acumen in claiming there might be an interest in life writing of "queer sexualities." We see qualifying and self-contradicting rhetorical moves similar to those enacted by Leslie Stephen. Where Stephen calls attention to his refusal of the autobiographical impulse, and protests against telling his story even as it unfolds over the telling, Sackville-West seems incapable of pinning anything down, moving from event to feeling in an outrush of passion, first self-recrimination, then defiance. Where Stephen insists that his only task is to "arrange" the material of life without "dropping into narrative," Sackville-West insists her text is not arranged at all: "There isn't a word of exaggeration in these statements—nothing, for that matter, in the whole of this writing is to be exaggerated or 'arranged'; its only merit will be truth, but truth as bleak as I can make it" (22). While these rhetorical gestures appear to suggest the inability of creating a coherent narrative, I would claim, rather, that such apparent incoherence is in the service of constructing a coherent imagining of *couplehood*. The narrative and rhetorical moves might be messy, but they are deployed to make something whole, and whole in its being in-process. Or, another way to think about it is through the rhetorical nature of telling. Sackville-West tells us "nothing" will be "arranged," but the crafting of a story, even (or perhaps especially) from life, requires arranging. This is the work of narrative discourse; and it should be contrasted with the arranging of Sackville-West's manuscript, the chronologies of and commentaries on her intimacies with Violet Trefusis and

Harold Nicolson, and the incorporation of letters, all assembled by the narrator-arranger Nigel Nicolson. The writer is telling the affects—recounting how the force of feeling through the body and experiencing the world through the affair overspills the confines of "story." Of course, this is the work of imagination. One can think of few things as messy in human experience as couplehood. It is not the work of this book to suggest otherwise. Rather, it is my contention that we attempt to use narrative to make the messiness of couplehood—the "mess within," in Peter Goldie's phrase—begin to make sense.

Sackville-West's narrative begins with her childhood and her meeting with and marriage to Harold Nicolson, but concentrates on her passionate affair with Violet Trefusis from 1918 to 1921, along with her deep feelings for Harold in the face of the possibility of losing him. The first few entries focus on youth, as well as a series of metaleptic commentaries on the purpose of the writing: whether it will be completed, whether it's worth doing, whether its author is a raging egoist. Trefusis herself interrupts, in the narrative present: "(My writing has been broken here by Violet telephoning to me; I scarcely know whether it was the Violet of fifteen years ago, or my passionate, stormy Violet of today, speaking to me in that same lovely voice)" (22). This parenthetical disrupts the narrative, much as lesbian desire has disrupted the marriage. Further, it disrupts temporality in its invocation of queer sexuality and its subversion of heteronormative narrative (cf. Roof). Marriage unfolds over time; it is events in time. As Joan Didion writes in her memoir of widowhood *The Year of Magical Thinking*, "Marriage is time" (197). But time does not apply to Trefusis. She exists outside of and compromises Sackville-West's own apprehension of time as it plays out in her married life, and in her desire Sackville-West resists the "chrononormative" temporality of marriage (Freeman 3).[9] In constructing time thusly, Sackville-West enacts a subversion of couple emplotment even as she deploys the work of relational life writing to affirm her couplehood with her husband.

Such starting and stopping, interruptions and disruptions, characterize this assemblage. Sackville-West writes, "I start writing, having spent no consideration upon this task. Shall I ever complete it? and under what circumstances?" (3–4). Key to the early moments of the narrative is the telling of mental activity, the reporting of what is and is not remembered, of "my head swirls with this writing" (12); and the judging of "doing all this part very badly, very confusedly" (23). Placed within these moments of origination for both the text and its author is an entry that turns to Harold, the husband: "I lay awake thinking about this writing, and watching the patterns that the moonlight, shining through branches and lattices, made upon my bed . . . I got a rather sad letter from Harold"—and I'll pause here to note that Sackville-West's contemplation of Harold is prompted by text, by an artifact of his own writing, a physical marker of his absence, an absence Sackville-West proceeds to fill—"He is the only person of whom I think with consistent tenderness. . . . He has complete power over my heart, though not over my spirit. It is real tenderness I feel for him. . . . All this makes the whole thing so agonizing and so puzzling" (13–14). The word "tenderness" recurs, serving as a cue for the ethical work Sackville-West is trying to do. Her writing about her marriage functions as a means to contemplate the affection she has for someone of utmost importance in her life, someone she persisted in hurting for the early years of their partnership and someone who has been part of her becoming and must needs be recognized. The thinking of Harold requires cognitive and emotional effort—"thinking" with "tenderness" that is "agonizing" and "puzzling"—and also prompts the telling of affects as an effect of the disruptive event of the affair.

Sackville-West's writing toward Nicolson is relational and ethical. It is an acknowledgment of his alterity, and how her affection toward him, and his toward her, prompt mutual affectivity and phenomenological recognition. This becoming is continual throughout the long Sackville-West/Nicolson union, and is shared by both partners even when confronted with the Trefusis affair (and in the face of other relationships on both sides in a semi-open arrangement). The two believed that "a common sense of values" and "mutual esteem" were essential for a successful marriage, a belief articulated during a 1929 recording for the BBC (190). Even as each member of the couple pursued other erotic engagements, openly with each other's knowledge, the two analyzed, discussed, and renarrativized their love in an ongoing way, most especially through their letters.[10] These letters, indeed, form a significant portion of Nigel Nicolson's narrative and commentary throughout *Portrait of a Marriage*, and he recognizes the affective heavy lifting these texts do to sustain his parents' union.

Sackville-West's outpouring is an empathic, affectual move that allows her to recognize her husband's alterity, and to acknowledge that he has done the same for her; they are together in their separateness. Despite the rhetorical gestures toward self-critique regarding the egotism of her project, it was necessary for her to come closer to an ethical relationship with the person she claims to love the most, the person she seems to have hurt. She writes, "I don't know how to go on; I keep thinking that Harold, if he ever reads this, will suffer so, but I ask him to remember that he is reading about a different person from the one he knew" (105).[11] The charge of the text is to enable him to see, know, and recognize that person, even as to show Harold, in his position as implied reader/narratee, that person is to inflict pain on the writer herself: "I hate writing this, but I must, I must. When I began this I swore I would shirk nothing" (34). Interestingly, the one part of the text Sackville-West *does* shirk is the telling of the wedding to Harold: "I hurry over this part, because it is the same for everybody" (38). The word "shirking," and its expressed anxiety over concealment, over failure to fulfill authentic and sincere narrative and rhetorical purpose, and to do the work necessary to achieve that purpose, appears again when Sackville-West describes dressing as a boy in her travels with Trefusis: "I have never told a soul of what I did. I hesitate to write it here, but I must; shirking the truth here would be like cheating oneself playing patience" (109). The rhetorical stance adopted by Sackville-West as teller in her narrative demands not only that she tell of intimate life but also that she establish and maintain intimacy with herself and thereby with her reader. Note also the contrast in what can and cannot be "shirked." The heteronormative ritual of the wedding may be shirked, "because it is the same for everybody," but the dressing as a boy may not, because it is "truth," and her transgressive desires must be borne witness to.

Part III of Sackville-West's text, where her dressing as "Julian" appears, has a much different feel from Part I. Part I continually pushes up against the constraints of chrononormative narrative temporality. The author feels she must narrate the past, in order to account for the present, but the present continually obtrudes: "I want to get on, I want to finish those years that might have been the life of another person. I want to get to the present" (41). Once the narrative catches up with the present, and enters the narrative present of the height of the crisis, the story rushes headlong through the telling of Sackville-West's and Trefusis's peripatetic and passionate travels through Europe, as they seek to escape the constraints of their marriages; Trefusis, especially, is told to be desperate to remove herself from her husband, Denys. Nigel Nicolson comments on this himself in Part IV, after his own recursive retelling of events, writing, "The end of the story can be told quite quickly. As Vita was writing her autobiography, the last scenes were being enacted, so that it became in its final stages a running commentary" (178). In this way, we see Sackville-West deploying one of the salient characteristics of modern (and queer) life writing, in that it deliberately refuses to be beholden to chronology, even as the logics of chronology, and of events, insist upon themselves.

Sackville-West, in Part III, offers fewer reflective moments, fewer of those instances of contemplation. Yet this narrative rush performs a different kind of ethical work. In imagining her husband as her ideal audience—"There is only one person in whom I have such utter confidence that I would give every line of this confession into his hands" (3)—and in thinking of her writing as a confession, an apologia for what she calls her "unnaturalness" (105–6), she uses narrative to create an opportunity for the recognition of otherness. Her couplehood with Violet Trefusis becomes a storyworld into which Harold might enter as implied reader, allowing Sackville-West to do imaginative work on his behalf; she invites him into that world in order to enable a process of shared meaning-making, paradoxically strengthening their own couplehood and forming a chapter of their story together. Further, it offers an alternative story to that constructed by the exchange of letters during the women's journeys, one which might mitigate painful memories. Yet the Harold Nicolson serving as Sackville-West's implied, even ideal, reader is in some regards itself a fiction: how can he play that role never even having read her words? It is part of Nigel Nicolson's work to show that Sackville-West's trust in her intimacy with Harold Nicolson was not misplaced. And it is part of our work to see that the imaginative effort Sackville-West expended on creating her ideal reader facilitated a way of worlding with her real-life husband.

As part of his effort in telling his parents' marriage, Nigel Nicolson builds a narrative structure to contain the unruly bodies, minds, and desires of Vita Sackville-West and Harold Nicolson, and arranges cues within that structure for how a reader is meant to construe the emotional life of the couple. This effort culminates in the final section of the book: Part V. *Portrait of a Marriage* regenerates the storyworld of the couplehood created by Sackville-West and Harold Nicolson; I refer to the couplehood as having a "storyworld" quite deliberately. The two through the telling of an evolving intermentality, the creation of mutual affectivity, and the performance of intersubjectivity through life writing craft a world, one that can be narrativized by the son and entered into by the reader. Studying this and other writings of couplehood allows us to see the emotional life and intersubjective connection generated through narrative by the members of the couple itself, by readers entering into and making for themselves the storyworld created by the couples in their worlding, and by biographers appropriating and arranging the material, discourses, and tropes of these lives in a new form of intimacy.

Nicolson's choice to frame Sackville-West's words with his own reading of his parents' marriage, especially their letters, places her inner life in a wider context, while also attempting to impose some coherence on an emotional world the writer herself acknowledges to be incoherent. Such a move demands of himself as reader and biographer as well as narrator-arranger, and of his audience, a suspension of judgment; his revelation of her emotional life and the ways it is intertwined with that of his father's has ethical implications and establishes his position vis à vis value judgment as a narrator (Phelan 33). We are asked to withhold censure until the whole story is known, to pause for an alternative perspective and possible interpretation offered by a sympathetic outsider. At the same time, however, one could argue that Nicolson's imperative to render the story coherent is possibly a violation of his mother's, and his parents', own unruly desires. The working through via intimate life writing toward an ethical recognition of alterity is in large measure the project of *Portrait of a Marriage*—for both Sackville-West, as the spouse tries to come to terms with the transformation of her intimate world through narrative, and for Nigel Nicolson, as the son in his framing labors and renarrativization attempts to negotiate and acknowledge the alterity of his mother and the unknowability of her intimate life within her marriage and without. Parts II and IV, indeed, are retellings of Parts I and III, with additional items from the family's private archive offering elaboration and context. Nicholson envisions this work of retelling as a form of sympathy, echoing back to us his mother's story, capturing her multiple voices (90). Interestingly, in intervening in his mother's story, Nigel Nicolson can claim greater knowledge than his father. Thus the ideal reader of *Portrait of a Marriage*, in some ways, remains a fiction, an imagined interlocutor conjured by Sackville-West in her writing of couplehood rather than the fully embodied and situated other that formed the real partner in the union.

Nigel Nicolson's casting of himself as an outsider to his own parents' marriage is crucial to his developing credibility as arranger as well as to his stance of sympathy. He points out frequently that his parents were loving but uninterfering; each member of the family had their own concerns and interests, and the freedom to pursue a private life independent of domestic duty (while still valuing domestic ties) was of the utmost importance. Nicolson writes, "How ignorant we were in our childhood of these events, seeing in our parents' marriage unruffled conjugal bliss" (182). The extent of the complexities of Sackville-West and Nicolson's life together was concealed from their two sons until adolescence, and even then it is treated as though it were quite simply none of their business. At the same time, as Amber Regis suggests, the work of *Portrait of a Marriage* is highly relational via the deployment of an especially responsive intertextuality (289). As a result, Nigel Nicolson is able to intervene in the arranging of the world of the couple through novels, letters, diaries, interviews, and remembrances much as the members of the couple did themselves, while simultaneously remaining outside showing us how to read it. Again, though, this might be disingenuous, and figuring out these multiple positions on the part of the biographer himself is part of the epistemological and ethical work of the text.

The narrator-arranger of *Portrait of a Marriage* thus upholds the centrality of the union and its intimacy, displacing the lesbian romance—or, perhaps more generously, seeking to accommodate it—through his emphasis on his parents' marriage and its storyworld, along with the work he does to render their shared narrative coherent. For instance, he describes the decision taken by the pair to pursue an open marriage, while also asserting that Harold "saw Vita as the companion of a lifetime" (138). Their voices dominate in letters and diary entries, moved to the side briefly only by Nicolson's own attempts to interpret and read those texts as evidence of the emotional life they shared. These attempts are cues for the reader, opening doors into the couple's world, providing a means to decipher a private language: "It was not 'his' struggle, but 'their' struggle" (145). At the same time, Nicolson has to capture Sackville-West's and Trefusis's pairing as well, the private language and space created in their attempt to escape into their own "world of two," a hermetically sealed universe of passion and heedless devotion. He quotes extensively from letters sprinkled with pet names—Lushka for Violet, Mitya for Vita—and from Sackville-West's novel about the affair, *Challenge*, composed with significant input from Trefusis, written while the two were in the midst of their affair, and published in 1924 (148–49). Yet for all of the power this attraction had for the women involved, Sackville-West's emotional life—as presented via the crafting of the emotional core of the book, via Nicolson's arranging of his mother's text and the texts of her union with Harold Nicolson—lies with her marriage, with Hadji (her pet name for Harold). Nicolson makes this visible in telling the end of the memoir, with his father reclaiming his mother, and then crafting the remaining sections of the book from love letters over the next forty years of the union. In doing so, the division he describes in an interpretive metalepsis that Sackville-West must have been feeling between her erotic and her married subject positions—"She could love Harold, she thought, and be 'in love' with Violet" (145)—is reconciled, and rendered coherent.

Nicolson has himself an emotional investment in telling the story of his parents' marriage, of reconstructing a private world to which he himself was never fully granted access. One has only to compare other tellings of the Vita Sackville-West/Harold Nicolson marriage, other versionings of her liaisons with Trefusis, and later with Virginia Woolf, to see that the problem of the biographer, the epistemological problem of appropriating and reconstructing intimate life narratives, gaining and granting access to that private interior space, is at the heart of a genre committed to representing affects and the worlds they make. This critical challenge will form the substance of our discussion in Chapter 5. In writing about the two women's husbands coming to fetch them from one of their elopements during the time covered by the autobiography, Nicolson writes, "I wish I knew more about that flight. How did Denys [Trefusis, Violet's husband] happen to have a two-seater aeroplane? From which airfield did he take off? When had he learned to fly?" (173). These seem odd questions to ask given the revelations of his mother's words. It is true that much is revealed in Sackville-West's autobiography, and as with any other intimate text, much can only be imagined. He concludes his telling of the husbands going off to fetch their wives with this: "We shall never know the truth—and what does it matter now?" (176). Nicolson's gap-filling goes just so far; the emotional life of his parents' marriage, their "world of two," is opened up in the pages of his book, more so than many other intimate spaces. Yet he recognizes, "Dimly we [he and his brother Ben] acknowledged that the part of their lives we saw was not the whole. What was the whole?" (195). Like the interrogative quoted above, Nicolson's sympathy with his parents, and desire to empathize, leads him to ask questions, and just as much leads him to accept that there may be no answers. Still there will always be something of the unknown.

The work of Part V is to perform some of the gap-filling necessary to comprehend the functioning of this couplehood, both in the aftermath of the Trefusis affair and in the long life remaining to the Sackville-West/Nicolson marriage. According to Nigel Nicolson, much of the intimate work was done through writing, and its realization allows him to attempt what Suzanne Raitt characterizes as a gesture toward generating an "apparently happy ending" (81). Nicolson writes, "In their marriage there was no bed, but both, being writers, found infinite pleasure in analyzing their emotions. . . . They wrote to each other thousands of letters, and these formed the warp and woof of their marriage, which was thus continuously enriched and rewoven" (192). Raitt takes up the consideration of the task of Part V as well, arguing that "the complex structure of their marriage required constant maintenance and attention," a "contract" that "had to be constantly reinvoked and confirmed" (87–88). This observation could hold true at least in part for all of the couples under consideration in this book. Collaging selections from his parents' letters in the assemblage of the narrative of their marriage, Nicolson no longer seeks to account for event—the kernel of the affair leading to a kind of resolution—but instead seeks to reveal the unfolding of a couplehood which itself became a story, through storymaking.

In her writing on the marriage of Virginia and Leonard Woolf, Natania Rosenfeld offers a way to read representations of conjugal life in Virginia Woolf's work as well as the performance by the Woolfs of their own couplehood. She notes, along the lines of Woolf's own thinking about subjectivity, that marriage creates "a single, ambivalent being. . . . Bodies cannot meld, nor brains join" (18). Yet the work of couplehood is done through "embarking on a self-created fiction," and for the Woolfs, "marriage . . . was a cowritten narrative, one work in two volumes" (Rosenfeld 18). As a number of critics and biographers, including Rosenfeld, have noted, the Woolfs deployed a variety of textualities and discourses in the creation of couplehood.[12] One of these is a shared language in which each referred to the other as a pet animal; Virginia Woolf was called "Mandril" and Leonard Woolf was called "Mongoose" (Rosenfeld 144). Readers have connected this intimate gesture to Woolf's idiosyncratic 1933 biography *Flush*, the telling of the life story of Elizabeth Barrett Browning's cocker spaniel, in order to suggest Woolf's phenomenological affinity with animals and the ways she uses it to interrogate intersubjectivity. Trekkie Ritchie Parsons makes such a move in her 1983 introduction to *Flush*, writing, "In all her loving relationships she protected herself by half pretending to be an animal" (xvi). I would like to put forth that *Flush* is also an attempt to narrativize the joining of a couple, the bringing together of "one work in two volumes." I claim that *Flush* is a couple biography. Not of Flush and "Miss Barrett" (as she is called throughout the book until her elopement), entirely, as Jennifer Mitchell argues, but of Miss Barrett and Robert Browning—Flush focalizes the biographical narrator attempting to tell the tale of the couple. Through this biographical narrator, Flush is rendered both a witness and an intimate excluded from the world of the "we" as it is made.

Flush has generally gone under-considered relative to other works in Woolf's *oeuvre*, although the development of animal studies as a field has generated opportunities for exciting new readings. Important analyses have also been offered by placing *Flush* in the context of Woolf's responses to fascism and to sexuality.[13] Most saliently, *Flush* has been read through Woolf's attempts to experiment with biography and its family resemblances to fiction. Max Saunders cites *Flush* as an exemplar of Woolf's engagement with "autobiografiction," especially ideas of (im)personality (442). In all of these interpretive fields, defining the power relations between subject and other via a critical intersectionality—human and nonhuman animals, class, politics, and sexuality—is key to grappling with the text. Yet we can also read *Flush* in the context of the sexual episteme shaping "the new biography"; furthermore, and important to our reading practice moving forward, in *Flush*, we find enacted key epistemological and ethical concerns at the heart of intimacy and intimate life writing. These interrelated concerns are three. First, the problem of how to know another life, and how to know the life of one we love before that life was joined with our own. Second, the problem of how to know another, in all their alterity, even in the midst of the deepest intimacy. Third, the problem of narrating the ontological transformation that occurs as part of falling in love and joining with another in intimacy.

Anna Snaith offers a useful recounting of Woolf's own encounters with Elizabeth Barrett Browning's poetry and the auto/biographical writing surrounding the poet, including Woolf's reading of Barrett Browning's love letters with Robert Browning and Woolf's attendance at a performance of

Rudolf Besier's 1930 play *The Barretts of Wimpole Street* (616); this is delved into further by Battershill (101). Snaith suggests that it was Besier's "focus on sensational biography" that prompted Woolf to "reclaim the writing obscured by that focus" (616). I would add that it may have prompted a different kind of biographical intervention, one aiming toward ethical reading of the subject rather than sensationalism. *Flush* functions as a couple biography on two levels: it tells the story of the relationality between Flush and his mistress Elizabeth Barrett, and, more pertinent for my purposes and the point of our focus, it relates the courtship and marriage of Barrett and Robert Browning.

Couple biographers narrate the living of parallel lives prior to encounter, that epoch when two lives are emergent but have yet to merge themselves. The separateness of each subject in the couple in the moment before their coming together is at its most pronounced; yet at the same time, the intersection demanded by the normative *telos* of the form is just over the narrative horizon. Lytton Strachey captures this in his 1928 dual biography *Elizabeth and Essex*: "When two consciousnesses come to a certain nearness the impetus of their interactions, growing ever intenser and intenser, leads on to an unescapable climax" (6). The biographer's story has already been told by the couple themselves. At the same time, however, certain aporia are inevitable. Opening chapters of couple biographies capture the story of a life before it is wedded to another, those years that can never be known to the other. Who were you before I met you? Who were you with? Who were you before our encounter changed you? These questions are posed most poignantly in another fiction with a human/animal love relationship at its core: Sigrid Nunez's novel *The Friend*. In Nunez's novel, an unnamed narrator has lost a longtime best friend, who has also been a former lover, to suicide. She takes responsibility for his Great Dane after his death and develops a deep intimacy with the dog over the course of working through her profound grief. She says, of both her friend and his dog, "It's not uncommon to wish to have known what a person you've come to love was like before you met them. It hurts, almost, not to have known what a beloved was like as a child" (170). This Levinasian problem of alterity is performed in the opening pages of a couple biography; they manifest the impossibility of possession. The past of one-half of the couple can only be narrated to the other half, and is incomplete. As readers, however, we have certain forms of access. We may not have access to the inner core of a couple's intimate life, Backscheider's innermost circle; but, via the biographer's telling, we may have access to parts of one partner's story that ever remain unknown to the loved other.

In *Flush*, Woolf enacts these aporia brilliantly. *Flush* begins with the dog's early life, prior to arriving at Wimpole Street to live with "Miss Barrett." Thus, we gain knowledge of Flush, but Miss Barrett's—and "Mr. Browning's"—early lives remain a mystery to the reader. In fact, Mr. Browning does not arrive until a third of the way through the narrative, and that very arrival is shrouded in mystery: he is "The Hooded Man," as the chapter telling of his coming into the life of Miss Barrett and Flush is titled. The early lives of each member of the couple are not told, and the limited focalized perspective of Flush—shared by the biographical narrator, but sometimes breached by that narrator's own perspective and voice—keeps us from entering fully into those lives and the intimacy that develops. Thomas Lewis in writing on the text refers to this as Flush's "angle of perception" (306); but, as H. Porter Abbott reminds us, taking *voice* into consideration alongside *perception*, both seeing and saying, helps pin down from where the narration is positioned (243). At times, the biographical narrator metaleptically intrudes into Flush's focalization, offering something like a more conventional omniscient perspective. This serves to foreground how much goes unknown, as well as the warp and woof (ha) of biographical telling, and is a heightened version of the knowledge problem inherent to all couple biographies, the first concern articulated above.

The coming together of Flush and Miss Barrett at the end of the chapter entitled "Three Mile Cross" brings forth another problem of significance, our second concern: whether the other can truly be known, and how the couple biography as a narrative form grapples with the issue of alterity. Woolf writes,

> There was a likeness between them. As they gazed at each other each felt: Here am I—and then each felt: But how different! . . . Broken asunder, yet made in the same mould, could it be that each completed what was dormant in the other? She might have been—all that; and he—But no. Between them lay the widest gulf that can separate one being from another. . . . Then with one bound Flush sprang on to the sofa and laid himself where he was to lie for ever after—on the rug at Miss Barrett's feet. (23)

Flush raises the question of whether the subjectivity of another person can be understood within the context of relationship, so close yet so distant in otherness. How can one tell the story of an intimate relationship from within, using the private language of the "we," and how can one tell the story of the "we" from outside? We may not be lacking in the capacity for speech, as Flush is depicted as being, but the deepest recesses of intimate life and interiority remain beyond the reach of language. Recall the words of Leslie Stephen from the *Mausoleum Book*: "Husband and wife . . . do not require the language of words" (90).

The third concern—the ontological transformation effected by the entering into an intimate love relationship—is the subject of the chapter entitled "The Hooded Man." It is Flush who focalizes the biographical narrative, and because of this choice in the realm of discourse, Woolf is able to make the mystery of this ontological transformation the subject of the text. In other words, because Flush, whom as we have already seen has figured the problem of intersubjectivity, is so far outside the emerging union of Miss Barrett and Mr. Browning (outside not only because of the human/nonhuman animal relationship but also because we are all outside, excluded from, the intimate union), the problem of how to narrate such a transformation, and how to access it from an outside position, is made entirely central. Once Mr. Browning's letters begin to arrive, Flush observes changes in Miss Barrett's demeanor; her altered state as manifested through embodiment is a key feature of the narrative, as Flush attempts to interpret the signs bodied forth: "Flush, watching Miss Barrett, saw the colour rush into her face; saw her eyes brighten and her lips open. . . . Flush had never heard that sound in Miss Barrett's voice before—that vigour, that excitement. Her cheeks were bright as he had never seen them bright" (55–56). For Flush, who must depend on physical perception, and the perception of the physical, to discern and apprehend internal states, these are markers of a changed relationship between himself and Miss Barrett, and the beginning of a new story. The narrator tells, "[Flush] could read signs that nobody else could even see. . . . Flush began to notice signs of change in Miss Barrett herself" (51–52). The reporting of Flush's mental activity, as Flush reports what he observes, takes over "The Hooded Man," and suggests a widening out of narrative perspective and voice. The growing disconnect in intersubjectivity between Flush and Miss Barrett is one of these "signs of change in Miss Barrett herself," and indicates the necessity of reading the narrative relationally, as well as for intermental activity. Flush is able to discern the ontological transformation "in Miss Barrett herself" in part because his relationship to her, and hers to his, has changed. Our ontological condition depends, in these texts of intimacy, on relationality; and it is the shift in this situation caused by Miss Barrett's falling in love that Flush experiences and has narrated for him, voiced through the biographical narrator.

The biographical narrator strategically uses the focalization through Flush to tell of the coming together of Miss Barrett and Mr. Browning; one phenomenological element of this perspective is Flush's experience of sound, particularly Miss Barrett's voice. There are few moments in the text where Miss Barrett's words are reported directly. Interestingly, there are a number of instances where her letters are quoted—something Flush could not know, suggesting again several layers of knowing and telling in the narrative, with a kind of metaleptic interruption of Flush's perceiving and the telling on the part of the biographical narrator. It is reported that Flush hears a change in Miss Barrett's voice as it joins with Mr. Browning's: "Now it gained a warmth and an ease that he had never heard in it before. And every time the man came, some new sound came into their voices—now they made a grotesque chattering; now they skimmed over him like birds flying widely; now they cooed and clucked, as if they were two birds settled in a nest" (60). Once again, the change in Miss Barrett is highlighted with "new" and "now," as earlier we saw the use of the word "never": now she is like this, and never before had she been like that. There are few temporal markers in "The Hooded Man," in contrast to, for instance, "Whitechapel," which tells of Flush being dognapped and places great emphasis on each terrifying day of waiting and wondering and trying to retrieve him by recording over the course of the chapter the passing of specific dates. Rather, the coming together of Miss Barrett and Mr. Browning unfolds in an ongoing present where the unfolding is understood not through time but through change in state. Time matters only insofar as "before" Mr. Browning and "after" Mr. Browning. In the telling deployed in the quoted passage, a series of figures are used to gesture toward the affect experienced by both the lovers and the confused and unhappy witness. There is "warmth" and "ease," but because they had never been there before, they are actually perceived as an unpleasant change by Flush (who seems at odds with his biographical narrator, a disconnect hinted at by word choice). For the two as their voices join, "two birds settled in a nest," one hears the delight of cooing; but for Flush, the sound must be "grotesque," and "over" him, signifying his exclusion from this new world of two. It is only when Flush realizes that if he loves Miss Barrett he must accept the presence of Mr. Browning that he is brought into this world: "We are joined in sympathy" (73).

Shortly after Flush is restored from his harrowing dognapping episode in the "Whitechapel" chapter, he realizes Miss Barrett is wearing a gold ring on her finger (103). While he does not apprehend the meaning of this signifier, the reader most likely does. The marriage of Miss Barrett and Mr. Browning is never mentioned outright; the narrator subtly gestures at it with the glimpse of the ring focalized through Flush, and the shift in referent that occurs a few pages into the penultimate chapter, "Italy," once the couple has eloped and left London: "'Flush has grown an absolute monarch and barks one distracted when he wants a door opened,' Mrs. Browning wrote" (113). This is the first time the change in name is noted, but the change in state has already occurred. Thus Woolf suggests that more is at work in the creation of a couplehood than the social niceties of convention or the ritual of a wedding. The work of making the two together, witnessed and told by Flush, has already occurred.

The theorizing and practice of relational life writing in the early twentieth century opened the way to discursive representations of intimacies which have had radical implications for how we write about love and desire. At the same time, these writings *are* constructions—and co-constructions—of the imagination, deployed intersubjectively between two people as part of a process of becoming. This collaborative work results in shared narratives that sometimes hold together, and sometimes break apart. In her introduction to the love letters exchanged between Leonard Woolf and Trekkie Ritchie Parsons—respectively, widower to Virginia Woolf and wife to one of the Woolfs' colleagues in publishing, a colleague who was also, later, one of their biographers—Judith Adamson asserts, "Every marriage is an invention with its own limitations" (xx). So we can say of form, as Caroline Levine has theorized—including narrative form and the forms of life writing. It is the work remaining to this volume to look at how those intimate inventions are made, where those limitations lie, and how they might be transgressed, as subjects in couples undertake the processes of becoming, of making a world, through narrative.

2

Worlding: Gertrude Stein and Alice B. Toklas

Gertrude Stein and Alice B. Toklas, who met in 1907 and remained together until Stein's death in 1946, are famed for their salon at the rue de Fleurus. Through their relational aesthetics, manifested in a kind of hospitality, they created a generative space in which sociability and aesthetic and relational experimentation are all intimately linked. They made a world. Their coupled world, their world of two, was integral to the making of this space, even, or especially, when, it was not visible or accessible to others. From the start of their relationship, Stein and Toklas used a shared discourse, and shared tropes, to facilitate the creation of a world, the story of two lovers making a space together, but full access to that space was governed by an inhospitality to everyone but each other. A consideration of the work of relational aesthetics, affects, and narrative storyworlding in Stein's texts "Ada," *A Book Concluding With As a Wife Has a Cow: A Love Story*, and *The Autobiography of Alice B. Toklas* and *Tender Buttons* alongside Toklas's *The Alice B. Toklas Cook Book*, will help us to further apprehend this work of worlding. Taking up the *Cook Book* as a text of mourning will lay some groundwork for our consideration of Sylvia Townsend Warner and Valentine Ackland in Chapter 3. And the closing section of this chapter, examining the afterlives of Stein and Toklas as engendered through the intimate life writing of biographers and artists adapting their lives in a variety of multimodal narrative forms—specifically Tom Hachtman's serial comic strip *Gertrude's Follies*—will enrich our sense of the work of worlding as undertaken by those outside yet invested in the arcs of the love affairs of others.

In the narrative of a couple, the final act—the one where half the pair has died and the other half is left to keep the story going (or begin a new one)—is singly authored. However, this is only one side of the frame; the other side is the life before the couple, the epoch in each of the individual lives where they run parallel until the point of intersection. The members of the couple are thus confronted with an ontological and epistemological quandary, one that I argue generates narrativity in intimate life writing: who were you before I knew you, and how does that story become part of our "we"? How does *your* story become part of *our* story?

Such a quandary originates Gertrude Stein's *The Autobiography of Alice B. Toklas*. Karin Cope tells the story of the book, which was conceived by Stein as an attempt to reconcile with Toklas after Toklas found out in 1932 about a past relationship of Stein's, occurring in 1903, with May Bookstaver, and the book that had emerged from that affair, *Q.E.D.* Toklas, apparently, was seized by a fit of jealousy, overwhelmed by a sense of being displaced in importance in Stein's life, and wounded by the revelation that Stein had had other muses; it is not hard to imagine that discovering that Stein had used another woman and another union as a source for writing would be deeply painful for Toklas. To reaffirm their relationship, Stein performed an act of validation, appropriation, possession: she told Toklas's life story.[1] Yet it is, too, Stein's life story, and it is the life story of their couplehood from the moment of encounter, their shared life in Paris, a life they built together. Shared friends are included; the past lover is deliberately not, except in the form of a "forgotten" "first piece of writing" (*Autobiography* 84–85). Stein remade the union through giving Toklas a version of her life that made Stein of primary importance, thus affirming for Toklas her primary importance in Stein's life. Cope writes, "Toklas may appear to be the satellite of Stein, but covertly, she is the architect of Gertrude Stein as anyone else may know her. In fact, the book, then, is a backhanded reassurance—and confession—that Gertrude Stein is entirely the possession of Alice B." (166). Even the practice of writing the *Autobiography* is a shared project; as Ulla Dydo notes, Toklas's hand is visible throughout the manuscript in the form of edits (*Gertrude* 539). The text opens up for both women to participate even as Stein appropriates Toklas's voice and life in order to bolster their relationship. Toklas's life *becomes* the life of the couple.

Before the *Autobiography*, however, is "Ada." A portrait of Toklas, "Ada," is the first literary portrait, portrait-in-writing, that Gertrude Stein produced. She describes the event in the *Autobiography*:

> I called Gertrude Stein to come in from the atelier for supper. She came in much excited and would not sit down. Here I want to show you something,

> she said. No I said it has to be eaten hot. No, she said, you have to see this first. Gertrude Stein never likes her food hot and I do like mine hot, we never agree about this. She admits that one can wait to cool it but one cannot heat it once it is on a plate so it is agreed that I have it served as hot as I like. In spite of my protests and the food cooling I had to read. I can still see the little tiny pages of the note-book written forward and back. It was the portrait called Ada, the first in Geography and Plays. I began it and I thought she was making fun of me and I protested, she says I protest now about my autobiography. Finally I read it all and was terribly pleased with it. And then we ate our supper. (*Autobiography* 113–14)

As in other narrative moments within Stein's work, the event being narrated is seemingly eclipsed by digressions. The event of the production of "Ada" is interrupted by Stein, voicing Toklas, talking about the food preferences of each, and communicating Toklas's definite opinion about how hot food should be served. In reading "Ada," the narrated response of Toklas is to imagine she is being made fun of; however, the emergence of pleasure in reading contributes not to the breakdown of intersubjectivity and shared experience but to greater connection: "And then we ate our supper." Such instances of pleasure are essential kernels of the Stein/Toklas emplotment and elemental to their storyworld. The telling of the "Ada" event is interrupted metaleptically by inserting the narrative present and Stein's "saying": "I protest*ed*, **she says I protest** *now* about my autobiography." Multiple temporalities (indicated in italics) and voices (indicated in bold) collide in the narrating of the "Ada" event, as do the thematics of two signal interests of the Stein/Toklas couple: writing and food, the latter of which will prove especially salient to our discussion.

In her extended reading of this scene, Anna Linzie notes "the juxtaposition and parity of food and literature, housekeeping and writing; the interplay of Stein's literary work and Toklas's domestic labor; and the subtle shifting of hierarchies and registers of authority" (14). I would argue that the digression, the sharing of the ongoing quibbles about supper leading to the reporting of Toklas's upset over suspecting she is the subject of mockery, is essential to the story of the sharing of the first portrait. As Ulla Dydo notes in her reading of "Ada," the portrait was composed shortly after Toklas joined Stein at 27 rue de Fleurus as her erotic partner and companion—her "wifie"—and the scene described in the *Autobiography* allows us access to the ways the two women shared work and life (*Stein Reader* 100). It describes an ongoing conversation—quarrel?—about the two women's preferences, a hint about their intimate life and the negotiations that are part of joining their two selves into a "we" (Linzie 16).

And, ultimately, it is telling upon telling, indicative of how storytelling, as Dydo argues, is essential to the erotic life of Stein and Toklas. The bringing together of multiple stories parallels the "join[ing]" of "hands" in the "little tiny pages of the note-book," where the two women copied the text out together (a phenomenon that recurs throughout the Stein notebooks) (Dydo, *Stein Reader* 100). Dydo writes, "Storytelling is about the intimate interaction between Toklas and Stein. Endless telling and listening to stories is the perfect writer's situation and the perfect lovers' situation, each enabling the other" (*Stein Reader* 101). In Stein, Toklas finds her ideal audience, and likewise Toklas serves that role for Stein. They each find a receptive person for their stories, a hospitality for their idiosyncrasies, and that receptivity, that reciprocity, is essential to the working of intimate narrative in erotic life. The *Autobiography* does not tell the story of the writing of "Ada": it tells the story of the *sharing* of "Ada." Integral to that story is the parallel story of the sharing of a meal, a story that recurs again and again throughout the writing of Stein and Toklas and is essential to their world (Linzie 14–16). Finally, the episode is also a narrating of Toklas's pleasure; she sets aside her protests and "was terribly pleased with it." Throughout Stein's work, we see writing serving the purpose of bringing pleasure, particularly to Toklas—Toklas, the ideal reader and narratee.

Stein's narratives often have their subjects receding into the background, only to be brought forward with a critical observation, or detail, or moment of reporting a thought, event, or instance of speech. "Ada" begins as narrative, and concludes as portrait, and it begins not with Alice B. Toklas, but with her brother and father. It begins not with an event, but with a nonevent: "Barnes Colhard [the fictionalized version of Toklas's younger brother Clarence] did not say he would not do it but he did not do it" (*Stein Reader* 101). The "it" of "he would not do it" is not immediately clear; it seems to refer to marriage, first to one girl who turns him down, and then to another girl, a rich girl marriage to whom Toklas supported. At the start, however, Toklas is outside the frame, and the first time we hear of "his sister," unnamed, is in the course of narrating that she "wrote to him that it would be a good thing," here, the "it" being marrying the rich girl. Thus Toklas, as "Ada," is a supporting player in the story of her brother's heterosexual coupling, facilitating but never visible herself.

How then can this be a "portrait" of Toklas? Once Barnes/Clarence is married, by the end of the third paragraph, he can disappear: "He had a sister who also was successful enough in being one being living. His sister was one who came to be happier than most people come to be in living. She came to be a completely happy one" (*Stein Reader* 101). Though this "one" is not named until the following paragraph, the fifth, clues exist to indicate that this sister is indeed the subject of the portrait, and that her story is the story of one who undertakes a meaningful process of becoming, who came to happiness, who came to the life well-lived, and that she came to this through love. She was one, and then, in becoming a part of "one," she "came to be" "completely happy." The pivot toward Ada/Alice hinges on becoming. "Being" is processural, and in the formulation of intimate life writing being put forth here, a beloved person can be important to that process—even if "happiness," as conceptualized and narrated as it is extensively by Stein as part of that process, is not always available, a consideration that will be significant for the discussion of some of the other figures taken up here.

At first, the sister is "successful enough," who then comes to "be happier than most people come to be," and it is "in living," in the process of living a life, that this happiness arises. The phrase "being one being living" is rich with the energy of becoming. Ada is "being one," she is "being one being," one entity who ends up being completed and happy by another, by the "hap" of encounter. Additionally, the condition of "being one" is to be "being living"; the gerund indicates process, and it also indicates that "being" and "living" are not necessarily the same thing. "One being" lives, is living as a self-contained entity that yet might connect not only through being and living but also through telling. Throughout Stein's work, to be "successful enough in being one being living," to "be a completely happy one," is the highest achievement, indeed, perhaps an imperative. This is so not only in *being* but also in *living*. To be a completely happy "one" depends on multiplicity. Stein's writing about intimate life bears the ethical weight found in Rosi Braidotti's formulation of becoming and desire, and evinces the possibility of happiness.

The sixth paragraph, the longest paragraph, focuses on the period after Ada's/Alice's mother dies and she is caring for her father. A number of keywords emerge over the course of this paragraph, and the length allows for an expansion of the text and the recurrence of the keywords such that a kind of rhythm is generated, a dynamic narrative propulsion. First, the word "then," creating narrativity through ordering of events over time as well as causality: "The daughter *then* kept house for her father and took care of her brother"; "The daughter, Ada they had called her . . . did not like it at all *then* as she did not like so much dying and she did not like any of the living she was doing *then*"; "Mostly *then* there were not nice stories told by any one *then* in her living"; "She told her father Mr. Abram Colhard that she did not like it at all being one being living *then*"; "Then every one who could live with them were dead and there were *then* the father and the son a young man *then* and the daughter coming to be that one *then*"; "The father said nothing *then*, *then* he said something and she said nothing *then*, *then* they both said nothing and *then* it was that she went away from them" (*Stein Reader* 102; emphasis mine). At first, "then" serves to order events in time; Stein as portraitist and narrator seeks to uncover the sequence of events that brought Toklas to her in Paris, a hap leading to happiness. Next, "then" functions to orient the reader in time, particularly with regard to Ada's *not* liking "being one being living"; at that moment in time, she is not herself, not the being she could be, living as she could be. Finally, "then" becomes a signifier of cause and effect as well as pointing to sequence: "Then it was that she went away from them." At that point in her life Ada/Alice moved to Paris, precipitated by discontent and precipitating the momentous change in her erotic affairs.

Along with "then," "them" is an important keyword, and one must think that Stein is playing with the similarity in sound. "Them"—father, brother, family—are other to the "one" that is Ada/Alice, and they are part of "then," the past. It is the emerging from the past, and the world of "them," that brings Ada/Alice into the world of Stein, where tenderness is possible. "Tender" is a third keyword, and is used recurrently to describe the letters Ada/Alice wrote to her father back home in California, and those he wrote in return: "The father was quite *tender* then"; "He wrote her *tender* letters then"; "He liked the *tender* letters she wrote to him"; "He wrote nothing and then he wrote again and there was some waiting and then he wrote *tender* letters again and again" (*Stein Reader* 102; emphasis mine). "Tender" is an essential word in the corpus of Stein, and the shift in the second half of the long sixth paragraph toward the repetition of "tender" is meant to show that Ada/Alice is now part of a new world where such feeling is possible.

The final paragraph of "Ada" reveals what made such feeling possible: telling and listening. "One" at the conclusion of the portrait becomes not the "one" who is "being one being living," not a solitary "one," but one who is discovered to be unique and who has discovered a unique other "one" in turn. Together these make a "one" in "we." The portrait of Ada/Alice thus becomes a dual portrait, the unnamed lover listening always: "Some one who was living was almost always listening. Some one who was loving was almost always listening. That one who was loving was almost always listening" (*Stein Reader* 102–3). "Living" and "loving" are separated by only one letter, and, for Stein, moreover, "living" has already been established as both a process of becoming and of the highest good. "One" who is "living" is also one who is loving.

A shift occurs, further, from "some one" to "that one"; this deictic shift moves us from the abstract and vague to the highly singular, a specific particularity that is part of finding and choosing intimacy. That intimacy, "living" and "loving," requires "telling": "That one being loving was then telling stories having a beginning and a middle and an ending. . . . Ada was then one and all her living then one completely telling stories that were charming, completely listening to stories having a beginning and a middle and an ending" (*Stein Reader* 103). Steinian ideas about narrative do not necessarily depend upon beginnings, middles, and endings. In fact, "Ada," ostensibly a *portrait*, not a *story*, looks more like a narrative than many other Stein texts that purport to be narratives. Indeed, it has a happy ending: "Certainly this one was loving this Ada then. And certainly Ada all her living then was happier in living than any one else who ever could, who was, who is, who ever will be living" (*Stein Reader* 103). Stein, in telling the story of her coming together with Ada/Alice, telling the importance of telling, is reaching for an arc—a beginning, middle, and ending—in order to show how the two have become *one*. "Completely listening" leads to a phenomenological and relational completeness, as well as a kind of certainty. One might see this in the repetition of "certainly," as well as the concluding phrase, which seems to echo the end of the "Gloria Patri": "As it was in the beginning, is now, and ever shall be, world without end." This "living," this "loving," is what brings happiness. Stein's narrator is able to give us access to the happiness of Ada/Alice, and the telling of the story is another instance of how telling is loving. At the same time, the form of the portrait allows for the telling of the life of the beloved, in all her lovable singularity.

The story of the couple, though, as told in *The Autobiography of Alice B. Toklas,* seems to consist almost entirely of other people comprising the Stein/Toklas network. The book is a pageant and parade of Stein's and Toklas's life in the 1920s and 1930s and the personages who moved through their salon. The deeply private world of their relationship is mostly elided. The writing of the *Autobiography* was an act of intimacy that yet in a seemingly limited sense depicts the women's intimate life together. Life writing is relational; the *Autobiography* enacts a relationality beyond the couple to, paradoxically, instantiate the centrality of the couple and their worlding process. Only the end of the *Autobiography* gestures toward that deep intimacy, the "mirroring" Georgia Johnston posits as a function of lesbian life writing:

> About six weeks ago Gertrude Stein said, it does not look to me as if you were ever going to write that autobiography. You know what I am going to do. I am going to write it for you. I am going to write it as simply as Defoe did the autobiography of Robinson Crusoe. And she has and this is it. (*Autobiography* 252)

Throughout the text, the "autobiographical" narrator "Alice B. Toklas" refers to Stein by her full name, a distancing move. Yet the final sentence of the book merges the two women: Stein has written the autobiography, it is the thing we have just finished reading, yet the thing we have just finished reading is Toklas's life, Toklas's text. The women mirror each other back to each other and to us, an ever-deepening *mise en abîme* of self-reflexive intimacy that holds us ever more at a distance.

Johnston makes the point that lesbian life writing deploys cloaking and masking as trope and device; it serves too as a mechanism to subvert heteronarratives (3). My interest in the *Autobiography* resides not only in its status as an exemplar of lesbian life writing but also in the ways it complicates our understanding of relational and intimate life writing. Stein calls *The Autobiography of Alice B. Toklas* an autobiography, but much of Stein's work as a whole demands that we question our assumptions regarding genre. Ulla Dydo notes about her "subjects," those of her portraits, "She wrote portraits of people whom her titles name, but they are not recognizable likenesses" (*Gertrude* 12). Thus, potentially at least two presumptions should perhaps be dismantled at the start: that *The Autobiography of Alice B. Toklas* is an autobiography, and that its subject is Alice B. Toklas. I propose instead that we read the *Autobiography* as the autobiography not as that of an individual but as that of a couple, of Stein and Toklas together. I propose, furthermore, that we consider the *Autobiography* not as Stein's attempt at "audience writing," at celebrity and fame, but as an experiment in intimate life writing emerging from her ongoing considerations of what constitutes narrativity.

Autobiography, like life writing and like narrative more generally, depends on some form of continuity, even when that continuity is being disrupted. Continuity over time and the ordering of the experiences of the subject shapes some aspects of readerly expectation. Our consideration of "Ada" shows that Stein, like other modernists, interrogates what we mean by life writing, by portraiture, by narrative, by telling. In "Regular Regularly in Narrative," Stein writes of the distinction between portraiture and narrative: "There is this difference between narrative and portrait a narrative makes anybody be at home and a portrait makes anybody remember me . . . a portrait and a narrative together makes it be one at a time" (*How* 229). The portrait, with its connection to remembering, and the narrative, with its connection to being in a place at a time, exist in differing relations to time, the present, and the past. Brought together, they manage both a still point and a simultaneity. Furthermore, narrative calls upon the reader to make a storyworld—to "*be at home*" in the world of the story—while portraiture calls upon the reader (or viewer) to recognize singularity. Both are at work in "Ada." We shall return to this phrase "*be at home*" in our discussion of *The Alice B. Toklas Cook Book*, and the ways the reader's desire to be welcomed into the world of the couple may indeed be refused.

I suggest, though, in addition, that we can read "one" in Stein in light of the monad she sought to create with Toklas: the portrait, the moment meant for memory, and the narrative, the "making" of bodies at home—the essential narrative of Stein and Toklas's life—together makes "it" *be* "one." Stein and Toklas's salon might be seen in light of hospitality to each other, the welcoming of each into the other's life.[2] The bringing together is an instant of creation, of making, and also of will, to make one do something. The "it" might be the two forms, and the "it" might be the couplehood, and the "it" is one at a time—not just each a discrete form, but coming together *at a particular time*, in a moment of encounter that is both singular as the instant captured by the portrait and extended over the duration and events of a narrative. *Or*, one can be a portrait, or one can be a narrative, one at a time—not both.

Ulla Dydo in her examination of Stein's writings on narrative, including *How to Write* and her lectures on narration, asserts that "Stein objects to the false coherence of chronological narrative. . . . Furthermore, chronological history breaks up continuous experience into separate events in time—plots—without immediacy and intensity. . . . Stein does not believe people are realized as cause and result. Regular narratives fail to seize identity" (*Gertrude* 146). How, then, can the work of life writing be achieved such that the experience of the subject is conveyed with "immediacy and intensity"? How can formative experiences be liberated from the logic of cause and effect? Reading the *Autobiography* through *How to Write*—specifically "Regular Regularly in Narrative"—allows us to see intimate life narrative differently, its conventions and its place in Stein's *oeuvre*. Early in the essay Stein offers what might be construed as a "definition" of narrative: "What is narrative narrative is the relation between there being there at once once and having their next not at once not once not now not merely but as much as after this which is what is placed after not before by that time not at this time how not only on their account" (*How* 226). First, narrative is *relational*, not only in terms of an ontological unit existing immediately *one time* (once) and in place (there) but also in terms of people: "having *their* next not at once," having the next thing that happens to the ontological units involved happening not immediately but later in time; and not necessarily only once, and certainly not now, as time needs to pass. Next, narrative is further defined by the relationship of one thing placed after another thing, not before, and not at this time—immediately—but at the appropriate time. Thus, narrative must consist of relationships, a being there (both an ontological unit and a process of being, as considered in the discussion of "Ada"), and a now and future (once, next, not now, not before, after) as being happens over time.

The arrangement of being over time, not necessarily enchained by the imperatives of chronology or hierarchy, is also essential to Steinian narrative. I would go further to say that we can think about intimate life narrative this way, called upon as we are to see it as narrativizing a space of encounter, becoming, multiplicity. Stein writes, "And might once in a while might it once in a while might it once in a while be not only more than there was any bettering of their chances in having changed changed to it believing that it was well arranged" (*How* 227). "Once in a while" repeats three times, enacting the telling of a narrative over time. Events do occur *once*, and then again, and then again, in a while. Additionally, narrative requires change, and arrangement:

"having changed" it was "well arranged." We might go a step further, recalling our discussion of "Ada," and suggest that change in Steinian narrative is improvement, "bettering," and we might also see that the process of narrative must require participation, the shared belief that the art of it is indeed "well arranged." All things in Stein's world are arranged: food on the table, pictures on the wall, words on the page. And, all of these arrangements depend on their arranger—Alice B. Toklas.

These arrangements, the generation of narrativity, are arousing. The word "aroused" appears several times throughout "Regular Regularly in Narrative":

> It always happened that it aroused them in the way that it was mentioned that they had their own arrangement for everything. . . . Who can now be aroused. They can by the narrative. . . . If seen two at a time there could be no difference of them reorganizing reorganizing their arrangement. . . . Who can now be aroused. They can by the narrative. . . . This will be what happens when very much as they like they are over pleased with what has happened and just like that at once. (*How* 222, 229–30)

Stein considers the role of difference in narrative, in creating distinctions among events and persons as well as distinguishing elements over time. Ultimately she envisions narrative not as predicated upon a false or artificial coherence, but in a union through arrangement. The two "seen two at a time" once they have reorganized their arrangement may be perceived to have no difference between them at all. Such a unity occurs in time, not over time but "at once." The pleasure in narrative is to be found in this unity, in the union. "Over pleased" is not a criticism of excess, but an appreciation of excess. To be aroused, to be "over pleased," to "replace one one of that one two replace two of that one there never having been two" is the aesthetic and affective purpose of narrative.

Thus when Stein says, "Who can now be aroused. They can by the narrative," the definite article "the" bears weight. "The narrative" is now not just narrative, it is *the* narrative of Stein and Toklas. Even as the narrative itself is definite, the "who," though, is elided. Were one to read the sentence "who can now be aroused" as the declarative it appears to be based on punctuation (full stop), thinking of "who" as a relative pronoun functioning as a subject, rather than the interrogative it might be based on thinking of "who" as an interrogation word despite the lack of appropriate punctuation (i.e., no question mark), one might understand this phrase to be commenting on an ontological unit, an agent, a person, who has the potential to be aroused—or who has perhaps been given permission to be aroused. At the same time, that person (Toklas?) is unnamed, an aporia. The playing with naming, with interpellation and with gaps, is a significant feature of the *Autobiography*. Perhaps, though, too, that text is "the narrative," the one that arouses, the one that makes two into one (recall Barthes's encounter): "A narrative of in union there is strength," as Stein writes (*How* 262).

The *Autobiography* is Stein's attempt to tell "in union there is strength." It is a phenomenological and relational act, as she proceeds to show the story of her life with Toklas through Toklas's eyes; and an act of empowerment, as she places the arranging of that story in the hands of the Toklas-narrator; and an act of appropriation, as she takes Toklas's story and makes it her own and that of their shared world. Sidonie Smith and Julia Watson read the *Autobiography* as relational, characterizing the book as "an act of dedicated speaking through the other that commingles the boundaries of separate identities into a shared subject" (*Reading* 36). Integral to this is the commingling of multiple narrative voices (Barros 179). Early on, the Toklas-narrator relates an episode wherein an American confesses an infatuation with Picasso's attachment Fernande: "I would, he said to Gertrude Stein, if I could talk French, I would make love to her and take her away from that little Picasso. Do you make love with words, laughed Gertrude Stein" (*Autobiography* 48). Stein's laughter may not be at the expense of the besotted American; it may be the laughter of recognition. For Stein does indeed make love with words; the work of the *Autobiography* is the work of union, of joining.

A look at the contents of the text might belie an interest in chronology seemingly at odds with Stein's writing in "Regular Regularly in Narrative": "Before I Came to Paris," "My Arrival in Paris," "Gertrude Stein in Paris—1903–1907," "Gertrude Stein Before She Came to Paris," "1907–1914," "The War," "After the War—1919–1932." The text as a whole is shaped by a recognizable chronological logic. However, what we are witnessing here is the bringing together of two separate lives. The first two chapters focus on "I" and "My," Toklas in the early part of her life, alone and then encountering Stein for the first time: "In this way my new full life began" (*Autobiography* 5). The first chapter of the *Autobiography* might be a retelling of "Ada," but the conclusion is much the same. (The very first chapter is the shortest, 921 words, only about one hundred words shorter than the portrait "Ada," which covers the same period.) The conclusion of Toklas's story is the creation of a "new full life," "happier in living than any one else who ever could," and the work of the narrative is to get us—and her—there.

The next two chapters concentrate on Stein, and are achronological: Stein in the years immediately before meeting Toklas in 1907, and then, reaching further back in time, her own "before" coming to Paris. The two women exist in parallel to each other, each having a "before." "Gertrude Stein Before She Came to Paris" is the central chapter of the book, bracketed on either side by three other chapters. This chapter is in some ways the aporia, the gap to be filled. Who was Gertrude Stein before she came to Paris? Allowing the Toklas-narrator to tell that story allows Toklas to appropriate it for herself, for her own story, thereby filling in a key epistemological gap with implications for erotic life: Who was my beloved other before they were my beloved? Not having an answer to this question holds the beloved continually in a state of otherness, of unknowability. To be able to answer the question through a narrative of union bridges this gap. The Toklas-narrator is given the ability to narrate events in which Toklas herself was not able to participate. This is a move essential to much intimate life narrative; lives running separately are construed to be parallel, their coming together predetermined, even inevitable. Thus here Stein breaks the chronology of the telling through analepsis—disrupting the temporal convention of autobiography—in order to create that narrative of union.

Even the chapter "Gertrude Stein in Paris—1903–1907," the narrative of Stein before Toklas, concludes with the interpolation of Toklas. In talking about the publication of *Three Lives*, the Toklas-narrator notes, "But this last was after I came to Paris." The Toklas-narrator—and the Stein-author—cannot help inserting her through a series of disruptions in chronology. The coming together of Stein and Toklas, the beginning of creating their life together, occurs after the problem of Stein before Toklas is resolved, in the chapter "1907–1914." This is the only chapter designated simply by a span of time. From this point forward, the text evinces an emphasis on "we"; the word "we" appears in the *Autobiography* 914 times. This span of time is shared, and despite the focus placed on people the two women knew—"Everybody brought somebody. . . . It was an endless variety" (*Autobiography* 123)—and the movement through a network of other relationships, Toklas and Stein are perpetually still, still points in the turning world, a "we." Over the course of the *Autobiography*, other changes are told: Paris during and after the war—"We once more returned to a changed Paris" (*Autobiography* 189)—friends falling out or dying, the restlessness of the postwar years. Yet there is no nostalgia, because the thing fundamental to the story, the couple, is unchanging. As shown in "Regular Regularly in Narrative," Stein's concern with time resides with thinking about events over time, events which are being over time. A lexical analysis of the *Autobiography* reveals patterns related to time remarkably like those in Stein's writing on narrative, as well as her other writing generally judged to be more "inaccessible" than the *Autobiography*. Time phrases that rely on deixis—"it was then that," "it was at this time," "it was at that time," "it was the first time," "it was about that time," "was not long after this that," "it was in these days that"—recur throughout. The Toklas-narrator has a simultaneously particular and general stance toward time, and is both within the events as they occur and distant from them. She is part of a "we," and the members of that "we" are fixed as events and time move around them.

Relationships outside the couple but integral to its existence—with Picasso, Matisse, Hemingway, the Whiteheads—serve another purpose. They create a kind of scrim behind which the intimate life of Stein and Toklas can play out, beyond the view of the reader. The Toklas-narrator says early on, "But to return to the beginning of my life in Paris. It was based upon the rue de Fleurus and the Saturday evenings and it was like a kaleidoscope slowly turning. What happened in those early years. A great deal happened" (*Autobiography* 89). The element of digression so essential to the telling in the *Autobiography* is to be seen here; the Toklas-narrator must keep directing herself "to return," because the telling of events in something like a continuous linear fashion is continually interrupted. This is because continuity does not matter; identity does (Dydo, *Gertrude* 149). Specifically, the identity, the shaping of Stein and Toklas as a "we," is the purpose, and the end, of the telling. The coupled voices make a couple (Gilmore 60). The Toklas-narrator anticipates our question—what happened—and notes that those events should be situated in time—the early years—but what matters is the what-ness, that *story* happened, and that story is the story of union. Thus the hierarchy of events to be told in autobiography is deliberately dismantled; anecdotes are relayed of "My Life with the Great" (*Autobiography* 251), seemingly to the exclusion of key events in the life of Alice B. Toklas and her being with Stein. The intimate life of the women together recedes as the Toklas-narrator follows other imperatives: "Before I tell about americans [sic] I must tell all about the banquet to Rousseau" (*Autobiography* 103). Stein is deploying the Toklas-narrator such that telling is designed to conceal.

Once Stein tells of Toklas's early life in the first chapters of the book, intimacy is told, in the second half of the *Autobiography*, through attention to Stein's writing and to the women's pleasure. These moments are few, emerging quietly almost as interruptions in what we might perceive to be the cavalcade of modernist celebrity; yet in the world of the two women, they are essential to the story they are trying to tell. The presence of "we" is quite visible in expressions of pleasure, expressions we might even read in light of Stein's claim for the arousing power of narrative. The Toklas-narrator says, "We did have a good time in England" (*Autobiography* 127); "We had an extremely good time" (*Autobiography* 127); "We were on the whole very pleased with ourselves. We had had a very good time" (*Autobiography* 128); "We had a very amusing time" (*Autobiography* 129); "We had a delightful time" (*Autobiography* 130); "We had a lovely time" (*Autobiography* 145). Pleasure is associated with and bounded by time, but pleasure is also how the Toklas-narrator understands and talks about time. Pleasure itself, arousal and the appetitive, become events themselves, perhaps as important, if not more so, as the events that precipitated the pleasure. And yet, what precisely constitutes that pleasure is withheld from the reader; the reader is let into the modernist salon, but not behind the closed doors of Stein and Toklas's intimate life.

The conclusion of the *Autobiography* is not simply Stein "offering" to write Toklas's autobiography. The offer to write the *Autobiography* is preceded immediately by *Toklas* offering to publish Stein's work: the story of the creation of Plain Edition and the first publication of *Lucy Church Amiably* (*Autobiography* 242). In reading the conclusion of the *Autobiography*, critics often emphasize the Toklas-narrator reporting: "About six weeks ago Gertrude Stein said, it does not look to me as if you were ever going to write that autobiography. You know what I am going to do. I am going to write it for you" (*Autobiography* 252). Reading Stein's "offer" to write the autobiography without Toklas's offer to start Plain Edition neglects the reciprocity catalyzing the shared project of making a life, and catalyzing the impulse to narrate that life and the shape it takes. The Toklas-narrator tells the origin of Plain Edition—her gift to Stein and her work—as part of the origin of the *Autobiography*.

Furthermore, the origin of the *Autobiography* is in Stein's designation of Toklas as "wife." As the Toklas-narrator describes the teasing that led to the creation of the book, she says Stein suggested titles like "Wives of Geniuses I Have Sat With" and "My Twenty-Five Years With Gertrude Stein." Despite the absence of an explicit "outness" in the text, these jokes are revealing (as teasing often is): from the start Toklas has sat with the wives, because she is a wife. Her couplehood with Stein is her life story—but so is it Stein's. Stein's writing of the *Autobiography* concludes with "And she has and this is it." The narrative brings us directly up to the immediate present of the couple, a couplehood and a narrative that continues beyond the frame of the text, beyond that last page. The final "it" renders the telling circular, pointing to the thing itself in the reader's hand. That "it" creates a self-contained unit, much like the couple itself.

Language, for Stein, is an embodied experience. The experience of the body, the appetitive, affective, and relational body, is the source for the two women's cocreation of the world. Further, and perhaps even more importantly, that language is shared, emerging from shared bodily experience and the ongoing engagement in a shared narrative. We can here extend our reading of Stein's writing, taking into account her continued return to the narrative of "that one to replace two of that one there never having been two of that one one of that one" (*How* 228)—a unity, a monad that comes from two coming together in a highly singular way—through attention to sex. Stein not only writes sex; sex and sexual pleasure are essential to her conceptualization of the writing process, something that will be made clear through attention to the narrative *A Book Concluding With As a Wife Has a Cow: A Love Story*.

I recognize that to assert the significance of sex to Stein's writing is to point out what is essentially a given in the study of her work. My interest in doing so here lies, first, in situating Stein within the theorizing of embodiment in intimate life narrative. Additionally, second, I am keen to show the development and workings of a shared, intimate vocabulary, one that can be used again and again over a corpus to tell the story of a couple's worlding. A number of commentators have examined the gendered discourse deployed by Stein and Toklas in their construction of their relationship—electing the use of "husband" and "wife"—and responses to this move have ranged from critical of the couple for perpetuating a patriarchal and heterosexist ideology in their coupling to, more recently, embracing Stein and Toklas for a radical performativity in their intimate life.[3] Diane Souhami, in her couple biography of Stein and Toklas, is among the latter. Souhami opens her chapter entitled "Marriage" with "Gertrude wrote a great deal about the delights of [marriage] with Alice. She called her gay, kitten, pussy, baby, queen, cherubim, cake, lobster, wifie, Daisy and her little jew. Gertrude was king, husband, hubbie, Mount fattie and fattuski"; Souhami continues, "For Gertrude and Alice love budded and flowered and grew more like a rose each day. . . . Their happiness and routines depended on no one but themselves and they were everything to each other" (111, 114). This latter point is echoed by Shari Benstock in her *Women of the Left Bank* (190). Souhami asserts that the world of Stein and Toklas could indeed be seen as a marriage; and, to our second point, uses language and tropes drawn from such Stein texts *Tender Buttons* and *Lifting Belly* to do so. In this move, we see what Ira Nadel suggests is key to "the biographer's process of understanding or interpretation of the life of his [*sic*] subject . . . [and how] we become aware of the presence of the biographer" (157). My interest lies in the discursive and narratological choices made collaboratively by the pair, as part of their lived everyday experience, their situatedness in ordinary life, as well as a broader concern with what *kinds* of stories are available to couples, as they seek to write stories from multiple and shifting positions.

A signature discursive choice in the creation of the shared intimate language between Stein and Toklas is the use of the word "cow." Before analyzing the importance of this to *As a Wife Has a Cow: A Love Story*, I would like to trace the work of Stein readers in making sense of "cow." As Anna Linzie notes, readers of Stein for decades understood "cow" to mean orgasms, particularly those given to Toklas by Stein. Ulla Dydo writes,

> Stein likens the creative act to the sexual act, associating it not only with lesbian sexuality but also with patriarchal gender. Again and again she writes notes to Toklas [found in Dydo's study of Stein's *carnets* at Yale] that describe making love to her in intimate detail and indeed *are* lovemaking. Always it is Stein, the husband, who makes love to Toklas, the wife, which culminates in her *having a cow*, or orgasm (the verb *to cow* also appears). Toklas's sexual fulfillment inspires Stein to write, which in turn represents sexual fulfillment for herself. . . . Toklas is both the beloved and the muse.

> As beloved, she induces Stein to create masterpieces of sexual fulfillment on the instrument of her body; as muse, she inspires Stein to create literary masterpieces with the instrument of language. (*Gertrude* 27–28; see also 50–51)

Dydo refers to notes made in Stein's *carnets,* the small notebooks that germinated much of her writing. Other notes, those collected by Kay Turner in *Baby Precious Always Shines* and meant singularly for Toklas, exhibit the use of "cow" as well. For instance, "An incredible sweet wife loved by an incredibly / loving husband. / He walked up and down and he did not frown / Not once. / He treated his wifey to have a cow now / At once. / That is what he did. / And now his eyes are closed with sleepiness, / And love of his wifey" (*Baby* [2918-8] 49). In a note such as this, a "cow" is given to "wifey," Toklas, by "an incredibly loving husband," Stein; the wife is given an orgasm by the husband, and "he," or Stein, takes pleasure in the giving of pleasure.

Yet the publication of Turner's edition, and certain notes appearing to have been written in a different context, raised for Stein readers the question of what is meant by "cow," an observation made by Linzie as she interrogates the critical givens around Stein and Toklas. In her introduction to the collection of notes, Turner asserts:

> More than a third of the notes demonstrate unequivocally that "cows" are Toklas's feces or stools. . . . Stein's attention to Toklas's bowel movements exemplifies, in a profound sense, the hallmark of married intimacy: one body entrusted to another, singularly known, cared for, loved, and desired in all its intricacies, all its successes—and all its failings. (25, 29)

This turn in interpretation might be seen in one note in particular: "Baby sweet Baby sweet cows and / cows baby sweet cows and cows / baby sweet cows and cows and cows // Large smelly cow" (*Baby* [2922-33] 95). What reads at first like the pleasure of orgasm in the conventional understanding of Steinian writing pivots after a break toward the scatological—its own form of pleasure.

Turner does suggest that "'cow' has a double meaning," that "it could be that she purposefully confounded the orgasmic and the excretory expulsions of Alice's body" (25, 27); however, for her, the preponderance of the evidence suggests that her revisionary understanding of "cow" should demand a new look at Stein's writing in light of the excretory. For Turner, the notes make the emphasis on the bowels explicit (27). I would like to pick up on Turner's suggestion, however, that we understand "cow" in Stein's work as having a double valence, that the bringing together of the orgasmic and the excretory is indeed called for. A reading of *A Book Concluding With As a Wife Has a Cow: A Love Story* is illuminated by such openness, echoing one of Stein's own notes: "Baby precious has a / cow baby precious now / has a cow baby precious / oh baby precious has / a precious cow now" (*Baby* [2919-6] 54). Above all, "cow" accumulates significance around creation, productivity, pleasure—the idea of the gift given freely in the ongoing hospitality of intimacy.

Recalling our consideration of *The Autobiography of Alice B. Toklas* and Steinian conceptualizations of narrative and genre, we begin with the subtitle of *As a Wife Has a Cow*: it is a "love story." What does a Stein love story look like? Ulla Dydo comments on Stein's reenvisioning of traditional narratives and love stories:

> Traditional narratives are love stories about boys and girls, men and women. Love stories conclude with weddings and marriages, which in turn mark regular, chronological family histories or patriarchal narratives. Stein rejects this narrative form. She is looking for love stories that are not determined by the patriarchy and not tied to rigid roles of gender and sexuality. (*Gertrude* 147)

As a Wife Has a Cow does not depend in any way on chrononormative time, nor on the teleological heteronormative imperative of narrative that demands an arc toward resolution. Like other Stein narratives, *As a Wife Has a Cow* calls for continuity, circularity. The nature of the wife in the story is to be loved and to be given pleasure; the story itself, the text itself, is a form of sexual pleasure and fulfillment.[4] Thus the first page of the "love story" opens with the repetition over two paragraphs of "All of it as to be a wife as a wife has a cow, a love story," and then over the next two paragraphs of "Has made as to be as a wife has a cow a love story" and "When he can and for that when he can." Recurrently, when "he," the husband (Stein), "can" "for that," he will and "has made." Possibility and creation, potential and making, and then giving between "he" and "a wife" provide the beginning of the love story.

The end of the second page and beginning of the third page attend to time and cause and effect, while eliding almost everything else: feeling, bodies, even cows. The repetition of phrases includes "not and now, now and not, not and now, by and by not and now, as not, as soon as not not and now, now as soon now now as soon, now as soon as soon as now"; "And in that, as and in that, in that and and in that, so that, so that and in that, and in that and so that and as for that and as for that and that"; and "Even now, now and even now and now and even now. Not as even now, therefor, even now and therefor, therefor and even now and even now and therefor even now. So not to and moreover and even now and therefor . . . ." The first set of repetitions seems to indicate a kind of deferral, the second and third a kind of cause and effect. As in much narrative, gaps are created to be filled, resolution is withheld and deferred in order to heighten desire, or "arousal" in Stein's discourse, and at some point, "even now," desire is achieved. What is significant is that the bodies giving and taking the pleasure disappear; the subjects of intimate life vanish.

When they reappear, it is as a "we": "We feel we feel." Throughout her writing, Stein moves from the general to the particular, to the singular. By the end of *As a Wife Has a Cow*, the "wife" is no longer "a wife" but "my wife." Stein writes:

> Happening and have it as happening and having it happen as happening and having to have it happen as happening, and my wife has a cow as now, my wife having a cow as now, my wife having a cow as now and having a cow as now and having a cow and having a cow now, my wife has a cow and now. My wife has a cow.

The narrative moves into the immediate present—"have it as happening and having it happen as happening," "my wife has a cow as now, my wife having a cow as now"—as the verb forms shift to gerunds. The final paragraph provides a form of resolution through continuous action, through ongoing becoming. Resolution here is not a coming to rest and closing off but continuous, almost rhythmic, movement. It is here we might read "having a cow," and the rhythmic repetition thereof, as waves of orgasm, or perhaps the peristalsis of excretion. The conclusion of this love story is "My wife has a cow": the achievement of pleasure, the fulfillment of desire, and the intimacy of possession.

Thus far this chapter has focused primarily on the writing of Gertrude Stein. In what respects can we then say that the worlding of the couple through shared discourse and narrative was collaborative and co-constructed? If we turn to *The Alice B. Toklas Cook Book*, written and published in 1954, after Stein's death in 1946, we see that Toklas drew deeply and in very complex ways upon their shared life and language. To a degree, the *Cook Book* may be read as a text of mourning, not unlike Leslie Stephen's *Mausoleum Book* or Sylvia Townsend Warner's *I'll Stand By You* or Don Bachardy's *Last Drawings*. Yet the *Cook Book* also perpetuates a Steinian interrogation of genre and its thematics in order to perform its work of intervening in and shaping the coupled world, even after and particularly in response to loss.

Scholars have considered the *Cook Book* in light of the intensive domestic and emotional labor performed by Toklas as part of her "marriage" to Stein.[5] As "Toklas" "writes" in the *Autobiography*, "I am a pretty good housekeeper and a pretty good gardener and a pretty good needlewoman and a pretty good secretary and a pretty good editor and a pretty good vet for dogs and I have to do them all at once and I found it difficult to add being a pretty good author" (*Autobiography* 251). The possibly Stein's pushing off of or resisting Toklas's imperative to write—Toklas's insistence that her cookbook was not an instance of authorship, not a claiming of that mantle from her deceased partner—has also been discussed by those grappling with Stein's self-proclaimed "genius" and what it means for theorizing queer or modernist authorship. Toklas famously answers the closing question in the *Cook Book*, "Alice, have you ever tried to write?" with "As if a cook-book had anything to do with writing." Is Toklas's refusal to name herself "author" a cunning subversion of Stein's project, a desire to assert an alternative form of writerly identity?

Toklas's couplehood with Stein as relayed in the *Autobiography* is her life story—but so is it Stein's. And pleasure—especially lost pleasure, and the mourning of lost pleasure and the world constituted by that pleasure—becomes the story of *The Alice B. Toklas Cook Book*. Through the embodied textuality of food writing and the genre of culinary memoir, or "gastrography" (Smith and Watson, *Reading* 148), Toklas uses the space of the *Cook Book* to engender a storyworld in order to mourn the end of her intimate life with Stein. Thus narrative in the *Cook Book* serves a commemorative purpose, and a means of working through the ontological shifts brought about by the death of the other and the passage of time.[6] As Smith and Watson suggest, "Life writing invoking food as both memory and metaphor may index a shift in subjectivity" (*Reading* 149). By reading Toklas's text through the "Food" section of Stein's 1914 *Tender Buttons*, as well as relevant excerpts from the Stein/Toklas love notes; and then considering the ways Toklas uses the narrative of the culinary memoir, or gastrography, and its recipes themselves to generate a storyworld, drawing particularly on the salient thematic of food, I propose to illuminate

Toklas's collaboration in making the "we" and her resistance to seeing that "we" breached. Toklas's writing of the *Cook Book*, looking retrospectively on her life with Stein, depends on the memory of lived experience in intimate space and time in order to maintain the "we," even after the "spouse" is gone—in this way, it is a text of mourning meant to maintain a radical relationality with the subject of the loss, namely Stein. In perpetrating this radical relationality with the subject of loss, Toklas refuses relationship with the reader. Toklas uses the form of the cookbook to conjure private pleasure in the service of elegy, repurposing tropes of hospitality that, when performed, are anything but hospitable.[7]

To start, I'd like to build on Astrid Lorange's theorizing of food in Stein's writing. Her understanding, and mine, of Stein's and Toklas's writing about food emerges from Leibnitz's and Whitehead's idea of the appetitive. (Incidentally, *The Autobiography of Alice B. Toklas* mentions extensive conversations between Stein and Whitehead during the First World War; Stein and Toklas were visiting England when war broke out, and were able to stay with Whitehead as return to France was impossible. So in some ways Whitehead's hospitality makes this reading of hospitality in Stein and Toklas available.) The appetitive is a forward-reaching, a forward movement, toward experience and perception; it is the desire for experience and perception that causes shifts in the subject and furthers forms of becoming. In Lorange's reading of this through Stein, the subject is a unity that contains multiplicities, a way of thinking about the subject that resonates with Braidotti's monad/nomad; appetition is the seeking out of experiences that might activate and transform those multiplicities, even create new ones, while the monad still remains an indivisible one. We might see this as another way of thinking about becoming, again along the lines of Braidotti, through perception and language. This is what this means for understanding Stein, according to Lorange:

> In the case of Stein, ordinary appetites evoke metaphysical appetitions. . . . For this reason, a sentence "about" food is in fact a sentence in which food is the subject of philosophical inquiry, since eating provides quite an explicit example of how entitities come to be in relation with, or come to occupy, or come to be occupied by, other entities. (81)

Writing about food thus becomes a way of writing about the body, and writing about the reaching forward and reaching out for experience and perception that formulates desire.

The "Food" section of *Tender Buttons* provides insight into what this language of appetition looks like, what it looks like to write bodily experience and the reaching out for sensation and perception, and how Stein's discourse shaped a shared experience of the world for herself and Toklas. *Tender Buttons* consists of three sections, "Objects," "Food," and "Rooms." "Food" is made up of titled prose poems, some of which are only a sentence; all of the titles or headings refer to food or meals (but not all the writing always seems to do so directly or explicitly). Interpolated throughout the food signifiers are lines evoking togetherness, separation, connectedness, pleasure, "intimate and private metonymic signification" (Garland 43). For instance, from "Roastbeef," which Sarah Garland characterizes as evincing "a bittersweet lexical field": "There are bones and there is that consuming. The kindly way to feel separating is / to have a space between. This shows a likeness" (38); "Bargaining for a little, bargain for a touch, a liberty, an / estrangement, a characteristic turkey" (39). Likeness and difference are essential concepts in Stein's thinking on narration. "Roastbeef," like other sections of *Tender Buttons*, offers up the creation of a storyworld via shared consuming as two distinct persons come together. The chronology of consuming—bones and then "that," or "that person" "consuming"—is reversed, a retrospective kind of pleasure. The space between two which indicates separateness is actually a tenderness, because it allows for the revelation of sameness and a reaching toward. Further in "Roastbeef," the negotiations that are part of intimate life are on display: "bargaining," bargaining for physical contact, for freedom, for separateness.

In lines later in the text, from "Apple," Stein offers a kaleidoscopic swing through what might be on the table, in the kitchen: "Apple plum, carpet steak, seed clam, colored wine, calm / seen, cold cream, best shake, potatoe, potatoe and no no gold / work with pet, a green seen is called bake and change sweet / is bready, a little piece a little piece please" (48). While the realm of the kitchen, of the domestic, is often seen as being that of Toklas's, as cooking was one of the many domestic arts and labors for which she was responsible, here the work with food is interrupted by Stein—"work with pet"—as she seems almost to be a companion in baking, baking which brings change (much like narrative) and which can also bring pleasure (much like narrative) should the beloved choose to give a piece.

What I find here as well are images and associations, reaching out while also resisting sentiment. I see the use of "please" throughout "Food" as a signifier of desire: wanting to please, and also expressing need. It is an expression of appetite, of desiring to fill emptiness with perception, with sense—even as language itself seems emptied of "sense." Stein writes in "Salad Dressing and an Artichoke": "Please pale hot, please cover rose, please acre in the red / stranger, please butter all the beef-steak with regular feel faces. / It was please it was please carriage cup in an ice-cream, / in an ice-cream it was too bended bended with scissors and / all this time. A whole is inside a part, a part does go away, a hole is red leaf" (59). The sexual language that is so much a part of constructing the story of the everyday world of Stein and Toklas is present, and is also essential to theorizing Steinian narration as comprising likeness/difference and separateness/togetherness. Was it the sitting together and eating salad dressing and an artichoke that prompted this moment of language? The lines begin with the transitioning of color from pale to rose to red, as one might imagine the rising of desire, the stages of arousal. For Stein, narrative prompts arousal, generates arousal, and is structured by arousal; here she seems to be narrating arousal. "Bended with scissors" is an image conjuring separateness as well as joining, as does "a whole is inside a part"—the whole that is Stein and Toklas is inside each of them as a part. The play on "whole" and "hole," a "hole is red leaf," may very well refer to the vagina here, the "hole" that makes the two whole.

Margueritte Murphy in her work on Stein has reviewed cookbooks published between 1890 and 1912 and found remarkable similarities between the paratactic style of the cookbook and Stein's work in *Tender Buttons* (391); Sarah Garland, too, reads the *Cook Book* alongside *Tender Buttons*, and also finds similarities between that latter text and cookbooks (37–38, 40). Toklas says in a 1953 letter to Harold Knapik, as she was collecting recipes from friends for her cookbook, "Recipes are just as symptomatic as anything else of the person from whom they come and Gertrude liked to say that any and everything was symptomatic" (*Staying* 277). The lines from *Tender Buttons* are symptomatic of a preoccupation integral to the "we" created by Stein and Toklas, symptomatic of Stein herself but also of the unit.

Stein's language, as Murphy points out, may owe much to the recipes Toklas read in the cookbooks given to her by Stein every Christmas (Souhami 231). It is not simply that Stein is preoccupied with the appetitive, the subject reaching out to experience. It is that Stein *and* Toklas share this preoccupation: in the making of their "we" and their mutual becoming, they came to conceive of themselves as a *one*, a unity, an indivisible unit. Stein and Toklas thought of themselves as a monad, a unified being cocreated through appetition, and that monad was emptied out with the death of Stein. This loss led Toklas to seek out and regain the appetitive through memory—not a reaching forward and out but a reaching back—in the *Cook Book*. In writing the *Cook Book*, Toklas deliberately chooses a language cocreated by herself and Stein, in order to commemorate the world they created. Rather than the *Cook Book* emerging from what Linzie calls a "negativity" (145), the not-writing of an autobiography, the *Cook Book* deploys food in a language of memory and the affects. At the same time, the position of Toklas in relation to the reader and the work of generating a storyworld is ambivalent, even resistant. The expressions of hospitality that are essential to the forms of cookbook and culinary memoir are in some ways undermined—rendered *inhospitable*—by Toklas and her grief. She writes,

> When treasures are recipes they are less clearly, less distinctly remembered than when they are tangible objects. They evoke however quite as vivid a feeling—that is, to some of us who, considering cooking an art, feel that a way of cooking can produce something that approaches an aesthetic emotion. What more can one say? . . . To return to our muttons. (*Cook Book* 100)

Toklas here does not talk of *food*; she talks of *recipes*, textual artifacts that point to the embodied pleasures of cooking and eating but, without the making and sharing, go unfulfilled. She acknowledges that feeling is more powerful than memory, and that feeling cannot be entirely articulated. Without memory and thus narrative, and without the articulation of feeling, the reader is left on the outside of Toklas's experience: "Some of us . . . what more can one say?" Toklas suggests that cooking produces an "aesthetic emotion," while also resisting the turn toward aesthetic relationality.

Karin Cope has made the point that Stein writes of mirroring, joining, and experiencing oneself in the body of the other, particularly in her collection of lesbian erotic poetry *Lifting Belly*. Being with the lover prompts other kinds of appetites. This is clear in the love notes written by Stein to Toklas and left around their apartment; these notes, already mentioned elsewhere in this chapter, evince a private language in which food plays an important role. In her introduction to the notes Turner makes the point that "Theirs was a marriage of total immersion in each other" (35). As one note says,

"Baby we *is* one / Baby we *are* so happy to be one" (*Baby* 2920-33; emphasis mine). The monad, the unity, of Stein and Toklas privileges the appetitive impulse, manifest, as Lorange puts it, in appetite. Stein writes in a series of other notes, "I say bless her night and day asleep and awake / sitting by the fire or making cake" (*Baby* [2920-22] 60); "But his wifey oh his wifey is good / And she is wooed. / By hubby as food and indeed / as everything" (*Baby* [2921-16] 85); "Sweet is sweeter than / peach preserve tomatoe / preserve or honey, Sweet / is sweeter than butter" (*Baby* [2923-3] 103) These notes bear language evocative of the language in *Tender Buttons*, in its associative and sensory nature. The notes reverberate with essential thematics and preoccupations central to the relationship, manifesting embodied experience, corporeal sensuality, and the affects of desire.

What might have been plenitude, pleasure, a shared sense of the appetitive in Stein's texts, and in the everyday notes that formed the text and texture of Stein and Toklas's domestic life, is rendered emptiness in the *Cook Book*. Immediately after Stein's death, Toklas wrote to Carl and Fania Van Vechten, "And oh Baby was so beautiful. . . . And now she is in the vault at the American Cathedral . . . and I'm here alone. And nothing more—only what was. You will know that nothing is very clear with me—everything is empty and blurred" (*Staying* 4). In authoring the cookbook as a form of intimate life writing, Toklas remembers, commemorates, and works through desire and absence; appetition becomes retrospective, and access is closed off. Toklas does provide recipes, a form which is in some ways singular and specific, but also iterative and recursive. Each iteration can conjure up the memory of another time the recipe was made and the meal was eaten. In Toklas's telling, these instances transform the individual through perception but also remind us that those instances were shared, generating an intersubjective space. Recipes are desire deferred and becoming: one moves forward through the making toward fulfillment. Here, however, the recipes are imagined and remembered moments of retrospective desire. More than one commentator has observed that many of the recipes in *The Alice B. Toklas Cook Book* are unmakeable.[8] They serve another purpose.

Toklas seeks to remedy the lack with an appetitive text reminiscent of Stein's own, but can only do so through memory, not as the "movement (or striving) of desire" toward *new* perceptions (Lorange 75). In Toklas's hands, the appetitive text is not a reaching out or forward but a continually recursive and retrospective look *back*; that is where desire lies. The prefatory note, "A Word with the Cook," gives some indication of the purpose of "mingling recipe and reminiscence":

> Partly, I suppose, it was written as an escape from the narrow diet and monotony of illness, and I daresay nostalgia for old days and old ways and for remembered health and enjoyment lent special lustre to dishes and menus barred from an invalid table, but hovering dream-like in invalid memory. (*Cook Book* n.p.)

The reflection on the mental activity of nostalgia, of memory, makes clear for Toklas the connection to the body, to corporeal and sense experience. The appetitive here—desire for the experience of dishes—is thwarted—barred from the table—and can only be found in memory—remembered health and enjoyment, dreamlike in invalid memory. The body here is cast in terms of disease, in the dis-ease of loss, rather than the sweetness and pleasure of Stein's writing.

The first mention of Gertrude Stein by name in *The Alice B. Toklas Cook Book* is toward the end of the second chapter, "Food in French Homes," around twenty pages in. Up to that point, the only gesture toward this most significant person is in the use of "we." A passing mention of the Second World War is included at the start:

> The crowded continent of Europe on which wars are fought inevitably suffers more privations than *we* do. Restrictions aroused our American ingenuity, *we* found combinations and replacements which pointed in new directions and created a fresh and absorbing interest in everything pertaining to the kitchen. (*Cook Book* 4; emphasis mine)

Here the first use of "we" is directed toward Toklas's American audience: Americans do not understand the deprivations of war, and I count myself among Americans right now as I address my readers. The second, however, refers to Toklas and Stein. Furthermore, the memory of seeking new ways of doing things in the kitchen—Toklas's particular "genius," as noted by Anna Linzie—is transformed into a shared appetitive moment: "new directions," "fresh and absorbing interest in everything pertaining to the kitchen."

This first mention of Stein is in the context of "an unusual lunch in an unusual setting" (*Cook Book* 23). Toklas proceeds to describe a *plein-air* "Gargantuan feast," with fish and ducks roasted over an open fire, before noting that there had been so many meals in so many French homes that they began to seem "indistinguishable" (*Cook Book* 25). This establishes Toklas's priorities in composing the cookbook. She seeks not to share tips for homemakers or the basics for everyday dishes. She is seeking to conjure the extraordinary, the intensely experienced as it manifests itself even in ordinary life. Her chapter focusing on American dishes is presented in the context of Stein and Toklas's visit to America in 1934–35, which she refers to as "the great adventure" (*Cook Book* 123), and about which she says, "I realized that the seven months we had spent in the United States had been an experience and adventure which nothing that might follow would ever equal" (*Cook Book* 135). For Stein and Toklas, the reaching out for experience is intimately linked with food, and for Toklas therefore food plays an essential role in the writing of that life and the commemorating of their creation of intersubjective space, their coupled world.

Dishes that are central to Toklas's experience prior to Stein are recast within their intersubjective intimate project. She writes in the chapter "Dishes for Artists,"

> When in 1908 I went to live with Gertrude Stein at the rue de Fleurus she said we would have American food for Sunday-evening supper. . . . So I commenced to cook the simple dishes I had eaten in the homes of San Joaquin Valley in California—fricasseed chicken, corn bread, apple and lemon pie. . . . At Thanksgiving we had a turkey that Hélène the cook roasted but for which I prepared the dressing. Gertrude Stein not being able to decide whether she preferred mushrooms, chestnuts, or oysters in the dressing, all three were included. The experiment was successful and frequently repeated; it gradually entered into my repertoire, which expanded as I grew experimental and adventurous. (*Cook Book* 29)

As part of coming to conceptualize the unity that is the two women's relationship, Toklas brings her experience into the kitchen and to Stein's table. The reaching back to her own singular past becomes a moment of appetition, as experiencing what she has already experienced becomes itself a new experience. And, again, we see the word "adventure"; here, Toklas remembers moments of appetition, of new experience, as well as of appetite, and reflects on how food brought her to her own new and shifting multiplicities, her own becoming, within the world of the relationship.

The *Cook Book* ends with Toklas recalling the end of their time at Bilignin, the country house they occupied during the summer and into the fall from 1929 to 1943; the chapter, "The Vegetable Gardens at Bilignin," focuses on Toklas's extensive gardening, as well as her canning and preserving (recall the lines from one of Stein's love notes). The fact that this sad leave-taking occurred during the war goes unmentioned aside from a reference to "the state of the world":

> Our final, definite leaving of the gardens came one cold winter day, all too appropriate to our feelings and the state of the world. A sudden moment of sunshine peopled the gardens with all the friends and others who had passed through them. Ah, there would be another garden, the same friends, possibly, or no, probably new ones, and there would be other stories to tell and to hear. And so we left Bilignin, never to return. (*Cook Book* 280)

Toklas concludes the cookbook with remembering that in that moment she could still imagine new experiences, new perceptions—new friends and stories—that the appetition shared by herself and Stein was still within reach. As the war goes unmentioned, so does what prevented the ongoing fulfillment of those desires: the death of Stein. The fruitful space of the gardens, the plenitude of that home—a house they acquired "ecstatically" (*Cook Book* 94)—dissolves in the backward gaze. Thus we might read Toklas's closing comment—"As if a cook-book had anything to do with writing"—as simultaneously desperate and dismissive. Writing is the only way to go back to those shared experiences, but it is in some ways so woefully inadequate.

Let us return to the point about the unmakeability, the unachieveability, the unrealizability, of Toklas's recipes. They do indeed serve another purpose—that of conjuring, of commemoration—but that purpose is also undermined. Both Stein and Toklas's writing of couplehood play with the boundary between accessible and inaccessible. As we have seen with *Tender Buttons*, Stein uses shared language and images to facilitate the creation of a storyworld, the story of two lovers making a space together, but never permits entirely full access to that space, thereby fuzzying our storyworld work. Likewise, Toklas's reminiscences depict meetings and shopping trips and managing servants, but we are given no access to what happens at the table. Toklas uses the performance of hospitality so integral to the genres of cookbook and culinary memoir, as well as a language foundational to her intimate life with Stein, in order to create a space that is actually inhospitable to the reader. In seeming to extend an invitation to the reader, Toklas withdraws from relationship. The cookbook commemorates the couplehood lost with Stein's death through an intimate archive of recipes (many of which are impossible to recreate), as well as reenacts retrospectively the modernist idyll of their salon, in order to close off readerly access to closeness, to intimacy, to hospitable space. Stein in "Regular Regularly in Narrative" writes that "a narrative makes anybody be at home." Not so in Toklas's narrative of the loss of Stein. We are invited in, but only so far.

What might be clear at this point is that forms of intimate life narratives might be seen as simultaneously transgressive, in that they explore areas of desire and sexuality not meant to be seen or spoken by others, and conservative, in that the couple is reified through the workings of the form. This is made especially visible in the couple biography, the constraints of which shape how we come to view narratives of couplehood (cf. Levine). My particular thrust here is how biographers read and reinscribe the texts of intimate lives. Put simply: How do we receive and respond to the writing of a private life, an epistemological and interpretive act that demands we read something that is founded on the impulse to deny access to outsiders?

Janet Malcolm's own dual biography of Stein and Toklas, *Two Lives*, seeks to (re)construct their coupled world from the overt and limited perspective of the outsider/reader, bringing intimacy into visibility by showing all the ways Stein in particular attempts to render it invisible.[9] Malcolm makes the point that Stein's unintelligibility is part of her impulse to textualize the "I": "Even the most hermetic of her writings are works of submerged autobiography. The key of 'I' will not unlock the door to their meaning—you need a crowbar for that—but will sometimes admit you to an anteroom of suggestion" (*Two* 38). The biographer takes as her work here the rendering and opening up of suggestion. For Malcolm, it would seem that more than many people, Stein understood the impossibility of representing intimacy, and weaves words around those private spaces in a scrim meant to keep outsiders firmly out. Malcolm's reading of Stein is a project of pulling back that curtain.

Thus she retells the story of the May Bookstaver incident already described. She writes, after the inclusion of the famous photograph by Man Ray of Stein and Toklas at home (itself a significant artifact of a peculiarly public intimacy of a piece with the David Hockney painting of Christopher Isherwood and Don

Bachardy discussed in Chapter 4, and the various representational artifacts collected from the Sylvia Plath/Ted Hughes marriage discussed in Chapter 5):

> The photograph is a kind of parody of the conventional society portrait of a husband and wife at home—it shimmers with the genre's sense of appearances being kept up and things not being said. The word "lesbian" was never publicly uttered by either of them about their relationship—as it was the custom of the day not to utter it. But the intensity of their love is documented . . . in one extraordinary instance, by a piece of literary vandalism. (*Two* 47)

Malcolm is writing not only of the genre of the husband/wife portrait; she is right to denote it as such, but wrong to call it "parody," given Stein's and Toklas's commitment to the conjugal roles they established for themselves (see again Hockney on Isherwood and Bachardy). She is writing of the couple biography itself, where one sifts through incomplete pieces of information, multiple perspectives and voices, an archive of uncertainty (points raised in her *The Silent Woman* as well, as we shall see). Things may have been said or not said, and what appeared in public may be quite different from what occurred behind closed doors. How are we to read what remains?

Part of Malcolm's reading Stein is to grapple with the writing and rewriting of the couple in text. In the *Autobiography*, Stein has Toklas perform this recollection:

> She [Gertrude Stein] wrote a short novel. The funny thing about this short novel is that she completely forgot about it for many years. She remembered herself beginning a little later writing the Three Lives but this first piece of writing was completely forgotten, she had never mentioned it to me, even when I first knew her. She must have forgotten about it almost immediately. (*Autobiography* 84–85)

This is, of course, *Q.E.D.*, the discovery of which sparked the creative atonement of the *Autobiography*. Stein accounts for this work that so wounded Toklas by telling Toklas "she must have forgotten it almost immediately," and by making Toklas say it so that she must acknowledge her own primacy in Stein's life. (Note that the word "forget" and its variations appear three times.) Malcolm uses the passage in the context of trying to figure out why Stein made strange and "disimproving" revisions to her *Stanzas in Meditation* (Malcolm 59), written the same time as the *Autobiography*, in 1932.

More importantly, she uses the passage—her reading of the passage—to come to terms with the covering and uncovering of the couple's life. After consultation with Ulla Dydo, Malcolm learns not only that the *Autobiography* was published to perform a public reconciliation with Toklas, intimated in the quoted passage and mentioned earlier, but that Toklas forced a private penance on Stein as well. The year 1932 was the moment of Toklas learning of Stein's past lover, as both Cope and Souhami point out, and Toklas made Stein excise all incidents of the word "may" from *Stanzas in Meditation*. Malcolm interviews another Stein scholar, Edward M. Burns, and records him saying, "The manuscript tells a terrible story. The force with which these words are crossed out. The anger with which this was done. Some of the slashes go right through the paper" (63). Toklas is read here as forcing Stein to erase a version of her pre-couple past, rewrite a new one in the *Autobiography*, and construct a present for their couplehood that places her at the center. Toklas appears, in Malcolm's telling, to insist that her partner has no past but the originary moment of their encounter; the life that ran parallel to hers before that crucial moment of intersection no longer exists.

Malcolm's *Two Lives* is not only a reading of Stein and Toklas's couplehood, lives separate but shared, dual and joined. It is a meditation on the problem of reading and writing intimate lives; it is a consideration of the challenge facing the biographer. She asks, "What does one know about other people's intimate lives?" (*Two* 63)—a question that emerges again in her mediation of Plath and Hughes life writing narratives, *The Silent Woman*. Later she answers her own question: "The instability of human knowledge is one of our few certainties. Almost everything we know we know incompletely at best" (*Two* 186–87). As Malcolm notes, Stein both invites and disinvites the outsider from reading her life, as does Toklas. The coupled, shared narrative is not always one in which others can "be at home."

It is Stein and Toklas's intimate life that Tom Hachtman takes as his subject in *Gertrude's Follies*, a serialized comic strip which ran in the *Soho Weekly News* in 1978 and then intermittently until 1982 in *National Lampoon* (under the editorship of cartoonist Sam Gross), *The Advocate*, and several alt-weeklies in New York and Los Angeles. *Gertrude's Follies* is clearly influenced by the underground comix of the late 1960s and early 1970s, and emerged from Hachtman's own response to the gay liberation movement. In an interview, he explains, "I was just thinking about how important it was for me to be living where I was—on Sixth Avenue between 27th and 28th Street in NYC. . . . The Gay Pride Parade used to go up Sixth Avenue and I know that this spectacle made me think about doing a comic strip with gay characters" (n.p.). Comix such as Hachtman's were in direct contravention of the "Comics Code," a set of standards established by the Comics Code Authority. First created in 1954 in response to the perceived dangers of representing sex, violence, drugs, crime, and horror themes, the code also sought to censor depictions of homosexuality. Part C, "Marriage and Sex," seeks to ensure, first, that "illicit sex relations are neither to be hinted at nor portrayed," and, then, states that "sex perversion or any reference to same is strictly forbidden" ("Comics Code"). A 1971 revision to the code loosened the restrictions on representations of violence, drugs, crime, and horror—but kept all the restrictive and censorious language related to sexuality. Comix like *Gertrude's Follies* circumvented the code via distribution through small press and alt-press publishers; since they operated outside conventional distribution methods, they were not required to seek the seal of approval from the Comics Code Authority.

Hachtman's strip was well received at the time of publication and beyond, so much so that his work was included in the 2011–12 exhibition *Seeing Gertrude Stein: Five Stories*, held by the Smithsonian's National Portrait Gallery. *Gertrude's Follies* presents a riotous view of Stein and Toklas's life together, one heavily infused with the ethos of the counterculture. (Naturally, pot brownies play a significant role.) The square panels, usually the 9–12 per page typical for comics layout, are crammed with wordplay, references to popular culture and modernist art and literature, and visual puns. Stein is depicted as rotund and playful, while Toklas is all angles (and looking not unlike the cross-dressing Corporal Klinger, played by Jamie Farr, from the television sitcom *M. A. S. H.* [1972–83]). They are surrounded by fixtures of Stein's salon—Picasso is a central recurring character—and their celebrity and social network form the basis for much of the plot as well as the gags. *Gertrude's Follies*, however, is worth consideration in light of our attention to how those engaged in forms of life narrative intervene in intimate worlds, generating storyworlds that extend the original boundaries of the "we." Despite Hachtman's being drawn to the comic potential of drawing Stein's celebrity, the couplehood of Stein and Toklas, including an exuberant celebration of their lesbian love, their queerness, is at the heart of his work.

Hachtman picks up on the two women's pet names for each other; throughout, Stein is "Baby" and Toklas is "Pussy." Indeed, several strips are devoted to the infamous episode, told by Ernest Hemingway in *A Moveable Feast*, wherein Hemingway overhears Stein in another room pleading with Toklas—"No, Pussy, no"—and is so horrified by the revelation of their lesbian (and possibly, he imagines, sadomasochistic) relationship that he flees 27 rue de Fleurus, never to return.[10] My interest here is in Hachtman's excavating of Stein's and Toklas's intimate life, separate and distinct from gossip and celebrity, and the ways in which he subverts Hemingway's tale and redeploys it in a ludic celebration of queerness, as well as to play with Stein's and Toklas's stature as icons of gay domesticity.

Over the three episodes devoted to the "no, Pussy, no" story, a row of small thumbnail panels occupy the very top of the page over the title panel. These depict Hemingway's overhearing of Stein and Toklas and his horrified response. Hemingway's panic over Stein and Toklas's lesbianism is thus placed at the margins, and the story becomes the two women bewildered at his naïveté, what might in fact be read as his homophobia. The second strip devoted to the episode begins, after the thumbnails, with a row of panels depicting Hemingway rushing through the streets of Paris in a state of panic. Each of these panels includes a narrative text box alternating the voices of Stein and Toklas commenting on the action in the panel: (Toklas) "Words from under Gertrude's door . . ."; (Stein) "keep ringing in his ears . . ."; (Toklas) "words he never heard before . . ."; (Stein) "confirm poor Papa's fears." A thought bubble follows Hemingway over the course of the panels: "Pussy no ringy dingy pussy no bong bong pussy pussy no no pussy no pussy no bing bing." All of the thought and voice bubbles depicting "no, Pussy, no" are inked in pink—a clear moment of visual play—and Hachtman draws increasingly on Steinian style as Hemingway's panic increases, bringing together sexuality and textuality, and capturing the melding of body and word. Perhaps it is this very melding that prompts panic, as well. Hachtman exploits a polyvocality here, as the two women's voices are brought together and mirrored in rhyme.

Halfway through this second strip, the narrative pivots to Stein and Toklas. The final panel showing Hemingway includes a voice bubble as he says to himself, "All these years . . . all these years . . . I didn't know they were . . . they were . . . GAY!" The subsequent panel, the last in the row, has Stein leaning out of the panel border, her finger pointing into the Hemingway frame and overlapping into the Hemingway panel, with the voice bubble: "Is THAT why he ran away?" The remainder of this strip, the final two panels, presents Stein and Toklas reflecting on Hemingway's homophobia in rhyming couplets. The series of strips devoted to the "no, Pussy, no" episode culminates in a panel depicting Toklas, Picasso, Henri Matisse, F. Scott Fitzgerald, Telly Savalas, Sherwood Anderson, Carl Van Vechten, and Stein doing the cancan and singing "No Pussy no pussy no no pussy." Here, the men in the Stein/Toklas circle join with the two women in something like a celebratory and (following Coffman) homosocial show of support (and a joke at Hemingway's expense). In Hachtman's vision, Stein and Toklas's lesbianism is known among their intimates, and one who refuses to see it, or accept it, must be expelled from the network.

Prior to this spectacle, one which both comments on Stein's celebrity and offers a laugh for the culturally savvy reader, three rows of panels depict Stein and Toklas in a domestic setting (Figure 2.1). The dangerous lesbians who set Hemingway off in a panic are actually sitting quietly reading, writing, and doing needlepoint.

Figure 2.1 Panels from *Gertrude's Follies*, 1979. Copyright Tom Hachtman.

An alternative narrative for "no, Pussy, no" is posited, a possible world of equal truth value. Over the course of each panel, Toklas asks Stein a series of questions, all answered with "no, Pussy, no": "Have you seen my gloves?"; "Wanna help with the trash?"; "Bananas on your cereal?"; "Been to the roller disco?"; "Free hang glider lesson at the Eiffel Tower?" This staging of domesticity provides a counter-narrative to the story of Stein's celebrity, and, albeit with humor, privileges the two women's intimate life. The punchline is the final of these panels: Toklas asks, "Did you cancel the big dance number?" and as Stein responds, "Pussy nooo!," she opens the door to the salon to reveal all of the men we see at the end. Hachtman thus reclaims the "no, Pussy, no" story for Stein and Toklas, a move which accomplishes two significant purposes. First, it undoes the appropriation of Stein's modernist celebrity performed by Hemingway in *A Moveable Feast*. Second, and more importantly for our work here, it counter-narrativizes Stein and Toklas's lesbian relationship, their queerness, opening that world up to us by enclosing it in intimate space.

The final strip of *Gertrude's Follies* leaves the two women alone together in Venice. Unlike many of the other panels over the course of the strip, the nine devoted to a stay in Venice are uniformly square but open and uncluttered, inked with a rosy pink wash. Stein and Toklas are drawn as playfully sexual, and the strip ends with three panels over which Toklas draws blinds closed. The final panel depicts the blinds fully closed, with a voice bubble saying "mmmm" in red ink. For all of the bawdiness of the strip as a whole, this final moment is surprisingly, sympathetically, and quietly intimate, leaving the reader outside the private world of the women.

In this last instance, in this afterlife for Stein and Toklas, we see Hachtman privileging the private, thus reinscribing—and reaffirming—the worlding of the two. In this coupled world of Stein and Toklas, things and beings very much come to exist through love. And those things and beings, and thereby the world, cease to exist in such rich plenitude through the catastrophe of loss.

3

Encounter and Loss: Sylvia Townsend Warner and Valentine Ackland

Biographers may wish to put the stories of couples—all couples—into conventional containers, imagining that no matter the idiosyncrasies of individual couples, there is only one emplotment. As numerous theorists of auto/biography have argued, genre bears the weight of ideology; Lauren Berlant's critiques of intimacy come to mind when thinking of relational auto/biography. Subjects such as Sylvia Townsend Warner and Valentine Ackland are in excess of a conventional container. We find instead an affective overspill that manifests in the compulsive creation of intimate life writing texts in a multiplicity of forms.

Warner and Ackland came together as a couple in 1930, and remained together until Ackland's death in 1969; Warner lived on until 1978. Ackland had other lovers, but none were as disruptive or as damaging as her affair with a younger American writer and activist, named Elizabeth Wade White, whom the two women met through their work in support of Spain during that country's struggle against fascism in the 1930s. The affair finally petered out in the early 1950s, but Warner and Ackland's relationship never entirely recovered. The narrative practice, the polymorphous discursivity, shared by Warner and Ackland bears resemblances to that deployed by Sylvia Plath and Ted Hughes, particularly in the recognition of the failures of the emplotment of intimate life, and gaps engendered through the reinscription of that emplotment in biographical writing. We might apply Sarah Churchwell's words about Plath and Hughes just as well to Warner and Ackland: "They used writing to conduct their relationship" (qtd. in Clark 5). In the present chapter, we will find that Warner and Ackland inaugurated their couplehood in part with the jointly produced collection of poems *Whether a Dove or Seagull*, an expression of their hope, ultimately to be thwarted, that the writing of both together would shape their coupled life mutually and reciprocally. Warner's greater success as an author in part caused the grief over this failed hope, articulated by Ackland in her memoir *For Sylvia* as well as in the diaries available in her and Warner's archives. *I'll Stand By You*, which captures the arc of the couplehood including the highly fraught period of the White affair in 1949–50; letters among Warner, Ackland, and White; and Warner's published diaries all show Warner in particular mourning the loss of mutuality brought about by Ackland's affair, especially the loss of Ackland's erotic focus.[1]

More attention has been paid in recent years to Warner's novels, although, as Janet Montefiore has pointed out, her poetry and short stories remain understudied ("Scholership" 789). With this greater attention to the novels has come further consideration of the life writing that constellates around Warner as well as Ackland, along with what Melanie Micir, drawing in part on Ann Cvetkovich, has termed their "intimate archive": "The accumulation and organization of material about the life of a partner where there are no immediate plans to publish or otherwise make public this material" (120).[2] What of the roles of biographers and editors as narrators, curators, interlocutors, particularly as they enact discursive and narrative practices or deploy tropes that reverberate with and route through the intimate texts they make public and use to generate their own? In her own biography of Sylvia Townsend Warner, Claire Harman writes of Warner and Ackland, "Though their lives may have joined up along their lengths, and remained so joined, their breadths remained oddly different and unknown and, like all wise lovers, they left a little strangeness between them, a little privacy" (*Sylvia* 113). Harman deliberately takes up language used by Valentine Ackland in that subject's own writing about her couplehood with Warner, a kind of "joining up," while also acknowledging the mystery inherent to intimacy. There are many such illustrations of the ways in which biographers use the discourse of the couples themselves to shape the writing of their lives from the outside. Recall the words of Ira Nadel, wherein through the selection and deployment of such discourse the biographer interprets and becomes present (157). The discursive performances of these subjects are appropriated as a way to enter their world, even as we are not entirely at home.

My contention throughout this book has been that the subjects of couplehood, in joining together two different, even divergent, lives, must grapple with the process of making story as well as managing strangeness as they undertake the work of becoming, creating a shared world. How this was achieved by Warner and Ackland remains underemphasized in the study of the Warner/Ackland intimate life writing. One who has considered this aspect of both Warner's and Ackland's respective life writing texts is Ailsa Granne, who argues that Warner in her letters to Ackland worked to create a version of Ackland that the latter would find reparative after the trauma of producing *For Sylvia*, which text Ackland composed in the midst of the worst period of the White affair. In her formulation of "catastrophic reading," Granne argues compellingly that "the presence of Warner in Ackland's life and the latter's lack of success as a published poet are linked and constitute Ackland's real tragedy" ("Fantasy" 778–79). For Granne, the two women were not engaged in a process of cocreation; rather, Warner sought to heal and maintain the relationship by "creat[ing] another world for Ackland" ("Fantasy" 783), even as Ackland suffered, as she writes, "appalling and disgraceful pangs of envy . . . to hear her [Warner's] happy typewriter . . . and know that she is able to work" (diary entry for October 18, 1951, qtd. in Granne, "Silent" 37). These tensions become even clearer as we gain access to Ackland's unpublished diaries through the work of Granne's excerpting and analysis. In February 1951, Ackland writes, "I shall not . . . ever again call myself a 'Writer'" ("Silent" 32). According to Granne, within the couplehood with Warner, even as Ackland continued to write, especially as she was taking as her subject her torment over her partner's success, creativity, and prolificness, Ackland felt she must be silent ("Silent" 35)—an interesting point given the significance of voice for Warner, as we shall see.

Key to my uncovering the mechanisms of the shared project of Warner and Ackland is an understanding of the forms of narrativity involved in their intersubjective creation of a shared storyworld and the telling of intermentality; the failure of these processes and the narrativization of that failure; and the recuperation of couplehood through a reimagining of those processes. Micir proposes the evocative notion that as an auto/biographer—of her own life and in her one substantial biographical project, a life of T. H. White—Warner thinks of herself, as she writes to William Maxwell, as living in "two tenses" (120; *Elements* 165); by this she means "a remembered past" and a present she is forced to inhabit without Ackland (Micir 120).[3] I would go further to claim that both Warner and Ackland make use of a perspectival and analeptic backward glance to negotiate loss, the negative affects—shame, guilt, betrayal, resentment—and the resulting ontological shift that come with betrayal.

Especially in life writing made during the 1949–50 White catastrophe, Warner and Ackland write out of the past from a fraught position in the present, and evince an "ambivalence toward the future," in the words of Heather Love, that emerges from a sense of failure (23). Love's "feeling backward" offers a way into the affective dynamic rendered by Warner's and Ackland's writing, and recuperation, of failed couplehood.[4] Warner writes in 1949, after the crisis of Ackland's affair and her own devastated emotional response, "The past rushed back at me, and I wept for a long time. . . . I dare not speak, I am so much afraid of imperilling what may already be about to fall" (*Diaries* 147). Acknowledging that I am convinced by the political efficacy we might draw from Love's work but do not engage that possibility explicitly here—as Love writes, "The public sphere is big, feelings are small" (11), and I remain fairly square within the more "small" throughout—I also see Warner and Ackland returning to the sites of past injuries for a kind of emotional efficacy in the face of present hurts, and to envision a future for their couplehood. The "ruined sociality" of the relationship (Love 22), what we might from the perspective of cognitive narrative studies deem a story of failed intermentality, necessitates specific telling, and thus worldbuilding, moves.

From the beginning of the Warner/Ackland couple in 1930 in East Chaldon, the two wrote together; it formed as much a part of their experience of couplehood as shared housekeeping, gardening, and political activity, but was much more fraught with resentment and misunderstanding. To mark their developing erotic and literary partnership, they decided to publish a collection of poems under both their names but without attributing individual poems within the book to either author. The "Note to the Reader" at the start of *Whether a Dove or a Seagull* says in part,

> No single poem is in any way the result of collaboration, nor . . . is the book collaborative. The authors believe that by issuing their separate work under one cover the element of contrast thus obtained will add to the pleasure of the reader; by withholding individual attributions they hope that the freshness of anonymity will be preserved. (n.p.)

Warner was always the more widely known writer, and the effect of the publication of *Whether a Dove or a Seagull* in 1934 was twofold, and unfortunate. Reviewers attributed all the "good" poems to Warner, which meant Ackland did not get nearly the recognition as an emerging voice the pair had hoped for; and they wondered why a successful writer like Warner would attach her name to an odd and uneven mélange of poems while also disavowing any specific authorship. Warner never really published poetry again, although continued to write it until late in life. Ackland published very little, and always struggled with overwhelming feelings of loss, impotence, and failure about her writing.

A second edition of *Whether a Dove or a Seagull* added a key at the back informing readers which poet wrote which poem in response to criticism by readers and reviewers; as Claire Harman points out in her introduction to a 2008 collection of Warner's poems, the inclusion of the key prompted a fresh round of vitriol, as reviewers accused them of disingenuously drawing more attention to the issue of attribution. For Harman, "Most of the reviewers seemed glad of the distraction provided by the 'experiment in the presentation of poetry'" since it seemed to "conveniently displac[e] the issue of lesbianism" (Introduction, *New* 6). I'm going to follow Warner's and Ackland's original intention here and talk about the poems as unattributed. In so doing, I can highlight the ways they saw the book as a joint production of their couplehood, each individual subsumed under the "we." Such a move also allows me to point out discrepancies in the "Note to the Reader," specifically the insistence that the book is in no way a collaboration. As Harman puts it, the texts in *Whether a Dove or a Seagull* "keep wanting to re-knit into a conversation between two intriguingly different voices" (Introduction, *New* 5). The shared project was meant to create space for Ackland as a writer, a space which was difficult for her to claim at the start and increasingly more so over the thirty-eight years of her relationship with Warner. Highlighting that the book is not a collaboration either mitigates the possible influence, diminishes the presence of the more dominant partner—or erases and silences the less dominant one.

For indeed, the book was a collaboration, and despite the note's assertions to the contrary, reviewers perceived the mutuality of the work. Humbert Wolfe described the collection as having a "strange unity" (qtd. in Mulford 43); the *London Mercury* said, "There seems to be a strong sense of unity binding together the individual minds . . . an intermingling of identities and imaginations" (qtd. in Mulford 43). Many of the individual texts do not have titles, so they blend into each other, creating an image or evoking a feeling that meets its response on the next page. The poems were written together, about Warner's and Ackland's burgeoning relationship, chosen and arranged to tell the story of their "we." In her dual biography of the couple *This Narrow Place*, Wendy Mulford identifies *Whether a Dove or a Seagull* as a kernel in the emplotment of the Warner/Ackland couplehood:

> The book is important, not because it does have any grand design but because it reveals the interaction and growth and feeling between two writers. . . . [The poems] grew out of a shared and mutually creative life together. . . . The voices of the two women speak to, slide past, touch upon, and explore the shifting growth of feeling in their relationship. (43–44)

Mulford's erotic language here is telling, as she deploys the tropes of and participates in the embodied nature of the women's discourse: "slide past," "touch upon," "explore." One might read the biographer's characterization of the women's poetic voices as bodily, their textuality as sexual. Mulford writes further that the "voice of the love lyrics modulates" between "pain and rapture" (44). Images and phrases recur and echo each other, a quality of their writing pointed out by Frances Bingham, creating a private language in a private world (qtd. in Davies 3). These poems, from this collection early on in their relationship, show the development of that private language.

The originary moment of encounter is what Seymour Chatman would call a narrative kernel in the story of a couple (53–56), an essential event required to move the plot forward, the instant of intersection and ontological shift. In the hands of couple biographers, the encounter can catalyze an arc, one that moves toward a teleological conclusion. Desire is fulfilled, narrative resolution is achieved, narrative and emotional closure found. That narrative kernel of encounter in the intimate life writing of the couple themselves, however, is often an event shaped much more by contingency, even mystery, or Ahmed's "hap." It is a fixed point in the couple's story, to which its members continually return, even as they are also continually becoming. It is both proleptic—the prompting of looking ahead to a future—and analeptic—reinscribed across experience via a looking back to the originary moment when the story began. Without encounter there is no story; without story the encounter is emptied of meaning. We might see this intuitively, in something as commonplace as the celebration of an anniversary, but each of the couples under study here make the telling and retelling, the continual reinscribing of their originary encounter, a central aspect of their shared worlding. They write their story over and over again, in a multiplicity of forms.

Warner and Ackland wrote and rewrote the moment of their coming together, their "bridal," throughout their life writing; they commemorated it each year with notes and presents. They conceived of it deliberately as the "anniversary" of their "marriage." In the 1930 diary entry telling of the moment with Ackland, Warner writes:

> And then we went to bed. Just as I blew out the candle the wind began to rise. I thought I heard her speak, and listened, and at last she said through the door that this would frighten them up at the Vicarage. How the Vicarage led to love I have forgotten (oh, it was an eiderdown). I said, sitting on my side of the wall, that love was easier than liking, so I should specialize in that. "I think I am utterly loveless." The forsaken grave wail of her voice smote me, and had me up, and through the door, and at her bedside. There I stayed, till I got into her bed, and found love there. (*Diaries* 69–70)

The next entry begins, "My last day, and our first. It was a bridal of earth and sky" (*Diaries* 70).[5] Note the retrospective, the constructed nature of this entry. We find not immediacy here—as seen in the "I have forgotten" and its subsequent parenthetical—but a crafted narrative meant to give meaning to the experience as well as position the moment as both an end and a beginning. Warner's entry offers hypotactic narrative cues related to time and sequence, carefully drawing out each instance of the encounter: "And then," "Just as." A gap is purposefully created between "There I stayed" and "till I got into her bed": what happened in the space between "there" and "till"? Warner is telling a story, not recording every titillating detail. The next day, a "bridal," is the commencing of their shared story—"My last day, and our first"—signified by the shift from "I" to "our," bearing erotic and ontological weight.

Ackland's voice is captured by Warner in one notable phrase—"I think I am utterly loveless"—and in fact the voice itself—"the forsaken grave wail of her voice"—is made present. The voice embodies Ackland's affects, and its siren call is what prompts Warner to enter. In this scene, Ackland is almost an *acousmêtre*, a voice whose source is unseen, bodiless until Warner responds to its need.[6] When we undertake our discussion of Warner's fixation on "presence" after the death of Ackland, we might find this observation worth recalling. For Warner, Ackland's voice is in part how Warner constructs the subjecthood of her lover. Her very utterances are her "I" (Lejeune, *On Autobiography* 9–10). Finally, Ackland's phrase gestures toward a feeling and perceiving of her own ontological state as being one of lack: love-*less*. The flagging of cognitive activity in "I think" is renarrativized by Warner into a gesture toward herself, one she meets, and one which opens the way for telling shared intermentality, for relationality; and which fills the absence, the "less-ness," expressed by Ackland.

Ackland's version of the story in *For Sylvia* is somewhat different, focusing as it does, in some respects, on revelation rather than resolution:

> I said sadly "I sometimes think I am utterly unloved." And Sylvia thought she heard heart-break melancholy in my voice, and with that passionate immediacy of succour which matches, through all her character, and makes her have the most purely beautiful heart I have ever known—perhaps that has ever existed—she sprang up and came through the connecting door and fell on her knees by my bed and took me in her arms. I do not know what happened then, except that in a moment or so she was in my bed and I was holding her and kissing her and we were already deeply in love—and never since have we ceased to love each other, and with each year of our joined lives we have loved more, and more truly. (*For* 123–24)

To start, the position of this kernel event in Ackland's memoir is toward the end, rather than at the beginning. For Ackland, the communicating of this event comes at the end of the telling of her own life story. It is not the beginning of a shared story; she undoes the narrative temporality, including order and chronology, demanded by (hetero)normativity (Matz 231). Ackland cannot necessarily look ahead to a positive future from this encounter, or even retrospectively construct such optimism from the originary moment, the "bridal," given the negative affects shaping both her looking backward and her pessimistic anticipation of the future (cf. Matz 234). This is where their shared story ends in the arc of *For Sylvia*, for Ackland's memoir takes us up to the moment of her being joined in the home she shared with Warner by Elizabeth Wade White. The narrativizing of "with each year of our joined lives we have loved more, and more truly," is thus not necessarily questionable but certainly highly constructed: the joining is in danger of coming apart. Ackland resists the *telos* of couplehood (Minich 60), as an essential feature of grappling with the future possibility of its failure.

In her telling, Ackland focuses on the character of Warner, instead of the sequence of events. Granne makes the point that Ackland's stance borders on the self-abasing—"the most purely beautiful heart . . . perhaps that has ever existed" ("Fantasy")—but one should consider purpose and audience in the telling. For her part, Mulford, too, notes the "strangeness" of the "account": "Part literary document, part confessional, part eulogy of, and plea to, Sylvia, without whom she knew herself to be lost" (33). Ackland insists on authenticity in her subtitle, "An Honest Account," while casting Sylvia as a character in a story told by an omniscient overt homodiegetic narrator (Chatman 196–97). The account is directed at and for Warner, but "Sylvia" appears as a character in the story she has up to a point shared with the "I," Valentine Ackland. Ackland professes to "not know what happened then," while filling in the gaps detailing intimate activity. And again, finally, the phrase that set the whole event in motion: "I sometimes think I am utterly unloved." This is markedly different from Warner's telling; Ackland's writing of the utterance appears retrospectively in a memoir almost twenty years after the actual event, while Warner's appears in a diary entry not only closer to the event but also with the patina of immediacy granted by diary-writing. Did Warner misremember? Did Ackland? I'm not entirely sure it matters, because I am interested in *telling*, not *truth*. So, I will close this part of the discussion by pointing out the difference between "loveless" and "unloved." The former suggests an absence to be filled; the latter suggests a negation. The latter also suggests a possibility for agency on the part of another: were someone, namely Sylvia, to take up the call to act and to love, Valentine would no longer be unloved, but loved.

Thus the ontological shift from unloved to loved would be effected. No matter the differences in the communicating of the event, each woman takes as the signal moment in that story such an ontological shift. To return to *Whether a Dove or a Seagull*, a number of the poems by the two share this transformation as their subject, and form multiple instances of textualizing the (be)coming together. In "Out, for a moment," the poet writes: "Out, for a moment, / Over your shoulder staring / At the angle of wall and ceiling, / I saw the room open—and I leant / Out from your arms, still wearing / Our love, our anguish of parting. / But the world has changed, the high air, the sky" (37). The transformative moment of love is here captured, the ontological shift of being made part of a "we": "The world has changed," and we find this new perspective in Warner's own life writing: "My last day, and our first. It was a bridal of earth and sky" (*Diaries* 70). The individual is "wearing / Our love"—enveloped in something made of two (a garment which protects? disguises? transforms?)—the shifts from "I" and "your" to "our," and the "world" changing, hearkens back to the diary noting an ontological shift into couplehood: my last day, our first. Gilliam Spraggs has observed this pattern as well: the "theme, of reciprocated passion and shared delight, recurs again and again. Words like 'we' and 'our' run like a thread through Sylvia's poems . . . a thread missing from the earlier volumes [of her poetry]" (115). One is no longer just herself, but part of a new entity.

Yet to presuppose coherence and completion as a result of this process is ontologically complicated, and to impose it upon a lover is potentially ethically problematic. Let's return to that "Note to the Reader." How did Ackland take that note? In a letter dated April 24, 1934, she writes to Warner:

> I have sometimes been gloomy about it, because I have been weighted down by a feeling that I should not have started on it at all. That I had injured you by having my poems with yours, and so on and so on. I have thought that the freak-fancy of having two poets in one book (mild frolic though it is!) had perhaps set many of your usual readers against you. . . . But I am sure of one thing, that I am far more pleased than sorry about the book—and—above all other things I am glad that we are together there. . . . I love it. It is most extraordinarily pleasant to me to think of this child of our love. A neat, tidy, quiet child—but a child of passion and truth, and, I believe, of sturdy life. (*I'll* 120)

This is a fascinating document of disruption, and there is no responding statement on the part of Warner. She says simply, in her interpolated narrative note in *I'll Stand By You*:

> Since then, I have come to doubt whether Valentine gained or suffered by a joint book. It showed her poems on the printed page . . . but on the other hand it carried a sort of cadetship implication (fatally reinforced by an entry in the Chatto and Windus list for 1934: Ackland, Valentine—see Warner, S. T.). . . . But at the time, we were pleased, even rather solemnly pleased. (*I'll* 114)

The tone is strikingly different, even given that Warner is retrospectively reading both the book and Ackland's letter in the process of collecting and annotating the letters in *I'll Stand By You*, while Ackland is writing closer to the moment with greater immediacy. Ackland suggests that she and Warner have not been able to talk honestly about the book; this comment appears as a postscript in another long letter about other subjects, and she seems to be taking advantage of a separation to speak freely (*I'll* 119–20). She notes that they interrupt each other, which inclines one to think she feels unheard—unrecognized both in the Levinasian sense with regard to her feelings about the book and in the literary sense through her work as a writer. There is the self-deprecating move "and so on and so on," as well as referring to the project as a "freak-fancy" and a "frolic."

Yet, finally, she makes a rather significant gesture: she refers to the project as their child. This, more than anything, more than the "Note," is a clear gesture toward collaboration, toward couplehood and its products. It is also an interesting counterpoint to Terry Castle's reading of Warner's "lesbian counterplots." Could it be that in making *Whether a Dove or a Seagull*, Warner was seeking a counterplot wherein the product of the couplehood is not the offspring of heterosexual union but rather a collection of lesbian love poetry? And then what would it mean for that attempt to fail, prompting the negative affect that Heather Love sees as underlying a reaching backward? That backward move is an integral part of both texts of guilt, loss, and mourning each woman creates in *For Sylvia* and *I'll Stand By You*. A clue to what it might mean can be found in a previously unpublished letter discovered when Warner's and Ackland's MI5 files were opened and then sent to their archive in the Dorset County Museum. In a 1935 letter to the editor of *New Left Review*, Tom Wintringham, Ackland writes that *Whether a Dove or a Seagull* was "a noble thing to do, but very stupid" (qtd. in Granne, "Silent" 45).

Such a disavowal undercuts Warner's stated notions that *Whether a Dove or a Seagull* is not a collaboration, not a shared reflection and record of their emerging erotic connection. For Ackland, it is not only a literary collaboration; it is a product of their love, and one of failure. Ackland further disrupts the narrative provided by Warner through the writing of *For Sylvia*. Those few critics who have taken up *For Sylvia* more substantively—namely Ailsa Granne and biographers Mulford and Harman—consider it in light of Ackland's position as the more "minor" of the two, characterizing her further as melancholic, negative, bordering on the possibly dysfunctional. The memoir was written quickly, and given to Warner on July 4, 1949, as Warner was preparing to depart their beloved home Frome Vauchurch so that Ackland could live there together with Elizabeth Wade White in a trial cohabitation. Warner would spend those weeks in a hotel near the train station at Yeovil; the fairly devastating diary entries from this period will be considered here as well.

Georgia Johnston posits that a key feature of lesbian life writing is its attempt to disrupt patriarchal narratives; this echoes Terry Castle's understanding of Warner's novels as crafting a kind of resistance to "compulsory plots." Johnston does not address Ackland's memoir, and I would suggest that we could extend Johnston's scholarship to account for Ackland's own disruptive force on the shared narrative of life with Warner. The memoir is not just an apologia for a life of infidelity and drinking, not just an accounting of what she sees as her deviance (and in this it echoes rather strongly Vita Sackville-West's *Portrait of a Marriage*, which Johnston does talk about). It is a story of disruptions and a disruption itself. In its "honest account" (its subtitle) it seeks to upset Warner's coherent narrative of their couplehood. It demands recognition via rewriting and rereading the couple. Presently I will argue that the affair with Elizabeth Wade White constitutes another disruption, one similarly textualized; and that Warner's writing after Ackland's death—her letters and diaries, and the archival project that became *I'll Stand By You*—comprises an attempt to manage the disruption which continued to rock her, and the even more profound alteration to her ontological state in the loss of her "wife."

In the painful midst of the affair with White, Ackland writes in *For Sylvia* of her early days with Warner, immediately following the telling of their first erotic encounter as discussed above:

> Our lives, for the next few weeks, scarcely knew night or day or any change in the hours or weather; we knew nothing except our joy and pleasure and the thousand-and-one, infinitely fine adjustments that we were each making, to fit always closer and closer to each other. . . . Time went on, and all the time I became more happy, and Sylvia did too, I think; and our lives joined up imperceptibly, all along their lengths, so that without thinking about it or arranging it, we remained together and could scarcely endure a day's parting, or an hour's. That is why, now as I write, I feel as though I were looking down into the pit of death [about to have White in their home, with Warner decamping for a hotel in Yeovil]. (*For* 124)

Ackland captures what it means to create a couplehood with Warner through the lens of a desperation engendered by deliberately endangering the world they have made. The "feeling backward" toward remembered happiness calls forth Ackland's situatedness in a present rife with misery, and the affects she feels compelled to tell from that position. This happiness came, for Ackland, from the process of generating a couplehood: "infinitely fine adjustments," "our lives joined up . . . all along their lengths" (language echoed—appropriated—by Harman, we might recall from the start of this chapter). If the happiness came from this shared process of cocreation in the course of falling in love, however, then in order to account for her present misery, Ackland must reach further back into the past and narrativize her shame and guilt over her own life outside the union. These manipulations of chronology are not the order of time but the "order of inquiry" (Lejeune, *On Autobiography* 73).

For all of the inner turmoil that forms the plot of *For Sylvia*—as Love writes, "In psychic life the trains hardly ever run on time" (11)—Ackland is preoccupied with the potential held by narrative to render patterns. Her prefatory note describes the account as a "record of blundering from shame to shame" (*For* 30), and the text begins by presenting the "'crisis' of the life" (*For* 31). We might read this literally; Ackland saw her life as carried forward on waves of multiple crises, beginning with her early lesbian affairs, her disastrous marriage to a man, a miscarriage and multiple sexual partners, financial worries, above all her "problem with drink," leading to the signal crisis prompting the book "for Sylvia," the infidelity with White. We might also read it narratologically: Ackland is aware of the ways in which narrative is giving her life shape, an arc, the artifice of coherence.

Mulford takes as her ethical responsibility as biographer the serious treatment of Ackland's crises within the "we."[7] She writes,

> Accepting that she was driven by the confessional urge to exorcise what felt to her like her heaviest sin, because it was bound up with the loss of her undivided love for Sylvia. . . . [e]ither one reads the autobiography as having a basis in reality, or one reads *For Sylvia: An Honest Account* as fiction, based on the writer's life. (154)

Mulford proffers the possibility that Ackland's *For Sylvia* is a fiction among fictions. She seems to be suggesting that this provides us with a way out: we don't have to take Ackland's version of things any more or less seriously than we might take another version (viz., Warner's). One "fiction" is not meant to be privileged over another (Mulford 154). This way of reading presents an alternative to those predicated on the necessity of identifying one member of the couple as "dominant," with that partner's voice holding the power to shape the narrative of the two. Rather, we consider the writing produced by the couple as a kind of polymorphous discursivity: an assemblage of multiple textualities taking multiple forms, some "fitting always closer and closer to each other," as Ackland puts it, some resisting and rupturing what the couple has made. In this case, Ackland narrativizes not only her own life but also the break made by her infidelity, thus revealing herself fully *and* offering insight into how much she has concealed. It will be for Warner to rewrite their partnership after the permanent rupture brought about by Ackland's death.

Prior to that rupture are gaps, gaps which create a sense of crisis. One, to be discussed further below, is that between Ackland and Warner in their erotic life. But this was precipitated by the shattering event of Ackland falling in love with White. The three women knew each other throughout the 1930s, beginning as friends joined in common cause during the catastrophe brought on by fascism in Spain. By 1938, however, Ackland and White had come together, and the relationship would cause tension between Ackland and Warner even as Warner agreed to give Ackland the freedom to pursue it. In doing so, she was not creating an "open marriage" scenario—she herself had no interest in the possibility of other partners; rather, she believed she was acting rightly and correctly, and that this was the most ethical way to sustain Ackland and maintain the integrity of their love. She writes in a diary entry for July 1949, "What she did, she did unwittingly, in innocence & too great trust in me; & since then she has still been the light of my darkened eyes, & the core of my heart, & my strength & comfort, & raison d'être, and all I have" (*Diaries* 133). We might understand this as Warner recognizing her beloved in her alterity, acknowledging the strange difference and distance between all lovers. Warner grapples with Ackland's desire as separate from herself and residing outside the world they have built.

However, for Warner, this process necessitates the working through of a painful shift in her ontological status, defined as her being and living is through her relationality with Ackland.[8] As Ackland and White prepare to live together at Frome Vauchurch (an experiment that lasted only several weeks) and Warner readies herself to decamp to a hotel in Yeovil, Warner writes in her diary for June 1949, "What I cannot begin to imagine is myself alone. The moment I think of that, I go out like a candle. I see a strange room. Scattered about it are things I recognize as mine. But that is all. There is no one in the room" (*Diaries* 132). Warner experiences the phenomenological effort of altering one's perception of oneself in space and in the world, and narrates the cognitive effort required to manage it: "cannot imagine," "recognize," and so on. Warner's attempts to imagine herself alone are evidence of her struggle. In fact, she disappears, and all that remains is strangeness. She can recognize her things, aspects of her material reality, but she cannot recognize herself in relation to them and the world.

As the affair progresses, Warner comes more to recognize her changed self and situation, and to recognize what her recognition of Ackland's needs is costing her. She comes to accommodate not only this vision of Ackland but also this perception of herself, writing,

> She lives and loves innocently with Eliz: because I am shaken with fears and doubts, ravished with physical and mental jealousy, and steadily murder myself in concealing it. . . . Alyse said that it was because of being sure of me that she was able to love Eliz: which is strangely akin to that enigmatic and shocking remark of hers that it was with the me in her she loved Eliz. (*Diaries* 142)

While she closes by expressing an inability to understand, her writing belies a profound insight into the ethical processes, painful as they might be, by which she has arrived at this moment. The couple as cocreated by Warner and Ackland allows Warner to do ethical work on behalf of Ackland at the very moment she feels most distant from her. At the start of 1950 Warner writes, "To be injured is not irreparable . . . what is irreparable is injustice and misprision" (*Diaries* 154). An unpublished poem from the same time bears the lines, "My Love is coming back, is coming back, I said: / My true and only love, falsed in another bed" (*New* 327). The falseness is something here being done *to* the beloved; or, the implication may be that the false love is not false but rather a false *version* of the beloved, and the true will return. The important thing is not to misprise the false love for the true. One might suggest that this is entirely self-negating behavior; but, we can read how Warner clearly articulates her situatedness, her mind, and these in relation to Ackland.

The polymorphous discursivity, the assemblage of life narrative, surrounding the Ackland and White affair is not without its own gaps, extensive as its textualities might seem. We observe in the quotations from Warner's diary that she refers to White as "Eliz," sometimes "Eliz:." I don't want to go too far in making hay out of Warner's refusal to write out the woman's name, but I do want to point out that until the work of Claire Harman, White was a prominent gap in the intimate archive of Ackland and Warner. She appears in Warner's collected letters, edited by William Maxwell and published in 1982, as a pair of empty brackets filled with white space: [ ]. The first and only letter to White in that volume appears in November 1936, with an explanatory note that simply reads "Biographer, living in Middlebury, Connecticut" (*letters* 41); the letter is about Spain. Harman's 1989 biography names White, and her 1994 edition of the diaries includes Warner's frequent and distraught references to "Eliz." *I'll Stand By You* also names White: Warner writes, simply, "Elizabeth was my doing," referring to the initial meeting that brought the young woman into their orbit (*I'll* 163). With the publication in 2012 of *The Akeing Heart*—letters among Warner, White, and Ackland edited along with interpolated commentary by Peter Haring Judd (White's cousin and godson)—even more of this gap has been filled.[9] Judd's work brought to light dozens of letters exchanged among the women, including numerous letters from Warner during the early days of their friendship, prior to the romantic entanglement, as well as while the affair was occurring.

The publication of *The Akeing Heart* calls for yet another revision in our reading of the Warner and Ackland narrative, and a further extension of its textual and discursive world. It renders one of the participants in the story of the couple less of a cipher, while she also creates gaps of her own. In writing in her journal of falling in love with Ackland, White opts not to name her new beloved even as she negotiates her own changed ontological state: "I know now and finally what love is and must be, that without [it] is only death, and that I am hopelessly, helplessly, inarticulately, and everlastingly in love" (*Akeing* 124). This journal entry is one of many interpolations around the letters in the volume; others include entries from datebooks, poetry, and telegrams, along with Judd's commentary and explanations. *The Akeing Heart* recalls Warner's own strategies of interpolation deployed as a means of narrativity in *I'll Stand By You*. It also enacts the polymorphous discursivity engendered by the affective overspill of the erotic situation. It belies White's claim to be "inarticulately in love"; such inarticulateness in practice seems to call forth a cascade of words as one begins to shape a new world.

Ten years before White arrived at Frome Vauchurch and plunged Warner into despair, she received a letter from Warner that articulated the ethical position the latter woman would maintain, even in her moments of greatest sorrow and jealousy. Warner writes in October 1939,

> You say that when you fell in love with Valentine you betrayed my trust. You betrayed nothing. You acted naturally and properly, and as a person of sensibility and poetry should behave. There is no betrayal in that. In a way, there would have been a betrayal if you had not acted as you did. . . . So let there be no more thought of betrayal my dear, it is a false and belying word, and *not appropriate to any one of us three.* (*Akeing* 214; emphasis mine)

In Warner's letter, we find her incorporating White into her couplehood with Ackland, and refusing to define their relationality in terms of betrayal. By doing so she does not have to account for her own changed ontological status: one who has been betrayed and must therefore radically alter her relationship to the beloved other. In this way, she negotiates the changed situation with the integrity we find in her diaries, and evinces a commitment to Ackland's being in process through another intimacy. But, at the same time, she does not entirely anticipate the impact it will have on her relationality to both Ackland and White, and on the shattering of her own subjecthood. We might therefore say, it is not entirely that Ackland and White betrayed Warner; it is more so that they became two, and Warner became one.

White's texts disrupt the clear progression we imagine we find in the narrative of the couple, in the way infidelity or betrayal disrupts the shared vision of the "we." Ackland's own letters offer a further disruption, as when she writes in 1939, "Probably I could promise complete fidelity. . . . But fidelity of desire is not enough to give you, because what I would necessarily be asking from you is everything you have to give. And in return I could not offer you what is probably the most important thing of all, security" (*Akeing* 223). In this letter, she explains that as much as she wants White, she has no intention of giving up Warner. In being unfaithful to Warner, she is being entirely faithful to White; but in refusing to give White the security she so desperately requires (a need for which she made Ackland miserable), she imagines her relationship with Warner to remain her emotional foundation. Moreover, and importantly, White insisted on security because she conceived of the relationship proleptically; she was always envisioning the future. Ackland, on the other hand, was entirely backward looking, and feeling. Her narrativization of her life with Warner required her to "feel" backward in *For Sylvia*, and it is her impulse to "feel backwards" that led her to maintain Warner's significance in her life even as that foundation was threatened. Ackland could not tell a story that progressed forward, which is what her couplehood with White demanded, according to White. For what it's worth, White is certainly not alone in imagining that the stories of couples must always be moving forward. That compulsion, after all, has driven everything from bearing children to the emplotment of "happily ever after" (one of the essential critiques of narrative emerging from queer theory, as Judith Roof has argued).[10]

In this regard, we find Ackland's thinking diverging from that of either woman in her life, and it is this which precipitates the failure of intersubjectivity that so devastated Warner. At the same time, Ackland recognizes the ways in which "Sylvia would understand. . . . She has always understood very clearly from her own point of view, of course, as all of us must understand like that—it's the only way; the process of 'putting yourself in someone else's place' isn't in fact possible" (*Akeing* 282). Maybe so; yet Ackland's judgment that Warner understands seems to be borne out by the writing, and, moreover, Warner seems to have done what she could to empathize, in many respects *by means of* her writing. (Recall Ailsa Granne's argument regarding the work Warner did to repair Ackland's catastrophe of self.) Ackland suffered a similar difficulty when White maintained her relationship with her own lover, Evelyn Holahan, which Ackland perceived as an infidelity which disrupted the "joy of creating 'you' and 'me'" (*Akeing* 287). Ackland's couplehood with White had its own narrative, the construction, the "joy of creating," of which was similarly jolted, and had to be similarly revised over time and text.

Harman notes that Ackland claims to have stopped writing in her diary after the White crisis of 1949–50, saying, "It is all written and re-written" (*Sylvia* 239). We know from the archives, and from Ailsa Granne's publication of excerpts ranging from 1951 to 1955, that this is not entirely true ("Silent"). Warner, on the other hand, continued to write and rewrite. In 1952, in a letter to Ackland (one of those collected in *I'll Stand By You*), she writes once again of their first encounter:

> My love, it was your sad viola voice that brought me in on what seemed then an imperative need to succour you because you were sad, and must be mistaken. . . . And not till I lay in your arms did I know that what I had gained was love, and that what I had sought, too, was love. And afterwards, O heavens: What a fidget I was in not to become a clog, a burden, an outstayer of welcome. And how I fought you with refusings of vows, and rejecting of contracts, and how I paid out such yards of free reins and long ropes that it is a marvel to me now that we didn't get strangled in them. (*I'll* 305)

Warner hearkens back to the sound of Ackland's voice, "your sad viola voice," and once more grants it the power of presence to bring her to Ackland's side. As Ackland is dying, Warner again preoccupies herself with her voice, writing to William Maxwell in November 1969, "One thinks one has foreseen every detail of heart-break. I hadn't. I had not allowed for the anguished compassion and shock of hearing her viola voice changed to a pretty, childish treble, the voice of a sick child" (*Element* 205). But this rewriting has Warner appropriating a key word from Ackland's own telling, one integral to Ackland's conceptualization of Warner's character: "succour." The processes of intertwining discourses observed in the writing of *Whether a Dove or a Seagull* continues, and seems to indicate that Ackland's writing in *For Sylvia* has shaped Warner's own vision of herself. Notably, that word "succour" appears still later, in an unpublished poem written after Ackland's death: "No succour. / You were dying of cancer; / No possible hope, no averting, no answer" (*New* 353), as well as in Warner's diary of 1970: "I felt guilty & appalled that I had not been of much succour to her" (*Diaries* 338).

That vision of herself is further altered, the effort of becoming continued, by taking up the status of lovelessness and applying it to herself, rather than allowing Ackland to maintain it: "What I had gained was love . . . what I had sought, too, was love." One must also read the new, retrospective element at the conclusion of this passage in light of the White affair. For Warner now considers that originary encounter in light of all that has transpired. She feels backward to find the instant of their love, but in order to do so she must recall what happened after. She must traverse that frontier once more, to use her own language from that same letter: "I crossed my frontier in a shift, my darling, and left everything but myself on the yonder side of that flimsy wooden door" (*I'll* 305).

At the time of this particular rewriting, Warner had been experiencing for several years the withdrawal of Ackland's erotic attention. While the original writing of this moment in her diary left out any specific details related to the physical aspect of the first encounter, this rewriting calls attention to Warner as sexualized. It is possible this rewriting engages yet another purpose: a reminder of Warner's own unflagging desire. From the early days of their relationship the corporeal played an important role in their developing story. Warner describes one evening in her diary for 1931: "It was our most completed night, and after our love I slept unstirring in her arms, still covered with her love, till we woke and ate whatever meal it is lovers eat at five in the morning" (*Diaries* 77). For Ackland to withdraw is to compromise this shared vision—inevitable over time perhaps, but no less traumatic if not mutual. As Warner describes it in 1949, on the eve of White's arrival, "She [Ackland] looks as beautiful now as when she was beautiful with love for me. The torment of the flesh is so much purer, so much nobler, than the torment of the mind" (*Diaries* 134). Warner's private writing throughout the 1940s and 1950s, and beyond, evinces both torments, and the physical persists long after the mental has been laid somewhat to rest. Claire Harman writes,

> How Valentine had come to the conclusion that Sylvia no longer wanted or needed passionate love puzzled her a good deal, but there was no changing it. Valentine interpreted all Sylvia's remarks in that light, and Sylvia herself had lost her spontaneity over such matters. 'She deceives herself about me far more than I deceive her,' Sylvia wrote. (*Sylvia* 239; the quotation from Warner comes from her diary for 1950, 161)

Ackland had come to construct a version of Warner devoid of desire, a version that was perhaps somewhat self-serving given her own need to maintain an erotic relationship with White as well as other women; and certainly a version divergent from the one they had shared from the start and which Warner still maintained.

Embodiment is a regularity of intimate life writing narratives. After the departure of White from Frome Vauchurch in 1949, Warner writes in her diary, "I lay with her [Ackland's] head on my shoulder, and I tried to warm her; and as she warmed, the smell of love came from her, that smell of corn and milk that I shall never smell from her again except love for another causes it" (*Diaries* 146). The erotic is cast as central in the making of a couple, based on the corpus analyzed in this book, bearing as it does the affects not only of love but of jealousy and anger. Furthermore, the representation and enacting of embodiment is necessary in the telling of erotic life at multiple key nodes: the telling of coming together, of betrayal, of breaking apart, of aging and loss and dying. Warner writes more frequently of the erotic in its corporeal, embodied form the more deprived of it she feels, and the more it shifts her affects in relation to Ackland. Harman offers some perspective on Ackland: "She still loved Sylvia, although a sort of physical embarrassment had grown up between them. 'So often lately I have felt longings towards her,'

Valentine wrote in her diary, 'and every time they have been quenched by self-mistrust. Maybe it is better so, after so long—I am getting old'" (*Sylvia* 243–44). This is in sharp contrast to the narrative of herself presented in *For Sylvia* by Ackland, the story of a prodigiously skillful lover sought after by men and women alike.

While texts such as *For Sylvia* and *I'll Stand By You* have received some notice in the study of life writing, more remains to be done. Both Mulford and Harman use Warner's diaries expertly in their biographies, particularly to capture the devastation wrought by Ackland's affair with White. Harman offers in passing, in her biography of Warner, that for 1970 Warner kept two diaries, "as if in acknowledgment of the two separate worlds she lived in" after Ackland's death (*Sylvia* 301). Micir too points out the two diaries, in an endnote, but does not consider them further in light of her discussion of "two tenses" (129). While Harman draws extensively on these texts, especially to capture Warner's grief, it is not until Harman's 1996 edition of the diaries that we see the full extent of this dual narrative, and they have yet to be considered as such beyond Harman's editorial explanations. It strikes one that not only do the two diaries signify two separate worlds—past and present, living and dead—they also enact the kind of affective overspill we have seen throughout the discursive worldmaking of Ackland's and Warner's couplehood. Warner's feelings are too much to be contained in one diary. This is a notable contrast to the period of 1933–45, which Harman characterizes as a difficult time for Warner, particularly starting in 1938: the *annus horribilis* of the beginning of Ackland's affair with White. Harman points out that almost nothing of Warner's diary is extant for this period (*Diaries* 93). The diaries provide a site for writing and rewriting that parallels the writing and rewriting of couplehood as finally collected in *I'll Stand By You*. Micir has shown, further, that the letters to William Maxwell during this same period allow Warner to construct a version of Ackland while also going through—and sharing—her private process of renarrativizing their union.

As discussed earlier in this chapter, the death of Ackland is not the first time we find Warner writing out of grief. The diaries and previously uncollected poems of 1949–50 speak of the grief engendered by the endangering and potential failure of the couplehood with Ackland. In the face of her best efforts to permit Ackland the freedom for her erotic pursuits, Warner struggles with her own ability to recognize her lover's separateness. She dreams of White as an "incubus," and writes of "grieving for the old courage" (*Diaries* 135). As she is left in Yeovil by Ackland in 1949, she writes, "I feel idiotic with grief, with care, with bewilderment, with exhaustion of spirit" (*Diaries* 136–37). Her own ethical decisions, her own sympathy for Ackland, causes her the greatest misery, told in a litany of negative affects, even as she is entirely honest about her "frankly base and hateful feelings . . . I can contain this also, and yet be myself" (*Diaries* 141). Here, as it does later, writing functions as a means of working through love and loss. Warner might be living in "two tenses"; she is certainly mourning more than two things. An excess of affects leads Warner to produce the multiple textualities, the narrative assemblages, we find in her attempts to memorialize her deceased partner, manage her altered ontological state, and retell the story of her couplehood with Ackland in such a way that affective gaps are filled. Those gaps, generated by the several losses detailed in this chapter—the pain of the affair, the end of Ackland's erotic interest, Ackland's death from breast cancer—and redolent with bad feeling, demand a renarrativization.

By bringing forth Ackland's presence through auto/biographical narrative, Warner grieves and comes to terms with her new status, bringing her own changed subject into being alongside Ackland's in a version of de Man's specularity (Marcus, *Auto/Biographical* 205). Micir shows how much Warner depended on her correspondence with William Maxwell in the months following Ackland's death as she began the work on the compilation that would become *I'll Stand By You*. In her writing to him, she puts forth a new version of her love with Ackland, one not thwarted by death (or betrayal). One letter, written two days after Ackland's death, has Warner saying, "I am passionately thankful that she is out and away, and that in a fashion we are back where we were, able to love freely and uncompromised by anxiety and doubtful hopes and miseries of frustration" (*Element* 205). Death actually provides a *return* to a more ideal form of love, one lost over the passage of time. For Warner, here, Ackland's absence in death offers a chance for renewal of love, and a better version of the "we." Warner continues, "Don't think I am unhappy and alone, dear William. I am not. I am in a new country and she is the compass I travel by" (*Element* 206). This metaphor is quite striking, signaling as it does Warner's recognition of becoming, of a changed ontological state: "a new country." In this "new country," Ackland *is* present, and a guiding force for Warner's continual becoming.

The language of presence—not haunting, but presence—reverberates throughout Warner's letters to Maxwell. She says, in a letter of February 28, 1971, "I spend most of my time in a strange straying conversation with her, not so much haunted as possessed" (*Element* 218). In a letter of November 26, 1969, she writes, "No, I am not alone. She is more living, more real, than I am myself. She pervades my days. But I can't talk to her . . . And I can no longer serve her. That is most annihilating of all" (*Element* 206). For Warner, Ackland is real; there is nothing of the uncanny about her presence, and indeed, Warner describes having a drawing of Ackland made on her deathbed (an act undertaken by Don Bachardy upon the death of Christopher Isherwood, as we shall see) as providing "the house [with] a centre again" (*Element* 206). It is Warner, instead, who finds herself "annihilated," as deprived and devoid of presence with the loss of her spouse. The word "deprivation" appears in a letter of December 16, 1969, as Warner realizes she will never be telephoned by Ackland again: "And for a moment the whole of my grief was comprised in that deprivation" (*Element* 207). Recall the significance placed on Ackland's voice by Warner; for her, the voice of her spouse had as much presence as any other bodily aspect, was itself a presence. As with the letters exchanged between the two women, mediums that might seem to signify absence—love letters, the telephone—in actuality body forth a beloved presence. Warner writes to Marchette and Joy Chute in March 1972, after the compilation of letters had been completed:

> A letter from William Maxwell this morning told me he had brought you the Valentine-Sylvia letters. . . . You will read them with love—as they were written. . . .
>
> We had no agreement about keeping them. We kept them, I suppose, because we loved too much to throw them away—it would have seemed a slight. They were preserved, not hoarded.
>
> Many of them were almost untranscribable: creased with being carried in pockets, kept under pillows, read & re-read. . . .
>
> Even now my desolation is enriched by her. (*Letters* 256)

In some respects this bodying forth is a function of mourning, as Warner "feels backward" through her grief. The letters are a physical reminder of Ackland, a way to recall touch as well as connection, and this is in large measure,

I think, why Warner turned to the project of *I'll Stand By You*, as the published assemblage is titled. The "feeling backward" of reading and annotating, and thus re-narrativizing in a space beyond loss, creating a space where Ackland can be fully present, is a conjuring enacted through retrospection. Ailsa Granne makes the solid point that the letters served a more complicated function during the course of Ackland's life with Warner, particularly during the White affair. For Granne, the letters from the period when Warner left Frome Vauchurch for Yeovil show "that Ackland prioritized Warner's epistolary over her physical presence" ("Fantasy" 781); further, we have only to recall the letters between White and Ackland, exchanged over the Atlantic, to see that Ackland longed for the presence of another as well.

Ackland's presence was brought forth by Warner's process, a process detailed in letters to Maxwell. This process involved rereading the letters, and crafting narrative passages to link and explain the work of the letters, what Warner calls "annotations." She explains: "Some of them [annotations], I find, need to be extended into snatches of narrative. David Garnett said to me long ago 'What you write best about is love'" (*Element* 213). These annotations are an extensive and self-conscious process of (re)narrativization, and brought her, as she says, "bliss" (*Element* 215). In describing the work of the annotations, Warner deploys joyful language: "I adore annotations" (*Element* 212); "Annotations have always been my besetting delight" (*Element* 213). As a reader, Maxwell responded after going through the letters in November 1970, "I will never again read the word *happiness* without thinking of them" (*Element* 214; emphasis mine). In this writing, Warner effects an affective shift as part of her negotiation of and precipitated by her ontological transformation. As we have seen, there is much in the writing and life of Warner and Ackland that led to *failures* of happiness. Thinking of Warner's reconfiguration of happiness might prompt us to return to Sara Ahmed's claim for the decentering of "happiness" in our cultural discourse as a way to locate other models. The process of annotating, and thereby rewriting, her relationship with Ackland allows Warner a "feeling backward" out of a place of mourning into a space where, as the quotation above indicates, "we are back where we were, able to love freely." Warner uses another metaphor to describe this process; she writes to Maxwell on September 27, 1971, "The letters [from 1936] onward are so sad and my memory of the last years still so raw that I had to take myself off and hide in plain hard work and useful futilities. I am perfectly well, but made of damp sawdust. If I were in an hour-glass, *I would stick*" (*Element* 225). Maxwell, in some respects at this point Warner's ideal reader, picks up the metaphor in his reply: "The only way I know to dry out the dampness of sawdust is by writing. It is the only cure, for the likes of you and me, for it doesn't matter what evil under the sun" (*Element* 225). Essential to Warner bringing her work to fruition is that ideal reader, one in sympathy with her mourning process and writing project—and one who sees that the two are integrally connected. Maxwell makes an explicit gesture of sympathy, "for the likes of you and me," while also mirroring her rhetorical gesture. Even as an outsider to the couple, Maxwell is able to enter into the shared world Warner is reinscribing through *I'll Stand By You*. She facilitates his creation of a storyworld through the narrativity of her and Ackland's worldmaking, and he is responsive to those rhetorical and affectual moves.

The taking up of the discursive moves that are part of the making and remaking of couplehood is a signature element of intimate life writing produced by biographers drawing on the archives engendered by these unions. For instance, Claire Harman activates her own entry into Warner's labors, and the resulting affective response, by using similar language of "presence" connected to "process." She writes:

> Valentine had said she would never leave Sylvia, and to Sylvia that assurance was everything; not a statement of intent, but a statement of *fact*. She constantly sought, and found, indications of Valentine's *presence*; a flight-feather lying by her chair, a letter in a book, a passage marked for her to read, Valentine's scent, suddenly, sharply on the air. . . . Sorting through the letters was not a comfort, but a wild excitement; she went to them "as if to an assignation" and through them entered into *a life parallel to her daily shadow-life*, a brilliant *real world* in which she and Valentine existed together, *where their love lived*. All losses were *restored* in that world. (*Sylvia* 300; emphasis mine)

Harman amplifies cues and accepts signals provided throughout Warner's writing for how to read the process of making Ackland's presence real. The working with the letters provides an infusion of erotic energy that had been lost during the later years of the relationship, and created "a brilliant real world." Harman too acknowledges that in her altered state Warner is living a double life, one textualized in the diary of 1970. The diary becomes a repository for the spilling over of pain and grief in order for the work on the letters to become "restorative."

In her editorial note for the diaries, Harman echoes Warner's language, calling forth the multiple lives Warner was living—the "two tenses"—as she negotiated a new phase of becoming. Harman characterizes Warner's experience of loss as "the extraordinary *other-life* of her bereavement," and explains that as editor she decided to present the diaries as "interlinked" as they cover "the same period of time," alternating between roman type for the sort of daybook that records everyday events, meetings with friends, work, and so on; and italics for the diary kept in a notebook that serves as self-reflection and narrativization of loss. Harman writes further, "Often the same incidents appear in the one and the other, written as if experienced by two different women. . . . The effect is very odd; the more intimate diary seeming as if it were written *underneath* the more conventional one, as if it were a lower skin of the same form" (*Diaries* ix). It is this "other-life," the diary underneath, that provides the space for working through the process of making the letters and their narrative. I consider *I'll Stand By You* as a way to reach across the "fold" in the diaries, separating one version of Warner's subjectivity from the other, as well as a way to reach across the "fold" separating Warner from Ackland. This reaching across alterity through narrative—"bring[ing] subjects into relationship with other subjects across this gap without conflating them, assuming their commensurability, or eliminating their distance" (Berman 40)—has profound ethical implications.

The italicized entry for March 4 provides some indication of this process, and how painful it was—and also perhaps how necessary for *I'll Stand By You* to come into being. Warner writes,

> I WAS WRONG. I traduced my own unwavering love. I sullied our marriage [by agreeing to the affair with White in 1938]. . . . So in /49 I was honest; I showed my misery. . . . What followed? Months of craving and laceration for her, and a wound which left her maimed. Last night I thought; I should have gone away. . . . Either way it seems I was to wrong her, whom I loved with my whole heart, having made that primal mistake in /38/39. (*Diaries* 340–41)

Warner retells the period discussed earlier, identifying a kernel of the story—the "primal mistake in /38/39"—which catalyzes a causal relationship leading to the agony of 1949—"a wound which left her maimed"—and a final process of counterfactualizing, of bringing into a being a possible world where Warner would have left, would have manifested sympathy and desire differently (yet equally flawed). In order to compose the restorative narrative of *I'll Stand By You*, Warner must retell this painful period accounting for the intersubjective failure of their union.[11] Remembering their time at Miss Green, the beloved cottage where their love began in 1930, in an entry a month later, Warner writes, "I was *inside* acceptance" (*Diaries* 342). In addition, Warner is able to renarrativize their couplehood to include the erotic, that which was lost in her later years with Ackland. In telling of erotic dreams, such as the one on May 22, 1970, Warner can return to that "brilliant real world": "She had brought the whole of herself back to me, all our years of bodily love and worship" (*Diaries* 345).

One element pushing against the reaching for acceptance is Warner's grappling, again, with her own profound desire, even need, for sympathy with Ackland. As we have seen elsewhere in this study—our readings of the *Mausoleum Book* of Leslie Stephen, for instance, or *The Alice B. Toklas Cook Book*—a fundamental issue with the memorializing of the spouse through narrative is that whatever sympathy may have resided between the two partners is eradicated by the way death effects a permanent removal of one from the other. In other words, the dead partner is rendered radically unknowable, making sympathy, or, in Warner's choice of phrase, "equity," impossible. It is not simply that Warner feels the pain of having not reciprocated a sense of dependence, "did not match her sadness with my own sadness" (*Diaries* 337), while it was still possible. It is that the plane of experience has been altered, and the sharing that is integral to the making of couplehood is no more. This emerges from her own awareness of the sense of deep inequity she is experiencing at being the one left alive: "There is no equity. She didn't want to die. I do" (*Diaries* 343). Sharing domestic space and routines, sharing rooms, sharing books and furniture and food, was a crucial component of the Warner and Ackland couplehood, as for others under study here. Countless letters describe cooking, gardening, house-moving—even the texts of Warner's novels have been observed to be especially invested in material reality, in the representation of lived-with objects (see Davies). From the very beginning of their relationship, making homes together was a form of making love, and remained so even when making love was no longer part of their lived experience. So when Warner must note that it was she who was meant to die first, it is to the transformed experience of the rooms that she turns: "Then I came back & looked at the empty places: the rooms looked raped" (*Diaries* 339).

Her perception of intimate space is so entirely changed, she must write it, from a phenomenological perspective, as a kind of violation. This is not unlike the scene from her diary in Yeovil, as she regards rooms that have become strange.

Rereading the letters, described by Harman in her biography, brings about for Warner the much-needed feeling of sympathy, in part due to precisely the erotic impulse they prompt ("wild excitement," "an assignation"). In the diaries, Warner is able to imagine a joining and completion not possible during the later years of Ackland's life, and made unavailable in death. Another dream, from which Warner awakes with her "body *resounding* with joy . . . warmed and kindled with the sensual reality of that embrace," prompts the reflection, "We were alive again" (*Diaries* 350–51). The dream, and subsequent telling, generates once more that "we" lost in death, and the equity of experience the lack of which is such a profound loss. The "we" is alive, restored, in erotic union, but Warner is also newly rejoined in a "we" with Ackland where they each transcend death together. The separation wrought by death is no more. Reading the letters during this time allows Warner to recoup one of their original essential purposes: manifesting the presence of the absent love, even to the point of erotic encounter. The turn these diaries take toward the erotic are even more notable; this kind of explicit writing is not to be seen elsewhere in Warner's private archive, but it does appear in the narrative interpolations created for *I'll Stand By You*, almost as though Warner were able to work through such writing in the diaries as she was preparing the text to accompany the letters. Thus Harman is apt in her characterization of these 1970 diaries seeming a "lower skin." They body forth the keen sense of sexual absence, and restore Warner to a moment when she was still the object of Ackland's desire. The diaries *allow* her the space to imagine herself to be so, which strikes me as entirely necessary to the concomitant narrative project of the letters and their annotations, pursued by Warner in parallel during this time.

I'll Stand By You begins with a narrative section which opens, "The course of our future life was determined by an unamiable farmer" (*I'll* 5), and concludes, "I was at home in an unsurmised love, an irrefutable happiness . . . We laughed as people do who have escaped, by a miracle, from some deadly peril and find themselves safe and secure" (*I'll* 16). The ultimate fulfillment of the couple, at least as Warner has been able to conceive of it after the processes of renarrativizing, and reclaiming, analyzed throughout this chapter, allows for the conventionally proleptic opening. (The unamiable farmer recurs throughout this first narrative to humorous effect; I have not made much of it here, but one of the pleasures of Warner's writing is that she is quite funny. Ackland, not so much.) Furthermore, Warner attributes their "happiness" to "hap"—she narrativizes the contingency of the encounter. The climax of this opening narrative is the coming together of Ackland and Warner, retold once more, this time with Warner taking on Ackland's word "unloved." In telling this tale again, Warner is able to deploy both a retrospective, backward look toward an origin story that had been shared so many times between the two and that formed a foundational component of their shared world, and a proleptic, anticipatory look forward to the letters that emerge from this union. She reclaims the story once and for all, and situates it beyond fixed and linear temporality.

Warner did mean for those narrative interpolations to facilitate the creation of a storyworld on the part of the reader, that storyworld being the world of her couplehood with Ackland, as we have seen in the discussion of William Maxwell's engagement with the project. Although there are gaps—including the protracted gap at the end of the compilation, as will be examined below—Warner means the narrative interpolations to do much of the work of gap-filling for the reader, fleshing out (in some cases literally) the exchange of private documents. For Warner, the letters make real the presence of Ackland; for us, the narratives make real the presence of the two and what they made in cocreating a couple. Once the union is established in the first narrative, the second brings us into its world—literally, as Warner uses an allusion to John Donne's "To His Mistress, Going to Bed":

> "O my America! my new-found-land." My America was a continent of many climates . . . a continent of all climates of love. . . . I had not believed it possible to give such pleasure, to satisfy such a variety of moods, to feel so demanded and so secure, to be loved by anyone so beautiful and to see that beauty enhanced by loving me. (*I'll* 24)

Important to the generation of narrativity is time: she describes how she "reversed the sun," with day beginning with the "ample" night (*I'll* 24), and the "ample" night being filled with admiring and lovemaking, altering the sense of its duration. Also important is Warner's telling of mental activity and affects: "To give such pleasure," "to satisfy . . . moods," "to feel so demanded and so secure." This is not necessarily a fusion text, to use Peter Rabinowitz's phrase—we are not sure how much of these activities and affects are shared by Ackland—but Warner's telling of her own experience in generating the space for the creation of couplehood is a moment of high narrativity and affective force. Warner also takes as a kernel in this second interpolation her first visit to The Hill House, Ackland's beloved summer home (*I'll* 24–26). In the telling of this episode, Warner brings us into Ackland's world in much the same way she herself was. The making of homes together continues to be important, particularly in the fourth and fifth narratives; the landscape, the furnishings, and the animals the two women share are presented in the thick description necessary to facilitate the making of a storyworld—but they also permit Warner to reenter that world made by herself and Ackland.

The progression of the narrative interpolations at the start of the relationship come fast and are numerous as Warner goes back to those early days. The third narrative captures the instance of their "marriage": "That night, our love-making had a new depth and serenity. When we woke she said it had been a marriage night" (*I'll* 47). This line makes explicit, through narrative telling, what has been seen previously in more private writing, such as letters and diaries; we find here the overlap and interchange among the multitudinous variety of intimate life writing. As the narrative continues, an outward turn is enacted, when the two women's work for Spain becomes a more important part of their life together, and then as the Second World War comes to drastically affect their existence. However, the eighth narrative, one of the longest, and the eleventh, one of the shortest, return to the turmoil within the relationship wrought by the White affair.

The eighth narrative appears at the end of the section of letters from 1937, and the text picks up again in a new section with letters from 1940; that section does not begin with a narrative interpolation, and thus there is a sizable gap. What occurred in that gap was Ackland and White falling in love, and Warner inflicting what she calls the "wound" and "primal mistake." Warner begins the telling with:

> We had been in our new house [Frome Vauchurch] for little more than a year when a new love exploded in it. I cannot trust myself to write a true account of the twelvemonth that followed. . . . What I remember is so infected by what I felt that it comes back with the obsessive reality/unreality of delirium.

> There are no letters, no diaries; a few sharply impressed incidents and the witness of poems (hers and mine) written during that year is all I dare be sure of. (*I'll* 163)

Yet Warner does proceed to attempt to tell what happened, collaging poems throughout—unattributed in many cases, in a move which replicates their practice decades earlier in *Whether a Dove or a Seagull* (but without a key). Some are Warner's, some are Ackland's.[12] The effect is to create a kind of dialogue between past and present selves, living and dead, faithful and not. The two women's voices echo back and forth to each across time and space.

In between, Warner lays out the events of that period, a telling of much greater duration than Ackland's own in *For Sylvia*—"If Sylvia had not stayed by me then I should have been damned in and out. I was lecherous and greedy and drunken, and yet I had two very serious loves in my heart, even then" (qtd. in *I'll* 168–69; *For* 134)—which Warner uses and then characterizes as a "summary," writing back to Ackland in commentary which suggests she "misrepresents" Warner's feelings in not accounting for Warner's own dependency (something we have already seen she believed she failed to adequately express) (*I'll* 169). The narrative in large measure proceeds by casting White in a fairly negative light, which serves as a recuperative, if not a reparative, move. By positioning herself and Ackland against White, Warner is able to reassert their union. She writes:

> If Elizabeth had loved her for what she was, none of this need have mattered. But love, which requires so little collaboration from circumstances, demands an agreement of tense. Valentine loved in the present. Elizabeth's love was pinned to a future conditional, to an amended Valentine she could safely call her own. If she noticed the discrepancy, she felt injured and sulked. (*I'll* 171)

This passage illustrates David Garnett's observation, cited above in a letter to Maxwell, that Warner was at her best when writing about love. She presents an understanding of love which depends on each member of the couple inhabiting the same temporality, and being able to narrate and thus create the couplehood from that site, that point of view. If tense is an essential feature of narrative, in the telling over time and from a particular position in time, then two people not in "agreement of tense" will not be able to create a shared story. This was gestured toward in the claim that Elizabeth Wade White's insistence on inhabiting her relationship with Ackland proleptically was the main source of their conflict. Warner, in creating *I'll Stand By You*, asserts that she and Ackland are able to live in the same tense, or, perhaps to recall Micir and the letter to Maxwell, the same two tenses. There is no discrepancy, but rather the Warner in the present memorializing Ackland who herself remains present, and the Warner in the past retelling a story shared with Ackland. We might recall from *For Sylvia*, though, that Ackland's own narrative acts did not always fit or facilitate this vision.

In contrast, the eleventh interpolation is short, much of it taken up with a four-stanza poem, telling of Warner's departure from Frome Vauchurch in 1949. Part of the work of this comparatively shorter narrative is to show Warner's laboring to "submerg[e] all traces of myself"; she continues, "It was as though we were impelled . . . to raise fortifications of anonymity round our love" (*I'll* 240). She draws explicit attention to her attempt to narrativize the unnarratable: "It was nothing like a happy ending" (*I'll* 240). This is in marked contrast to the very beginning of the first narrative, and the early subsequent interpolations, which look brightly to a future that could be imagined. The eleventh narrative ends with Ackland and Warner parting, an undoing of any happy ending that might have been available as a result of the "hap" of another lover. It would take the work of years, and writing, to right/write an ending that might be restorative, reparative—and in some ways, it required the death of Ackland herself.

There are thirteen narrative interpolations in all, but they cease with the letters of 1952. The penultimate narrative describes the sputtering end to the White affair. Ackland lived until 1969, and she and Warner wrote letters until 1968; *I'll Stand By You* includes writing from all of those years, ending with a final letter from Warner in which she says, "Never has any woman been so well and truly loved as I," on the back of which Ackland inscribed: "This letter is my greatest treasure and must be carefully preserved and given back to Sylvia if I die" (*I'll* 386). Why did Warner, with her professed love of annotation, stop with 1952? I will posit that those years bore traumas and losses that for Warner were ultimately unnarratable, and which may have been almost impossible to incorporate into her idea of their shared world. These include much of what has been brought forward in our study of her private writing: the loss of erotic interest from Ackland; the residue of the White affair and the subsequent attempts to recalibrate the relationship; Ackland's rediscovery of the Roman Catholic Church (which Warner greeted with incomprehension and some hostility); and Ackland's numerous illnesses culminating in her breast cancer and death. Warner's own private writing details her responses to these difficulties, but she elides them from her story of her couplehood with Ackland as put forth in *I'll Stand By You*. Perhaps they were seen as endangering what they had, and needed to go unwritten in order to maintain Warner's vision of their union. Perhaps she chose to maintain the couplehood by resisting moments in the story that would compromise its integrity. Perhaps they are simply unspeakable, and while the two women discuss these difficulties in their letters, Warner refuses to incorporate them into the narrative she has charged herself with making.

A further possibility is that Warner sought, finally, to keep those highly significant kernels of their story private and inaccessible, because the challenges they presented to the couplehood were the challenges of unknowability. Her response to the intersubjective and epistemic crises of loss of desire and thus connection (in Warner's mind) on the part of the lover, infidelity, a spirituality at odds with Warner's view of the world, and illness and death, is to *not* narrate the ways in which these rendered Ackland unknowable to her. Warner thus enacts the ways couples and their inner, and inwardly cocreated, world remain unknowable to us. Claire Harman gestures toward this in her introduction to Warner's diaries:

> Publication of a diary puts the reader in charge, and the writer at his [*sic*] mercy, a reversal of the usual order. But the stained notebooks which sit ready to go back to their museum cupboards still contain their pressed flowers and love notes between the pages, still smell of the damp house at Frome Vauchurch and carry their coffee rings, cat's paw marks, traces of cigarette ash, tear stains. The diary retains its privacy and essential meaning, unknowable to us, as Sylvia anticipated. (Introduction, *Diaries* xii)

Harman takes her cues here from Warner, first in recognizing and detailing the reader's situatedness, the world beyond the mind, and the material reality of private documents. These texts tell a life, and they are of a life lived. Next, though, she also acknowledges that the world made by Warner, and by herself with Ackland, remains unknowable. I believe this statement of Harman's applies just as effectively to *I'll Stand By You*, a document meant to be read (and indeed was by Warner's friends before being consigned to the archive until such time as those involved were deceased) in a more intentional way by those outside than the diaries perhaps; but the epistemological problem that lies at the heart of intimate writing still holds.

I would, however, say this doesn't simply lead us down the path of interpretive emptiness: it's not that we're left with no clear account of intimate life. Rather, we are invited back into the space of the intimate archive, where multiple versions of people's lives are available for us to seek, to find—not to yield to one fixed way of reading, one clearly defined arc of a life—but to encounter a proliferation of "I"'s and "we"'s in conversation with each other, and with us.

4

Time and the Other: Christopher Isherwood and Don Bachardy

In September 1979, writer Christopher Isherwood and artist Don Bachardy had been lovers and partners for twenty-six years; they would remain together for another seven years, the relationship dissolved only by Isherwood's death in 1986. In the fall of 1979, Isherwood was seventy-five, Bachardy, forty-five. Over the course of their sometimes tumultuous relationship, one of the ways they anchored themselves, each steadying the other, was to find opportunities for artistic collaboration. Isherwood, who had worked as a Hollywood screenwriter almost since his arrival in America in 1939 (accompanied by the poet W. H. Auden, who remained behind in Brooklyn), would suggest screenplays for he and Bachardy to work on together, including a 1972 made-for-television film adaptation of Mary Shelley's *Frankenstein*.[1] Attempting to formulate stage and film adaptations of Isherwood's novels *Down There on A Visit* (1962) and *A Meeting by the River* (1967) also generated creative connection between them (particularly during Bachardy's 1968 trips to London where he was pursuing an affair with a theater director, about which more to come).

It was Bachardy who, in 1979, proposed a collaborative project: a portfolio of his drawings accompanied by text written by Isherwood, ultimately titled *October*. Considering the prospect, Isherwood writes in his diary for September 17, 1979, "It's a crazy project because it will surely be almost impossible to relate the text to the drawings. Don has a sort of mystic faith that the drawings and text will do this of themselves—and who shall say he's wrong?" (*Diaries 3* 618). Isherwood was a lifelong diary-keeper, and indeed encouraged Bachardy to begin keeping one.[2] The "some sort of text" by Isherwood meant to accompany Bachardy's drawings emerged as a quasi-diary, a kind of performance of a diary; it was written during the month of

October 1979 separate from Isherwood's usual diary (there are no entries in the usual diaries for October 1979), and then heavily revised from November 1979 to May 1980, with publication in 1981.

Isherwood's choice of words in talking about what became *October* is telling: "crazy," "mystic faith," "almost impossible." During this period in their relationship, the mid to late 1970s, as Isherwood confronted old age and mortality, he came to believe that "this is certainly one of the happiest times of my life" due in large measure to great contentment and connection with Bachardy (*Diaries 3* 484). He writes in 1975, "I wouldn't say that I am enormously confidential with Don, that we talk everything over all the time—no, it isn't like that. But we are *continually exposed* to each other; we are no longer entirely separate people" (*Diaries 3* 484). In 1981, he writes, "This is such a strange period in my life. In some respects one of the very happiest, because of Darling's so frequently demonstrated love—the basket [their home, a reference to their animal nicknames/personae] is a paradise of loving snugness, and, throughout the day, we exchange dozens of looks and words and kisses and hugs" (*Diaries 3* 667). Isherwood's diaries provide a space for the performance of intersubjectivity in discourse, showing the relational self in process. One of the most remarked-upon features of Isherwood's work are the versionings he performed among his fiction and his life writing; and ultimately he stopped writing fiction entirely later in his career, turning solely to autobiographical writing, a development commented on by Katherine Bucknell ("Who" 23–24). In entries contemporaneous with what became *October*, he communicates to himself—and possibly future readers, including Bachardy—the intimacy deliberately made and shared by the two men. "The basket" of "loving snugness" is the world the two have created, and language of merging recurs—"we are no longer entirely separate people"—not only in Isherwood's diaries and the letters he exchanged with Bachardy but also in biographical writing on the couple as well. In seeking to enter the world created by Isherwood and Bachardy, we adopt the ways of representing them that they have made for each other.

Bachardy's "mystic faith" in the *October* project would not be misplaced, and the work of that book would open their world to viewers and readers. At the same time, Isherwood's diary indicates that the "diary" he was charged with creating to accompany Bachardy's drawings was weirdly constructed, a chore, even as the stakes seemed to be rather high to his partner. After Bachardy completed more than the necessary number of drawings—forty-six, more than the thirty-one planned, one for each day of the month—he read Isherwood's "diary" over and over again in order to provide suggestions for revision (*Diaries 3* 621). Meanwhile, Isherwood writes on February 14, 1979, "This is the kind of chore which I can only accomplish by brute willpower; something in me is resisting it. . . . I suppose what I resist is the lack of design, the irrelevance of these entries" (*Diaries 3* 627). This entry happens to be on the day of their anniversary: February 14. We might read this as a coincidence, but it strikes me rather as the kind of narrative design that characterizes the entire relationship, beginning with the coming together of the couple on Valentine's Day. The work of intimate life writing for Isherwood is integral to the sustaining of intersubjectivity, and to the world he has created with Bachardy. It has required design and arranging, in contrast to the public performance of *October* which at this point still had not found its shape or voice.

As Isherwood is writing that working on *October* is a "dreary empty chore" (*Diaries 3* 630), Bachardy, over the course of reading the revisions, offers his own critique, picking up on precisely the problems Isherwood is perceiving with the project: "The other day [Don] declared that all the stuff I have written for the *October* book is of inferior quality and obviously made-to-order" (*Diaries 3* 631). A comparison of Isherwood's private diaries and the text of *October* reveals not inferior writing but a different tone and rhetorical position. The *October* diaries are consciously reflective, particularly about Isherwood's perceptions of the generation of a queer identity and the positionality of gay men in society, and more regularly depend upon a narrative moment.

The interleaving of drawings and diary throughout *October* simultaneously creates and resists a narrative of intimacy. Bachardy is strangely both present and absent in the drawings; literally, he does not appear, while Isherwood's chatty voice fills the pages, and the faces of figures like Gore Vidal, Mary Steenburgen, Joan Didion, and John Gregory Dunne gaze out at the viewer. Bachardy's signature is not even present: it is his practice to have his subjects sign their own portraits, to signify the collaboration he believes is taking place between painter and sitter. The original printing of the book, by the art publisher Twelvetrees Press in Los Angeles (which has published other books of Bachardy's drawings), featured the title in all capital letters on the cover, with only the last names of the men involved beneath. On the back is a quote from October 2, describing the process of Bachardy creating the one drawing of Isherwood in the book:

> Don often describes his work as a confrontation. He himself, with a pen gripped in his mouth ready for use when it is needed instead of a brush, reminds me of a pirate carrying a dagger between his teeth while boarding the enemy. He seems to be attacking the sitter. So now I counterattacked. Summoning up all my latent hostility, I glared at him unwaveringly, with accusing eyes. While he was working, he didn't seem to be noticing this. Yet he recorded it. The finished drawing is scary; my old face is horrible with ill will. Most satisfactory. (*October* 8)

This description seems at odds with how Isherwood writes about the two of them snug in their basket, how he thinks of Bachardy as a "refuge" (*Diaries 3* 489). The paratextual framing of the book with this cover might strike a reader as resisting attempts at an intimacy that might be thwarted or incomplete. Yet there is a version of intimacy here that allows for access to a version of the Isherwood and Bachardy coupled world. Isherwood reveals a deep knowledge of Bachardy's practice: "a confrontation." He then gestures toward his willingness to collaborate with Bachardy in the sitting: "So now I counterattacked." When he concludes, "most satisfactory," he might mean that it was satisfying to "summon up all my latent hostility," but he might also mean that the end result, created in collaboration with his lover, was most satisfying, even if it meant he himself looked "horrible with ill will."[3]

Important, too, is the narrative event of this drawing. The first entry in the diary of *October* begins with Isherwood reflecting on the death of his brother Richard the previous May and concludes with the following passage:

> The beginning of October is a joyful, hopeful, inspiring time of the year for me—it always has been. For me, born so late in the summer, autumn is my spring. This is the season which I associate with fresh work-projects in their earliest, most creative phase—the phase of discovering what the project is really about, rather than how I can execute it. (*October* 8)

The book opens with a kind of aesthetic decorum: the beginning of the book paralleling the beginning of the month, bringing promise and creativity and fresh ideas. Yet Isherwood, in his reaching for "design," seems wholly cognizant of several ironies here. First, it was the execution of *October* that was the struggle, in the process of discerning what his purpose is as a writer: "I am evading the iron question which I try to live by as a writer: *Why* are you telling me this?" (*Diaries 3* 627). To what end are the entries in the "diary" of *October* being communicated, and to whom? Then, the image of Isherwood on the recto facing page of the book opposite this passage—"horrible with ill will"—seems opposed to the "joyful, hopeful, inspiring" tone of the entry. The next entry is the story of Isherwood being "confronted" by Bachardy in the sitting. The telling of this event undermines the establishing moment of the first entry, and positions us within the complex dynamic of the Isherwood and Bachardy relationship.

As a whole, *October* relies upon a kind of semipermeable membrane between self and other, inside and outside, public and private. Isherwood's entries show someone deeply involved in his own interiority, while Bachardy looks outward to others. In Bachardy's drawings, it is the faces, the eyes, the gaze that are most prominent and rendered with the most detail; he rarely shows a sitter in profile. (There is only one such composition in the book.) The sitters seem to have been allowed into the world created by the men, by their text, and then proceed to challenge the reader/viewer who seeks a similar kind of access. Torsos, lower bodies, and legs often appear to dissolve into the white space surrounding the human figure, creating a ghostly effect that has the figure at once grounded and floating. Two male nudes are an exception, with the genitalia rendered in the same detail and drama as the face, resulting in what Armistead Maupin has called a "coupling of Bachardy's probing psychological style with his unembarrassed eroticism" (49).[4]

Each drawing is dated, beginning with October 1, 1979, and ending with October 31, 1979. The passage of time over the course of the drawings, signified by these dates, creates an alternative, parallel narrative to the diary text. In fact, Bachardy has said of his own drawings, "A drawing is a time exposure; the mood changes and evolves" (qtd. in Whelan 14). The story of Bachardy becoming an artist is central to the narrative the two men created about their life together, their couplehood; it is told numerous times in numerous interviews, many of them published in venues directed at gay audiences, such as the *Advocate* and *Christopher Street*. It was Isherwood who encouraged Bachardy to attend art school, who supported him in his pursuit of gallery showings, and—at least at the start—facilitated his *entré* into the world of actors, directors, writers, and artists who would become his subjects. The imaginative, creative, relational commitment by Isherwood to the becoming of Bachardy, to the beloved as a being in process, is central to the becoming of the couple itself, and also the source of much of its tension. A few years after Bachardy's beginning forays into art, in 1960, Isherwood writes in his diary:

> I believe more firmly than ever in Don. I believe in his talent *and* his character, and I believe he will evolve into the kind of person we both want him to be. I believe, furthermore, that he has taken giant steps in this direction already. . . . He is becoming more and more independent in the only way that matters—inside himself. (*Diaries 2* 26–27)

In the deliberately and intentionally collaborative text of *October*, a project instigated by Bachardy, Bachardy uses his drawings to tell another version of that story, a micronarrative unfolding over a month. Each figure is an event, providing another moment of revelation into the character of the artist, his process, and his commitment to his own endeavor for its own sake, for his own sake, and for the sake of the relationship that made it possible. In other words, it is not simply essential to *October* that Isherwood's text and Bachardy's drawings speak to each other, nor that Isherwood narrates a working life so integral to their erotic life. It is also essential that Bachardy *show* the story of how his couplehood with Isherwood is necessary for his becoming and flourishing as an artist, *show* the effects of Isherwood imagining a version of and life for his lover.

In talking about Bachardy's work, Isherwood writes, "This is his way of encountering people. What he requires from the sitter is live motionlessness—'live' being the operative word. *He wouldn't take the smallest interest in a corpse, even a quite fresh one. For his purposes, it would be no more good to him than a still life or a landscape*" (*October* 58; emphasis mine). In considering the entire corpus of Isherwood and Bachardy's intimate life writing, this comment becomes proleptic. As Bachardy undertook the project of drawing Isherwood as he was dying, published as *Last Drawings*, he created a new way of encountering his partner. We will consider this in more detail later on, but for now it is worth pointing out that Isherwood, in his knowledge of Bachardy and in his telling, anticipates the final collaboration between the two.

After the death of Isherwood, Bachardy himself became Isherwood's reader, reading the diaries backward. John Boorman reports that Bachardy said that he couldn't wait until he got to the point at which they met (*Chris & Don*).

The beginning becomes the end in Bachardy's rereading; narrative pleasure is found in enacting an alternative to teleological emplotment and its fulfillment, an act catalyzed by loss. The end of their thirty-plus years together meant that Bachardy's status within the relationship shifted. No longer only a coauthor or co-narrator, he becomes narratee to the Isherwood-narrator, a stance Isherwood spent his entire career creating.[5] In several instances throughout the diaries, Isherwood imagines Bachardy reading the text after Isherwood has died. On August 23, 1960, Isherwood writes, after Bachardy has accused him of being dominating, "I do believe he still imagines I might willingly leave him—which is ridiculous and unthinkable. I have never felt so involved with anybody. And *gladly* involved. (I'm aware that I am writing this so Don may one day read it when I'm dead. Well, Don, I *mean* this!)" (*Diaries 2* 899). Isherwood engages in an act, an instance, of specularity along the lines theorized by de Man. He imagines his own demise and Bachardy as his reader. Then, he brings into being *Bachardy* as a different reader in the future than he might be were he to read the diaries now. What Bachardy will realize, one day, is that Isherwood was already able to tell a story that did not involve the two separating, even during their most fraught periods. Isherwood's practice here undoes a queer negativity regarding futurity, reading instead along the lines of Snediker's "queer optimism."

This enacts what Rosi Braidotti theorizes as the recognition of an other's becoming, one that requires creativity and imagination. By interpellating Bachardy in the diaries, through Isherwood's writing and Bachardy's reading, Bachardy is written *and* read into a different version of subjecthood. Philippe Lejeune writes that "the diary is both a retreat and a source of energy in each person's dialectical relationship with the world, which he uses to construct and sustain himself as an individual" (*On Diary* 164). Isherwood uses his diaries to construct a subject, but he also uses them relationally, reaching across a "fold" in narrative time and space, to construct the subject of Bachardy and/in his otherness. In so doing, the diaries become a space wherein Bachardy's processural being, his becoming and his otherness, can be recognized through time. Isherwood reads, and writes, with and through a reparative love.

The reading of the diaries, Bachardy's encounter with Isherwood's telling of their life together, is one of the few endeavors, erotic, creative, or otherwise, the two did not share. After Isherwood's death, Bachardy gave several interviews in which he described the experience of reading the diaries without his lover.

In one of the first, in 1990, even before the publication of the diaries (which prompted a number of new interviews, as did the publication of their collected letters, *The Animals*, and the release of the film *Chris & Don: A Love Story*, both of which we will turn to shortly), Bachardy says,

> When he died I started reading all the journals he'd left behind and that was a wonderful experience for me. I'd never read them before, other than the parts he'd published. So here was a history of our relationship written by this wonderful writer over 30 years. It was an extraordinary experience for me, and a lot of it is written directly to me. He knew I would read it one day. (Lee 43–44)

Bachardy takes pains to note that reading the diaries—"wonderful," "extraordinary"—revealed to him how much alike their views on the world and their experiences of it were, as well as how kind Isherwood had been to Bachardy's younger self. By now we have seen numerous instances throughout the corpus under study where intimate partners use language residing in the field of kindness: kindness, tenderness (in Sackville-West as well as Stein and Toklas), succour (in Warner and Ackland). These choices, to my mind, tend to generate the perception on the part of a reader that a form of ethical recognition is at work, an imaginative embracing of otherness.

The reading, and then publication, of the diaries, also prompted Bachardy to reflect on his own authoring and narrating of their life together: *his* diaries, which Isherwood never read and which have yet to be published. He says, "When I finished reading his journals I started re-reading my own. That's the first thing that hit me, that I'd never shared mine with him. . . . I never let him just read at his leisure, and it's one thing I very much regret" (Lee 44). Bachardy's admission raises an interesting point about the ways in which members of a couple engage with privacy, either the private life of the couple or the private space or experience of one of the members, and how they conceive of their own work of intimate life writing. As noted in the discussion of *October*, Bachardy is present through the figures of his sitters; and, in a number of interviews, interlocutors note that Bachardy is a more private figure, less inclined to self-disclosure and revelation than the more famous, and more notoriously self-revelatory, Isherwood. The sharing of the diaries, possibly with the person for whom they were meant all along, prompts one to ask: Were Bachardy's journals meant to be only his all along? If, as Jeffrey Reiman argues, privacy is essential to personhood (310), then how do we conceptualize the personhood of the singularity within the context of the intimacy, the intersubjectivity, of the couple? (cf. Eakin, *How* 161).

In the 1990 interview with Lee, Bachardy claims that he and Isherwood very rarely had conflicts over power. This is a bit disingenuous. To admit power struggles and conflicts over will in the public fora provided by venues for general readers, like the *Advocate*, or more specialized readers, like *Journal of Homosexuality* (where the 1990 interview was published), would perhaps compromise the story the two men were trying to tell. Yet the publication of a few excerpts from Bachardy's diary in a 1999 issue of the *Harvard Gay & Lesbian Review* illustrates, or at least hints, that the work of generating a narrative of couplehood, and the ways readers consume those narratives, is more complicated. One excerpt, from 1957, is the result of an argument between Isherwood and Bachardy over whether a friend should be allowed to use their home while they are traveling, a house that Bachardy, at this time of great insecurity and tension in their relationship, believes he has no right to share: "Chris's great disguise is that of someone who is without a will, who has only disinterested love to give. Without a will! Sometimes I can see nothing else but that ruthless will of his, as tall, as awesome, as immovable as a mountain" (Mendez 18–19). This struggle of wills, these conflicts over a perceived imbalance of power, are manifest in Isherwood's diaries; it remains to be seen whether Bachardy's own journals will offer similar access, but what is worth noting until then is the varying shades and nuances of the performances given by Bachardy since the death of Isherwood and as the creative work of the couplehood has been revealed. What work is done by the surviving lover once the other is gone? What autonomy from the shared discourse is that one permitted? What new versions might they share? Isherwood and Bachardy lived as "out" gay men, but the coming out of different versions of their relationship continues to unfold over time.

Part of the process of creating a couplehood, worlding a "we," is understanding the other as subject, and as other. Revealing over time, reaching for and recording access to mental and affective activity are essential components of making subjects. In the personae developed by Isherwood and Bachardy—The Animals, also taken as the titles for both their collected letters and the adaptation of those letters into a long-form serialized podcast—such creative and imaginative work was enacted. Such play is a means for Isherwood and

Bachardy to recognize each other's difference, their alterity, enacting ethical relationship through the imagination. (This is not unlike the "Mongoose" and "Mandril" of Virginia and Leonard Woolf's marriage.) The Animals recur throughout the diaries and letters produced by the couple over the course of their entire relationship, and make an appearance in *Chris & Don: A Love Story* as well. Isherwood is a drudging old workhorse, Dobbin, and Bachardy is a skittish and temperamental white kitten, Kitty.[6] They live in a "snug" "basket," their home, more specifically, their bed, and to curl up together is the greatest comfort. For Isherwood's biographer, Peter Parker, as well as for the editor of his diaries and the letters, Katherine Bucknell, the creation of The Animals hearkens back to Isherwood's nursery days and his love of Beatrix Potter's animal tales (Parker 548; Bucknell, Introduction, *Animals* x). However, we might also read this as the conjuring of a world within a world.

Over the course of the entire corpus of letters, it is worth noting that in the main, The Animals present a playful kind of intimacy, a ludic imaginative world of two. One of the ways this manifests is in the use of little drawings, sketches, and the inclusion of magazine cutouts, all depicting Kitty and Dobbin. Isherwood would attempt sketches of Dobbin that were generally not terribly successful, given a lack of talent at drawing as well as an arthritic thumb. Bachardy cut pictures out of magazines of playful, wide-eyed kittens and enclosed them in the envelopes to Isherwood. Readers of the Isherwood/Bachardy relationship have noted the imaginative and affective work deployed in the creation and sustaining of The Animals. In an essay about the making of *Chris & Don: A Love Story*, filmmakers Guido Santi and Tina Mascara describe the phenomenon as "a language of love" (29), and in their work on the film they created a series of animated sequences to capture the Dobbin and Kitty "plot." That plot runs parallel to the plot of Isherwood and Bachardy's own life together, permitting a working through of the conflicts that emerged over the course of that life. This process is a way to emplot the excess of affects generated within the relationship: one plot is not enough. Peter Parker writes in his biography of Isherwood, "Like all such play-acting between lovers, this was a mythology that remained essentially private. . . . It was also a refuge from their own more complicated and antagonistic relationship" (548). Isherwood's diaries and the letters collected in *The Animals*, as well as the serialized podcast adapted from those letters, illuminate the cultivating of this mythology. It not only permitted the two men to maintain their intersubjective connection; it also gave them a way to understand, record, and tell mental and affective activity which otherwise might have proved too challenging to their relationship.

The use of nonhuman animal personae speaks not only to the desire to remain childlike and innocent to each other. In her introduction to *The Animals*, Bucknell characterizes the "'pet' personalities" as "a camp that allowed Isherwood and Bachardy to masquerade and to play about the serious matters of love and commitment and thereby to reveal themselves more fully to one another"; their salient characteristics were "simplicity" and the ways they "embodied the instinctive life" (Introduction, *Animals* ix–x). Bucknell is a fine reader of the letters—and the driving force behind the adaptation of the letters into long-form podcast—so I'd like to extend her discussion here. Concomitant with the desire to "reveal themselves more fully" is a recognition that each to the other is mysterious. Bachardy remained mysterious—fascinating, intriguing—to Isherwood for their entire lives together; I would argue further that one of the reasons Bachardy was drawn to draw Isherwood during his final illness and death was precisely the ways his demise was rendering Isherwood more mysterious as he receded from life. Late in life, during an interview, Isherwood said, "Love is tension. What I value in a relationship is constant tension, in the sense of never being under the illusion that one understands the other person. . . . He's eternally unpredictable—and so are you, to him, if he loves you" (Leyland 105–6). Rather than simply creating anxiety, although at times it did, the inherent unknowability of the other gives the Isherwood/Bachardy union its energy. The desire for knowledge of the other, and a recognition of becoming both mutual and not, was itself a form of connection.

Thus the creation of The Animals allows a space to explore unknowability. A phenomenological understanding of the personae lets us see that each man in deploying his role draws attention to the particular way he sees the world and the relationship. Bucknell notes that Kitty and Dobbin are often deployed in the third person, as a way for Isherwood and Bachardy to distance themselves from the possible sentimentality engendered by their use. In an early letter, dated November 10, 1961, Isherwood writes to Bachardy,

> Perhaps neither of the Animals tells the other enough how much he loves him. But it is very difficult, during all of the day-to-day moods and fuss, and

> the constant preoccupation with cream and hay. The Animals must just have faith and remember the times when they're apart from each other, because then it immediately becomes absolutely obvious that there is no treasure but that furry love. . . . What Kitty must particularly remember is how very proud Dobbin is of him. (*Animals* 102)

This letter shows the way Kitty and Dobbin extend the domestic everyday world Bachardy and Isherwood have created, as well as how that everyday world is transmogrified by the use of the personae. The use of the third person allows one man to speak to the other, as well as to himself, and it also permits recognition of strangeness, of the weirdness of the other in intimacy.

It is when The Animals personae are ruptured that the perspective shifts, and these ruptures are often caused by Isherwood feeling compelled to note that sometimes Kitty and Dobbin are inadequate to the affective and intersubjective task at hand. In those instances, Isherwood cautions against sentimentality and how it falsifies authentic mutual affectivity (even or especially when those affects are negative), and against a too-easy assumption that intimacy can be sustained through a cheapening of the performance. This is most clear in the period of 1962–63, one of the darkest in their relationship. Bachardy was struggling to emerge professionally, and was engaged in an affair with another man. Isherwood left their home in Los Angeles for a brief time, to live in San Francisco; it was from this experience that *A Single Man* came about, a one-day novel that tells the story of a gay man left bereft by the sudden death of his younger lover in a car accident. Bachardy, in fact, had quite a lot of input into the writing and revising of that novel, including devising the title. In these letters, the refusal to use Kitty and Dobbin, and the commenting upon that refusal, becomes a way to negotiate the difficulties present in the relationship, the erotic conflicts, and the failure to connect. One wonders if the creative energy that went into the work of Kitty and Dobbin went instead into the making of the novel. Isherwood writes on March 11, 1963,

> I am so saddened and depressed when I get a glimpse, as I do so clearly this morning, of the poker game we play so much of the time, watching each other's faces and listening to each other's voices for clues. And then you say, for example, Dobbin's in a strange mood, and then things start to get tense. . . . Our relationship is really so very very strange. No wonder it gives us trouble. I mean, I often feel that the Animals are far more than just a nursery joke or cuteness. They *exist*. (*Animals* 125–26)

This letter serves as an opportunity to record and report the failure of intermental activity between the two. The event of Bachardy's leaving prompts Isherwood's attempt to re-narrate the intermental and dispositional conflict that occurred. The letter also evinces Isherwood's awareness of the work the two men perform in creating the personae, and how that work can fail, rendering their enacting of the relationship itself fraudulent: "playacting." The rupture of intersubjectivity creates a sense of despair, and sets in motion an attempt to repair that rupture through telling the intermental rupture of the personae themselves, breaking out of the story seen in the earlier example and showing them for what they are, a cocreation borne of intimacy. To undo it is to save it. Finally, Isherwood points explicitly to the ways the two are and remain unfamiliar to each other, and to the nature of the intimate relationship as itself "strange." They scrutinize each other for "clues," they make themselves unfamiliar to each other, and only distance can bring true knowing.

The Animals have found another life in a long-form serialized podcast, released in 2017, produced and edited by Katherine Bucknell, and featuring Alan Cumming performing Don Bachardy and Simon Callow performing Christopher Isherwood.[7] Excerpts from the letters published in the book collection are interpolated with Bucknell's own commentary which provides some biographical context and background necessary for following the letters, but also offers reflections on her work as an editor and shares information she has uncovered—hitherto concealed by her own previous editing of the diaries as well as by Isherwood's biographer Peter Parker but made available in the published collection of letters—regarding Bachardy's affairs with Paul Millard and especially Anthony Page. The podcast is of interest for three reasons. First, it provides further insight into our understanding of the narrative regularities of stories of couplehood, and how those regularities emerge via letter-writing as a form of intimate life writing. Next, it allows us to consider how these regularities work across media, thinking through the adaptation of the letters into the form of the serialized podcast, as part of a broader concern with how multimodal narrativity works in intimate life narratives. Finally, it offers the opportunity to further investigate the place of the editor or biographer in the work of couple narrative.

The imaginative world of The Animals furthers the intimacy of the men in the couple, creating a space for mutual affectivity which also serves as a bulwark against the threat of betrayal, and a refuge to which each man can return as he pursues freedom within the relationship. The readings of Cumming and Callow capture these affects through the modulation of voice. When reading parts of the letters dealing with gossip, friends, and the whirl of socializing and work, the tones and inflections of the voices of the actors range from gleefully confidential to arch. Cumming in particular deploys a kind of breathlessness, especially when reading the letters Bachardy wrote to conceal his affairs with Paul Millard in New York and Anthony Page in London; these letters are a litany of busyness intercut with references to a poor kitten ruffled and overwhelmed. Bucknell reads these letters as masquerades meant to mislead Isherwood, allowing Bachardy to cover his tracks while making travel plans to meet lovers, creating what she calls "a loophole in time" (Ep. 2), reminding one that Laura Kipnis has argued that infidelity warps the experience of time as lived by those in the affair. In the case of both actors, moments of true poignancy are revealed at the sign-off for each man's letters, all ending with the animal persona and many with endearments. Their voices drop to a level of concentrated intimacy as they repeat "kiss kiss kiss." The performances of Cumming and Callow capture the range of emotions experienced over the course of each letter, and over the course of the letters as a whole and in their adaptation to the serial form.

The course of those letters as collected texts do not always have the coherence we associate with narrative. There are gaps never filled, particularly in moments where reciprocity is absent, such as the period in 1968 when Bachardy was with Page in London writing to Isherwood, and Isherwood never replied in the expectation that Bachardy would return any day as he continually promised. One needs to turn to Isherwood's diaries to uncover his responses to the turmoil of that period. This was a clear instance of Bachardy using a performance of overwhelmed busyness in order to conceal a deception. But the rendering of these episodes *into* episodes—into the serial form—creates a coherent narrative beyond what is available in the form of the collected letters. This is achieved by two means. First, the podcast employs the classic conventions of the serial narrative dependent on temporality, including prolepsis.[8] Episodes end by looking ahead to future events in the life of couple, including those that occur beyond the frame of the narrative created by the time span of the letters (1956–70). The letters, and Bucknell's commentary, occur over a clearly defined period of time. Second, Bucknell's interpolations go far toward generating the coherent narrative necessary for the medium of the serialized podcast; at the same time, the acknowledgment that this is one duration within a much longer arc is essential to the narrativity of the couple. For instance, at the end of Episode Three, "I Want to Talk Cat-Horse Again," Callow reads an excerpt from Isherwood's diaries (sometimes used throughout the podcast in order to provide context, and always read by Callow) in which he ponders the possibility of selling the house should he and Don break up during the difficult period of 1962–63. Bucknell then rejoins the narrative, looking ahead to Isherwood's death and Bachardy's *Last Drawings*. The point is made that the two men lived in the house together until Isherwood's death—and the home is still Bachardy's—but the episode itself is also situated in the longer arc of the couple's life.

As the title of Episode Three might show, Bucknell has named each installment of the podcast after a significant event in the life of the couple, lifting phrases from the letters or referring to major moments in their work life. In the process of adapting the letters to the podcast, this is another way in which the perception of a coherent narrative is generated. Bucknell's own commentary serves this purpose, too. One example is provided by Episode Six, "David Hockney's 'Giant Portrait'"; this painting, a dual portrait of Isherwood and Bachardy created in 1968 and now regarded by many, as Bucknell puts it, as "a seminal public image of a successful gay relationship," is considered in more detail momentarily. For now, we will look at this episode in light of the work of the editor, in this case, the editor as producer and force behind the adaptation of the letters into a coherent narrative. The Hockney portrait is mentioned in five letters collected in the book *The Animals*, four of which are devoted to speculation as to who might buy the painting. Isherwood's diaries do not mention sitting for the portrait at all. Yet the "giant portrait" is not only "giant" in that the two men had a painting of great scale made by their friend who also happens to be a significant contemporary artist; it is also "giant" for what it means for the cultural representation of gay couplehood. How are we meant to narrativize this moment, operating at the intersection of public and private in the couple's life, and so essential to their (self-) representation? More than many of the episodes, this one depends on Bucknell filling in gaps. She does so by reading Bachardy's letters through Isherwood's diaries as well as his unpublished day-by-day agenda, and then bringing in another key voice, one privy to the intimate world of the two men, and in fact charged with conjuring a representation of that world that has gone on to be read by many seeking access to it: Hockney himself. Bucknell provides a visual analysis of the painting, as well as an interview with the artist, now in his eighties, his voice quiet and frail-sounding. We learn that Isherwood sat alone for the portrait, which was completed through looking at photographs of the two together. (Unlike Bachardy, Hockney often works from photographs rather than from life.) We also learn that Isherwood did not record sitting for Hockney in his day-by-day agenda or in his diary, and that the work on the painting is not discussed in the letters. Hockney corroborates that Isherwood knew that Bachardy was having an affair, and that that involvement was the reason Isherwood was posing for a dual portrait of the couple *alone*; Bachardy himself was in London with Anthony Page. The filling in of these gaps serves an interpretive purpose as we regard the painting, and creates a narrative event where one did not previously exist, constructed and told via the interventions and arrangements of the editor functioning in the role of biographical narrator.

Finally, the commentary provides insight into the work of the editor or biographer as she struggles with the epistemological problems presented by the forms of the couple narrative and of intimate life writing. Bucknell takes as a major theme of her work on Isherwood and Bachardy the unknowability of the life of a couple and their world, a theme echoed by Janet Malcolm in her biographical writing on Stein and Toklas and Plath and Hughes. Bucknell and Malcolm provide an interesting counterpoint to others such as Diane Souhami or Claire Harman, the latter two of whom deploy rhetorical and discursive moves and tropes drawn from their subjects in order to arrange the life according to the world the couple has made. The first type of biographical narrator overtly engages through metalepsis the epistemological problem at hand; the second type is overt in its arranging, as the biographer seeks to render the world of the couple, even as it covertly attempts to disappear behind that which it has rendered. My analysis here leads me to probe Ira Nadel's formulation of the biographical narrator: "expressive" (first person), "objective" (omniscient), and "interpretive" (limited) (176). Recalling H. Porter Abbott, we see here that Nadel articulates the relationship between *saying* and *seeing*. As has been suggested, what biographers see—or know, perspectivally and aspectually—determines what they say and how they say it. Moreover, these cannot be separated from the rhetorical position taken up by the biographer, or their discursive performance of relationship both with reader and subject.

Bucknell narrates her own struggle to understand the couple, to piece that world together and enter into it. In the introductory episode, "Introduction to the Animals," she describes her work as entering "a secret world," where she "pried and snooped" as the letters "beckon[ed her] deeper into their world" to uncover "the mystery of their relationship." The interpolated commentary, thus, *becomes* a narrative of the biographer working through her own lack of knowledge, her own experience with the intimate archive which she desires to see hinting at an epistemological completeness, as well as narrative coherence *and* closure, that nevertheless remain elusive. Intimate life writing, then, also invites a consideration of the biographer herself as a processural subject, becoming in unknowing. For instance, in Episode Two, "Something Bad Has Happened," focused on Bachardy's affair with Paul Millard, Bucknell describes going through the material artifacts—the letters, with their rusting paper clips, fragile air mail envelopes, and clippings of pictures of fluffy kittens—and realizing that Bachardy had sent a telegram saying he had arrived in New York several days after he had actually arrived: a way to disguise a meeting with Millard. In Bucknell's collaboration with Bachardy as part of the production of the podcast (for which she had his full cooperation and participation), he agreed to the sharing of this revelation. This move prompted a move in response: the editor's interrogation of the rules of the Isherwood/Bachardy relationship, a relationship she believed she had understood and to which she had full access. She asks herself, what is the "decorum of a semi-open relationship"? What this question is really asking is, what do I not know, and what are the rules governing other people's intimate lives of which I am unaware and to which I have no access? How can my apprehension of the relational—mine and others—be incomplete, and is that its very element?

The discursive creation of intersubjectivity undertaken by Isherwood and Bachardy means they are highly conscious of perspective, of point of view. This is rendered explicit in the various portraits of them taken throughout their couplehood. One of the first, the so-called engagement portrait, taken shortly after they met in 1953, has the two men (Isherwood still boyish, Bachardy seeming barely older than a boy) looking directly at the camera and smiling broadly. The image conveys the sense that they have taken ownership of the relationship, as well as the particular form or genre of the portrait in order to insist on recognition, even acceptance. This iconic representation of gay male companionship overwrites Isherwood's earlier self-representation as denizen of Berlin's demimonde, the Isherwood-narrator of *Goodbye to Berlin*. At the same time, Isherwood's embracing of queer companionship, even domesticity, permits him to delve further and further into the process, via autobiography, of coming out in his writing.

The 1971 memoir of Isherwood's parents as a married couple, *Kathleen and Frank*, is critical to that process, alongside the 1976 follow-up, *Christopher and His Kind*. This is the point in his career where Isherwood ceased writing fiction; his last novel is the 1967 *A Meeting by the River*. Before we turn our attention to *Kathleen and Frank*, Isherwood's foray into the couple narrative that might shed light on how the narrators of such texts work, we will pause on another iconic representation of Isherwood and Bachardy's gay couplehood already mentioned: the dual portrait made of the two by David Hockney in 1968. Hockney made the painting while Isherwood was working on *Kathleen and Frank* (and while Bachardy was pursuing his affair in London with Page).

The 1968 Hockney painting is currently in the Tate Modern; a lithograph Hockney made from the painting in 1976 resides in the National Portrait Gallery, both in London. Isherwood's biographer Peter Parker treats the painting and its creation extensively, noting its grand scale (seven feet by ten feet) and its iconicity (651–52). Essential to note about the painting is the gaze, and the use of perspective: Isherwood's head is turned in profile to look at Bachardy, who looks out steadily at the viewer. As mentioned earlier, Bachardy had to be painted from photographs. Isherwood's expression is enigmatic, leading the viewer to wonder what he must be thinking in regarding his lover; yet we might also realize here that Isherwood is regarding an absence. As Bucknell notes in the episode of *The Animals* dedicated to Hockney's work, "How did it feel to be the lone subject of a double portrait?" (Ep. 6). Bachardy looks straight ahead, toward the viewer, but his face is half in shadow. Jaime Hovey's work on queer literary portraiture might provide another insight into how we read this painting. Hovey writes that "queer self-consciousness . . . undermine[s] normal and conventional expectations about the relationship of gender and sexuality to social behavior and artistic expression" by deploying a "self-conscious self-observation—seeing one's self seeing one's self" (13–14; recall our discussion of Stein and Toklas). Isherwood perhaps regards Bachardy here as a way of "seeing one's self seeing one's self," a self-reflexivity integral to the work of cocreating the couple. Yet, then again, it might seem that it is that self-reflexivity that Bachardy, here, resists. The painting conjures an intimate space, a "stable," "luminous" space, as Bucknell observes—carefully arranged armchairs balanced symmetrically behind a coffee table, books and fruit adding to the sense of equipoise—yet it also raises the specter of the epistemological dilemma at the core of representations of couples: their fundamental unknowability. Such unknowability shifts constantly from one subject to another, its perspective never fixed. Hockney himself seemed to realize this: later drawings he made of the couple use the same composition, except in one aspect. In the 1976 lithograph, it is Bachardy who turns to regard Isherwood, as the older man gazes out at the viewer, expressionless save for a mysterious hooded look around the eyes.

The episode of *The Animals* devoted to the Hockney painting has Bucknell emphasizing that Isherwood was working on his own "dual portrait" of his parents at the same time Hockney was working on the dual portrait of his friends (Ep. 6). Bucknell raises some compelling explanations for why it is that Isherwood never discusses the Hockney painting in his diaries, but one thing is clear: the arduous work being done on *Kathleen and Frank* is discussed in detail. Isherwood published *Kathleen and Frank*, a dual biography of his parents and their marriage, in 1971. The text is an assemblage consisting of Kathleen's diary entries, Frank's letters, and interpolated commentary by Isherwood, in which he refers to himself in both the present and retrospectively looking back on his childhood as "Christopher." This text is also the first instance of Isherwood admitting openly in his own published work that he is gay. The exploration of the heterosexual romance of his parents—resulting in two children and by all accounts happy, however brief due to Frank's death in the First World War—prompts the author's own coming-out, both as a form of self-examination and as a form of resistance to the dominance of the processes of heteronormative erotic emplotment.

Isherwood's mother Kathleen kept a diary from the age of twenty-two until her death at the age of eighty-eight; his father went missing, presumed killed, in 1915 at Ypres, during the First World War. The letters are Frank's, starting with his courtship of Kathleen, including their long engagement and his service in the Boer War, and ending right before he led his regiment, the First York and Lancaster, into battle. Isherwood did not read Kathleen's diaries until she had died, and they did not discuss the contents during her life. Again, I am not really interested in the extent to which Isherwood's work here does or does not have referentiality in the "real world." What I am interested in is the narrativity of this text, and all the texts under examination: the ways Isherwood deploys particular narrative strategies to tell the story of his parents' intimacy, and what the epistemological and ethical consequences of those strategies might be. I see Isherwood's project of intimate life writing, in the case of *Kathleen and Frank* as well as in his other works, as highly narrative, namely in the use of strategies of ordering and arranging, temporal and generic artifice, metalepsis, distancing; as well as performing a self-conscious textuality, deploying multiple levels of discourse and voice through different textual artifacts (letters, diaries, quotation, etc.).

To start, we can read Isherwood's work in *Kathleen and Frank* as a kind of orchestration, and Isherwood as the arranger. This operates on a different level from the Isherwood-narrator, "Christopher." His own self-referentiality exemplifies the tensions among author/character/narrator/implied author, since Isherwood is simultaneously biographer, implied author (or arranger, explicitly given his selection of his parents' texts as well as through his interpretation of said texts), and character—he is "Christopher," son of Kathleen and Frank. As he writes in the Afterword to the book, "Christopher's project had become theirs; their demand to be recorded is met by his eagerness to record. . . . Perhaps, on closer examination, this book too may prove to be chiefly about Christopher" (*Kathleen* 510). He takes on a posture of knowing things he couldn't possibly know, positioning himself in his parents' intimate world—as well as distancing himself, as both biographer/archivist and as son who arrived after the fact.

We might then ask: how are Kathleen and Frank seen to construct their own intimate life, and how does Isherwood intervene? How does Isherwood, or "Christopher," create access points into his parents' narrative of intimacy? What are the effects or consequences? Early in their relationship, during a period of tension wherein the pair is unofficially engaged but encountering resistance from Kathleen's father (dubbed by Frank as "The Great Ignorer"), Frank's letters manifest a teasing that veers from the playful to the hostile. Kathleen's draft letters—the only that survive—show her attempting to elicit declarations of fealty, and her diary entries barely mention Frank at all. During this period, the gaps in both knowing and feeling that result from the text comprising *his* letters and *her* diary entries are filled to a certain extent by Isherwood in his hybrid role as narrator/arranger/archivist, yet an imbalance remains that is rendered all the more poignant when Frank's voice is silenced by his death in the war. A period in the fall of 1900 is narrativized by Isherwood in an interpolation thusly:

> The very fact that Kathleen made these drafts may mean that she felt she was playing a game of skill. . . . This is a phase of frustration, mistrust and sexual hostility between the two of them. Neither is content with the status quo; it is beginning to exasperate them both. How long will the war in South Africa drag on? How long will the Ignorer continue to ignore their relationship? How long will Emily's [Kathleen's mother] health make Kathleen feel guilty about leaving her? The answer seems to be: indefinitely—which for lovers is as bad as forever. (*Kathleen* 118)

Isherwood narrativizes and interprets, arranging with artifice; narrative functions as interpretation. We know how the story of Kathleen and Frank ends—with a successful marriage, children, and a tragic untimely death—but Isherwood deliberately creates uncertainty, suspense, and tension, that emplots courtship and marriage in a wholly conventional way. Furthermore, he inserts himself into the tension that they themselves are trying to mask and unmasks it. Their tension comes from a desire for intimacy that cannot be expressed and is being thwarted; he peels this back and makes the questions and uncertainty explicit, saying the unsayable. He renders himself the narrator of their story, directing us to ask questions in order to participate in the plot, even as he himself is the resolution of their story in his being their offspring. His very being punctures the pretense of suspense engendered by "Christopher" and the Isherwood-narrator. If this reads as an ironic critique of heteronormative emplotment, it would not be wrong to say so.

In deliberately emplotting his parents, taking the conventions of the marriage plot and using them to create an artificial tension, Isherwood provides an opportunity for resolution, and for offering an omniscient view of two people working through their messy erotic lives. He writes, speculating on what kind of "breakthrough" had occurred to change the tone of the letters from teasing to ardent beginning in 1901:

> If one tries to imagine the scene of Frank's proposal to Kathleen in 1898, one can only do it in terms of their inhibitions. . . . Their so-called engagement was actually a kind of literary charade: they were playing a Mr. Browning and a Miss Barrett who talked poetically of elopement but would probably never elope. . . . Once Frank had forced Kathleen to admit that he was not only a "dear friend" but a live human animal of the opposite sex, he could

> quote all the poetry he wanted without turning back into a charade character. Their engagement was now a real engagement, and neither the War nor the Ignorer nor Frank's lack of money was any longer a reason for despair; these had become mere material obstacles which could keep the lovers apart for a while but could never cause them to leave each other. (*Kathleen* 140)

The reference here and above to "lovers" gestures toward Isherwood's ironizing of the container in which most readers would seek to place the story of his parents, a late modernist, even Stracheyan, ironizing of the emplotment he deploys. Here Isherwood sets in contrast two proposal scenes, for a dual effect. First, he is resolving the tension established earlier, through the resolution common to the marriage plot, but he is also elucidating the process of dismantling the scripts that were obstacles to their real intimacy. He shows us how thinking of the other as a character actually limits intimacy, the references to poetry and "charade," Kathleen's inability to see Frank as an embodied man.

Part of the work required in arranging and narrativizing his parents' intimate archive is to tell the intermental activity essential to the intersubjective functioning of the union, and to its representation. Such work becomes clear in the contrast between these earlier texts and Frank's letters sent home during the First World War. Whereas the letters of 1898–1902 require a great deal of interpolated commentary, the letters of 1914–15 stand on their own as Frank uses the past and the history he has shared with Kathleen to connect with her across distance. Of particular note is the letter he sends on March 10, 1915, their twelfth wedding anniversary:

> We have had some ups and downs, haven't we, but I hope on the whole that you will be able to feel that it has been a happy time. I think you enjoyed the actual day itself a great deal more than I did, but I can never feel thankful enough to you for what you have been and are being. . . . I am with you in spirit, but that is nothing unusual. . . . I shall be thankful when we can sit down together over the fire again in a home of our own. (*Kathleen* 444)

The rhetorical gestures Frank makes in this letter, language related to thinking, feeling, hoping, as well as the conjuring of a shared vision of shared domestic space, serves to commemorate—analepsis—as well as to anticipate—prolepsis. Another contrast from the earlier periods of the book may be found in Kathleen's diary entries. As a married woman and mother, as a soldier's wife with a husband at the front, they put forth different preoccupations, of course, than the entries of a young woman: children's outings, schooling, and illnesses as well as housekeeping rather than dances and serving as a companion to one's demanding mother. More importantly, though, is the presence of Frank in the entries, as Kathleen writes openly of her "dread and anxiety" (March 13; *Kathleen* 445), and how her "heart sinks" (May 2; *Kathleen* 457). The world the two have created over the years serves as a space of refuge, but is also revealed to be precarious. Above all, "Christopher," the Isherwood-arranger/narrator, recedes into the background, leaving the couple to interconnect on the page without interpolation as the inevitable rupture that is Frank's death looms closer.

Once this rupture has occurred, what remains are Kathleen's diary entries, the widow without a "we." These detail her attempts to discover what happened at Ypres, her accepting of the official designation "missing, presumed dead," the process by which she endures. On May 22, 1915, she writes, "No news. It seems an everlasting silence" (*Kathleen* 465); the text itself replicates that silence, the silence of Frank. The 1915 entries are affecting in their recording of grief, particularly inflected by an awareness of time. On June 25 she writes,

> I don't know how the rest of the day passed, except that time seemed to have stood still and there appeared a vista of endless hopeless days of loneliness ahead . . . everything reminds me of him, the places we used to go together, our outings and the way he had making everything nice and all his thousand kind and thoughtful ways . . . one could bear the parting when one had the future but now there seems nothing but the stabs of pain from each happy memory. (*Kathleen* 471)

This notion of "vistas of endless hopeless days" recurs throughout the final pages of *Kathleen and Frank*, and the wife who looked constantly to the future pivots dramatically in her view and thinks only of the past. Recall Joan Didion's comment: marriage is time. Without her husband, the wife cannot think of a future. The heterosexual orientation toward temporality and futurity comes undone. Time stops, and can only go backward. To think of the future would be to bear the acknowledgment of her own altered ontological state: a widow, alone surviving a dead husband, no longer a wife.

As the son of Kathleen and Frank, Isherwood takes it upon himself to record their life together, as well as his place in it. His view from that place must be limited (recall Nigel Nicolson's role in *Portrait of a Marriage*), and the concluding pages of the book reflect upon what it means to be the product of a couple, to try to understand that world and that story, and to resist the ways that story determines one's own. Isherwood also uses those concluding pages to tell the rest of Kathleen's life, the many more years she lived as Frank's widow. The conclusion of *Kathleen and Frank* consists almost entirely of Isherwood's narrating, with few instances from his mother's archive. His interest lies almost solely in the couple, and how he might read himself as its realization. He sustains the third person, remaining there as his voice and perspective predominate; her story, their story, becomes his.

Isherwood and Bachardy worked throughout their relationship to flourish their becoming as part of sustaining intimacy. Given the age difference and Isherwood's extensive experience starting with Berlin in the 1930s, allowing Bachardy the opportunity for similar exploration, sexual and otherwise, was seen as essential to the survival of their couplehood, even as the negative affects of betrayal, jealousy, fear, and loss had to be managed. As noted earlier, Bachardy became a reader of the narrative of his and Isherwood's life together via the diaries. Yet even before Isherwood's death, before Bachardy became the steward of their story and worked to ready the diaries for publication, he was aware that Isherwood had had a robust erotic life prior to their meeting in 1953, and that writing that life had played a crucial role in Isherwood's discursive becoming as a gay man and as an author. Isherwood's diaries after his coming together with Bachardy show numerous instances of metalepsis, wherein he comments on Bachardy's reading of the diaries in the diaries, and the ways these textual objects shape their narrative together as it unfolds. For instance, on July 5, 1956, he writes:

> Don returns again and again to the examination of my character—with the furious impatience, indignation and fascination of one who studies a book which is full of matters vitally interesting to him, but which is very badly and ambiguously written. What *does* the goddam author mean? (*Diaries 1* 627)

The metaphor of reading is telling: a regularity of intimate life writing narrative is that each member of the couple picks up the story in the middle as part of creating the new story of the couplehood. Isherwood discerns the young Bachardy trying to take hold of the story and make it his own.

Sex, sexual life and experience, are a regularity of couple narratives beyond the thematic, not simply as event but as a structural feature of the discourse;

it signifies a coming together, a merging of narrative threads. In the story of Isherwood and Bachardy, this is what "snug" means: a coming together, a shared story in which each man can participate. But, each has to be willing to sacrifice "snugness" in order to allow for autonomy. Much of Isherwood's diary records the story of his struggle with Bachardy's otherness, and the need to foster for his lover an autonomy that becomes then a new kind of intimacy over the course of the narrative of their relationship. On November 27, 1962, Isherwood writes:

> We are still deeply fond of each other and I quite expect we shall go on living together, after a period of adjustment. Most of the freedom Don is looking for could actually be achieved right here, living with me. He doesn't realize that yet. Okay, he can find it somewhere outside and then come back. (*Diaries 2* 244)

This entry is reminiscent of The Animals: Don is Kitty, leaving the snug basket and exploring, but always able to come back to the space the two have created. The diary tells the imaginative work performed by the two men to create a space where each has autonomy and "snugness," but it also records the creative—and ethical—labor required to recognize the other, and to see that intimacy is a willingness to flourish the other even in their unknowability.

Even many years into their relationship, this creative and ethical work was still required as the two undertook becoming, and as the shared story threatened to rupture. In 1978, Isherwood writes,

> Nearly had a serious row with Darling because I saw him looking into one of my old (1956–1958) diaries which was open on the desk. . . . Don says I spoke to him as if he were "a chambermaid" caught snooping. I carefully explained to him what is the truth, that I was afraid he might find some slighting reference to himself—there are several in all those early diaries—and not be able to forget it. And I reminded him of that travel diary of his, covering our trip to Asia in 1957, which he let me see, having probably forgotten that it contained a most wounding outburst against the misery of our relationship at that time and his longing to be free of it. I have never forgotten how much I minded, when I read it. (*Diaries 3* 600)

Both Isherwood and Bachardy accounted for each other as readers, participants in their shared narrative as coauthors and as readers. Isherwood speaks of Bachardy as a reader by recalling his own position as a reader, and by instructing Bachardy in the best way to read. The telling of the scene also illustrates the pain of unknowability, as Bachardy rejects the characterization of his looking at the diary as "snooping." The polymorphous discursivity of Isherwood and Bachardy's relationship means that each one can always go back and reread—and that each one is perpetually reinterpellated and reinscribed as reader and author, narrator and narratee.

Last Drawings, the published portfolio of Bachardy's series of portraits created of Isherwood as he was dying of prostate cancer—introduced by excerpts from Bachardy's diary from that time and including drawings done in the hours after Isherwood was deceased, before the body was taken—documents the final act of cocreation by the two men, and shows the central significance of corporeal experience, of embodiment, to that cocreation. It is the final chapter in the narrative that is their life together, and it reveals how essential embodiment is to intimate life narrative. Of course, these were not the *last* drawings ever done by Bachardy, who continues as of this writing to have a full career as an artist, but the gesture toward finality is certainly meaningful. *Last Drawings* serves as a kind of memoir of widowerhood, a working through of a changed ontological state as the beloved person dies, leaving a bereft lover.

Last Drawings is a companion text to *October*, in that it positions Isherwood and Bachardy as collaborators (Mager 133). Whereas the earlier publication functions as a record of shared erotic and creative life, *Last Drawings* is a record of the end of that life; the then-silent Bachardy becomes the voice we hear. Entries selected from Bachardy's diary at the time provide the introductory text to the book, followed by ninety-seven drawings presented without interruption in a clearly chronological order, and closing with an interview with Stephen Spender and a note from the artist detailing how the work was done. Following Bachardy's usual practice, the portraits are signed by Isherwood himself and dated, until about halfway through. The last portrait to bear the signature and date is from October 20, 1985; Isherwood died on January 4, 1986. At that point, Isherwood was too weak and dazed to sign the drawings; the disappearance of the dates seems to render the drawings outside conventional temporality, even as the narrative of Isherwood's dying continues in order through the portraits. Recall the comment from Bachardy cited earlier: "A drawing is a time exposure." The drawings lose some of their detail, consisting of fast, heavy strokes, fading outlines, and white space. The viewer watches Isherwood become a ghost, become less present, as the pages turn. The individual portraits of the dying man, taken together, form a narrative, the extended duration of the event of dying, and each moment comprising that arc.

Bachardy's journal entries detail the work, not his feelings about the death of his lover. He echoes Isherwood's own diary entry in *October*: "In *October* Chris, referring to my insistence on working with live sitters, writes: 'He wouldn't take the smallest interest in a corpse, even a quite fresh one.' Well, only *one* quite fresh one, which I suppose is the exception which proves the rule" (xviii). This tone is representative, and the move toward intertextuality significant. In places he refers to himself as "ruthless," a "bastard," describing himself forcing Isherwood to sit even when the pain becomes too much. But he recognizes the challenge he has set for himself: to draw pain, to capture how the loved body, the dying body, tells a story, and how the telling of that story demands a new and radical form of recognition. The perspective on the body shifts over the course of the drawings. Sometimes the viewer seems positioned next to the body, seated alongside a bed with a head on a pillow. Sometimes the viewer is above, looking down at a mouth agape, into the blackest dark space. Some of the drawings are more expressionist, while in some the figure seems about to be swallowed by white space. As the drawings progress over space and time, one bears witness to a kind of emptying.

If we return to what we know about Bachardy's practice—that working with a sitter is a form of collaboration, of impersonation, of inhabiting a body—then we can read his work in *Last Drawings* as an attempt to participate in Isherwood's pain, his dying. It is an attempt at deepest empathy, at recognition, an attempt to transcend the not-knowing that we must face when someone we love is dying and there is no way to understand what that is like, no way to sustain intimacy in this other becoming. On December 1, 1985, Bachardy writes that the drawings are "the most intense way I know of to be with Chris. It is the only situation now in which we are both truly engaged" (xiv). After Isherwood's death, after the final drawings of the corpse, he writes:

> Since I only draw and paint people and always work only from life, my working experience is one of identification with my subject. While Chris was dying, I focused on him intensely hour after hour. I was able to identify with him to such an extent that I felt I was sharing his dying, just as I'd shared so many other experiences with him. (xviii)

The drawings then become a way to finish the story, to tell the dying. They are created over time, the limited time remaining, rendering a new kind of chronology within and beyond temporality. They become a way to manage the irrevocable disruption in the narrative the two men shared, and become a narrative themselves.

Bachardy's story has continued beyond the death of Isherwood, but that story is still intimately connected with the dead partner. The documentary *Chris & Don: A Love Story*, released in 2008 and directed by Guido Santi and Tina Mascara (themselves married), picks up with Bachardy and makes narrative out of the vast archive the two men created together.[9] Framed by Bachardy as an old man—a strategy that allows us to "mourn with one the heavy loss at the death of the other," as Lois Cucullu puts it (20)—scenes from the present day are intercut with footage from home movies depicting the life Isherwood and Bachardy made together. Also included in the visual storytelling are animated sequences bringing Kitty and Dobbin to life. Like many couple biographies, the film pursues the story of Isherwood's life in the years before meeting Bachardy, and then, after the moment of encounter when their lives intersect, continues as the story of their couplehood.

Santi and Mascara pick up on Isherwood's—and Bachardy's—impulses toward intimate life narrative as a form of discursive becoming. In their essay on the making of the film, they write,

> We wanted to present their story more as a memoir, a private diary, rather than a more traditional documentary. . . . [Don] started reading Chris's diaries immediately after Chris died, beginning with the most recent volumes and working his way back to the beginning, when they first met. Chris's diaries [read in voice-over throughout the film by the actor Michael York] also come back in the end, so they serve as the bookends and the spine of the story. (29)

The many scenes of Bachardy reading the diaries, as well as the voice-over performing their words, point to the importance of reading and writing the subject, and the couplehood, for the two men as a form of worlding. Bachardy himself also narrates, including in voice-over, adding another level of narrativity. Their couplehood was brought into being via discourse, each man participating in the endeavor of worlding through writing and reading themselves together. Finally, as the relationship comes to a close, the film creates the perception of narrative and emotional closure, and coherence, drawing from life.

Critical to the world of the documentary is the space created by Isherwood and Bachardy, their "snug" domestic setting—their "basket"—used extensively and skillfully by the filmmakers. The house is small but does not feel cramped, and the effect is one of being invited into a private, intimate space. We are positioned via numerous exterior shots of their bungalow, and sequences of moving throughout the house. The film begins with the camera tracking through hallways and rooms, the walls covered with art and photographs and book-lined shelves; the camera follows Bachardy through the space. The film ends with Bachardy going to bed—giving the impression that the film has taken a "day in the life" approach, even as time has extended back in order to tell an entire life and capture the arc of the love affair. As Bachardy lies down alone, the moon shines into the window, and he makes the comment that he feels the moon is Chris watching him. The moment is reminiscent of an entry from *October*:

> I don't really mind lying awake, especially if Don is asleep beside me. . . . Our bedroom is beautiful and restful at night. . . . Don and I used to have a persisting clash of wills: He wanted the curtains drawn back from both windows, so that the light in the room would grow naturally with the coming of dawn outside. I used to protest that I couldn't possibly get to sleep unless at least one of the curtains was closed. . . . And then, one night—I can't remember when or why—I agreed to try having both the curtains drawn back. And this was suddenly all right, my self-will had mysteriously relaxed. . . . Nowadays there are no curtains on the windows. (*October* 18–21)

Throughout Isherwood's diaries we find the importance of houses and home, and throughout the letters we see the longing to return home whenever either is away. In this instance from *October*, the bedroom—a site of the deepest intimacy, where both men often talked of sleeping entirely entwined, and where Isherwood would claim that he and Bachardy could communicate in their sleep—is an arena for willfulness, a willfulness that characterized their relationship, and also the "relaxing" of "self-will" that comes with love. Moments of tension and relaxation, almost systolic and diastolic in their nature, appear throughout Isherwood's and Bachardy's narrative. In this final scene from the film, the entry from *October* is not referenced explicitly, but it is coherent with the narrative as a whole, and transformed, not a moment of conflict but a reparative moment of peace and connection.

The home as depicted in the film is also a kind of multimodal archive. First, home movie footage is used extensively (so extensively that one wonders whether Isherwood and Bachardy had a movie camera on them at all times). Early on in the film, we see Bachardy reading Isherwood's diary in an over-the-shoulder shot; the film cuts to home movie footage of the two men in Venice, with a voice-over of text from Isherwood's diary performed by Michael York. In this moment, as throughout the film, the footage essentially serves as a flashback prompted by *the act of reading* the diary. By incorporating and appropriating Isherwood's diaries into the story of the couple, by having Bachardy shown reading the diaries—casting him as Isherwood's *ideal* reader and narratee—they become an essential feature of narrativity and function in the cocreation of the story. This process of co-construction even involves the viewer. The visual archive, in conjunction with the textual archive, serves an analeptic function, allowing the viewer to participate in memory. It permits access to the private world of Isherwood and Bachardy, while also reminding us that it is indeed private. In another early scene, where we learn of the originary encounter which catalyzed the Isherwood/Bachardy relationship, Bachardy performs a voice-over layered on home movie footage of the two men on the beach, then heading up to the house. Isherwood pauses at the top of the stairs leading up to the house and turns to the camera; lush flowering trees are visible behind him, his face is smiling but mostly in shadow (Figure 4.1). As the scene unfolds, Bachardy reminiscences in a voice-over of the weekend that "provided the first night Chris and I spent alone together." The voice-over ends and soft piano music by Miriam Cutler plays on the soundtrack. After a moment, music playing, Isherwood closes the door to the camera, that fleeting instant of access gone.

The scene works to manifest the significance of encounter, as well as synecdochically to comment on the work of the intimate archive. We are let into the world of two briefly, it is conjured by text and memory, but our access is limited and fleeting, our glimpse into the intimate world only that—a glimpse—and our knowledge incomplete.

Another element of multimodal narrative used by the film consists of the animated sequences featuring the Animals, Kitty and Dobbin, created by Katrina and Kristina Swanger. Reviews of the film treated this decision with

Figure 4.1 Film still from *Chris & Don: A Love Story*. Christopher Isherwood closing the door on the viewer.

mixed responses. Stephen Holden in *The New York Times* describes the film as a whole to be "tender" and "extremely touching," with the animated sequences developing the Animal personae, while Noel Murray for *The A. V. Club* called them "cloying." In choosing to create animated sequences of The Animals, Santi and Mascara participate in that fantasy, and allow the audience access to the world of the personae. The cartoons allow us to draw interesting contrasts with *The Animals* podcast, as well, and the performances by Alan Cumming and Simon Callow, as previously considered. Cartoons provide an exaggerated look at the all-too-human qualities seen in the letters collected in *The Animals*, and allow for insight into the childlike view each was able to have of the other when deploying the personae. The animated cartoons also do pick up on what Isherwood himself noted was a kind of sentimentality—a sentimentality that could be strategically withheld, as in a diary entry containing a draft of a letter copied down and dated January 27, 1962:

> Won't write a Kitty and Dobbin letter. That's sentimental. Though it's a beautiful poetic sentimentality. But I think we can still talk to each other by our own names—I mean, even when we're not mad. I realize I am deeply selfish. You admit that you are. But that doesn't stop me loving you. (*Animals* 114–15)

This letter was never sent, almost as though Isherwood could not finally bring himself to rupture the world of Kitty and Dobbin. It required such creativity, as Rosi Braidotti might suggest, to render that world authentically, witnessed in Isherwood's own drawings to Bachardy, and to maintain it. Rendering it for the viewer in cartoons is meant to reinstantiate that creativity, to gesture explicitly to a private world of the imagination. To return to the conclusion of the film, with Bachardy retiring to bed, the last moments are a final animated sequence, depicting Kitty curled up on the bed with Dobbin waving from the full moon hanging in the sky. This might be read as that "sentimentality," but it also might hearken back to the use of Kitty and Dobbin: to work through difficulties that Isherwood and Bachardy could not manage in their "human" form. The radical shift in ontological status that comes for the survivor of a dead lover or spouse might indeed be one of those difficulties that require intense imaginative labor, something the film seems to recognize.

Scenes of Bachardy reading letters and diaries, poring over drawings—including the drawings that make up *Last Drawings*—accrete into a performance of the intimate archive. We have already considered what it means for Bachardy to participate in the intimate archive as a coauthor, narrator, and reader. Surrounded by the artifacts of memory, we are invited in with him. Here, Bachardy goes back into the world of The Animals, and through the over-the-shoulder shot, we are admitted. At the same time, we are held a bit at a distance; we are in the darkness behind Bachardy, his hands and his artifacts in a pool of light formed by a desk lamp, encircling him in that private world.

The problem of the biographer is one of access, of knowledge, and biographers focusing on couples face particular challenges engendered by intimate life and intimate life writing. Writing about intimate life, uncovering the biography of a couple, enacts the problem of not-knowing, the challenges of epistemology. The period of the Isherwood/Bachardy relationship in 1962–63 is exemplary in this regard; this was a very challenging moment for the two men. Not only was each miserable erotically and creatively—infidelity and betrayal, anxiety over work and professional direction—each was creating misery for the other as well. Santi and Mascara prompt Bachardy to go back to that time, the signal moment in autobiographical discourse of coaxing. This coaxing creates an instant where we, too, are briefly suspended in a state of not-knowing. In this scene (Figure 4.2 and Figure 4.3), a medium close-up of Bachardy, centered alone in the frame in the present, is intercut with a still

Figure 4.2 Film still from *Chris & Don: A Love Story*. Don Bachardy reflecting on 1962–63 in the present.

Figure 4.3 Film still from *Chris & Don: A Love Story*. Don Bachardy as a young man.

black-and-white photograph of him as a young man from that difficult period. The two images consist of an identical composition, and there are six separate cuts, using a dissolve effect.

Bachardy is silent as he reflects, with the black-and-white functioning as a visual representation or signifier of mental activity. The intercutting serves also to create a moment where past and present exist simultaneously; the young man suffering at that time exists in the same instant as the old man in mourning. Thus a kind of emotional coherence is generated across time, through visual and narrative coherence. Not only are the two images almost identically composed, they are also strikingly reminiscent of many of Bachardy's own portraits: the head-on challenge or confrontation of the sitter's gaze (especially the tension in the young Bachardy's face and neck), the openness of arms that seem paradoxically unwelcoming. All these years later, Bachardy withholds his thoughts and memories of that time from the audience, keeping at least part of the archive closed.

Another significant part of the archive closed—for now—is Bachardy's own diaries. Yet with the material currently available to biographers, editors, and interviewers, one finds in Bachardy a willingness to participate in the project that is narrativizing the Isherwood and Bachardy couplehood. An analysis of introductions, prefaces, forewords, and afterwords shows that those intervening in the story of this couple in various forms of intimate life writing deploy the same rhetorical choices and tropes the members of the couple themselves do in their own private intimate life writing. For instance, in her introduction to the first volume of Isherwood's diaries, Katherine Bucknell writes that Isherwood's and Bachardy's life

> became so thoroughly intertwined, and they shared one another's projects and concerns so intimately, and with such a strong emphasis upon self-reflection and self-examination, that the project of living and working together became in itself a kind of artistic undertaking. . . . Their shared life . . . has iconic significance as a model of homosexual love and companionship. (Introduction, *Diaries 1* xxxix)

Words clustering in fields related to intimacy, such as intertwining, sharing, merging, appear throughout writing about the couple, as do similar anecdotes (such as how Bachardy came to develop an accent similar to Isherwood's, even though he had been born and raised in Los Angeles, not England). As we have seen in our discussions of David Hockney's rendering of the two, as well as in the deliberate construction of a kind of "out" gay couplehood, Bucknell is indeed correct in identifying both the intentional performance pursued by Isherwood and Bachardy, and the ways that process engendered a kind of iconic status for their pairing in the public eye. Their creative life as well as their couplehood became their "vocation," as Bucknell puts it in the introduction to the second volume of diaries (Introduction, *Diaries 2* xv). Thus the work of narrativizing the couple, begun in the collaborative generation of discourse and the creation of a world, is completed by those who take up the work of life narrative from the men themselves.

And, thus, the Isherwood/Bachardy couplehood has an afterlife all its own. The readerly and writerly need to return to the world of these two transcends the ways in which they were icons of gay love and partnership in their moment. What lends such couples the power to generate this kind of afterlife? What about their archive sustains story in such a powerful way? These questions will preoccupy us in the final chapter of this book, as will the problem of narrativizing lives, and afterlives, beyond the discourse, the ideology, of the happy ending.

5

Gaps and Closure: Sylvia Plath and Ted Hughes

It seems fitting that this study end with an examination of Sylvia Plath and Ted Hughes. They made their life together through words; the two together and apart engaged in a vigorous textual and discursive practice, telling and retelling the story of their coupling. However, they are particularly of interest because of the ways biographers—and critics who tend toward biographical readings—continually reinscribe and reinstantiate that story while also offering strenuous critique of the practice itself. The couplehood of Plath and Hughes depends upon the deliberate deployment of narrative practices of intimate life writing, practices which are often the focal point of any work of analysis on the poets. In other words, they provide a rich corpus—but so do their biographers.

Life writing on these two poets has proven to be an endeavor of such indeterminacy that any biographer, from Janet Malcolm in her classic take on the very nature of biography in *The Silent Woman* to Jonathan Bate and his attempts to navigate the life of Hughes in the face of resistance from the estate, must explicitly account for it.[1] My reading in this final chapter, therefore, will focus on selected exemplars of intimate life writing from Plath and Hughes, including Plath's journals and Hughes's letters. It will also concentrate on an analysis of the galaxy of biography and critical archive study that has emerged around them, and the ways the narrative practices that are part of this galaxy contribute to the polymorphous discursivity surrounding the couple. What we find is that biographers are continually drawn to these scenes of textuality, reinscribing their own narratives and schema onto those scenes. David Herman defines schema in the context of cognitive narrative studies as what happens when "previous experiences," such as those engendered by reading, form "structured repertoires of expectations" about "current experiences" (89). Rather than revealing all we can know about a subject, such work instead reveals the limitations of knowledge, and the stance of knowing as in fact a rhetorical and discursive performance. Ultimately, the narrative regularities at work in intimate life writing allow for particular forms of discourse in the telling of couplehood, desire, and intimacy.

The limitations of knowledge, of intimate knowledge, are at the fundament of the Plath/Hughes story. Essential to their understanding of themselves as a couple is the construction of a shared world, the idealization of what they perceived to be an entirely shared mind. The rupture generated in the marriage by Hughes's infidelity is the "hap" that undid their (possibly) "misdirected" happiness (Ahmed 220). It is the "hap" that, in their shared commitment to the imperative of "happiness" brought about by "oneness," they perceived to foreclose all possibility. This led to an epistemological and ontological crisis, a revelation of insurmountable difference where previously there had been fusion. The story is well known to scholars of Plath and Hughes, and to many general readers, but, in brief: upon meeting and marrying in 1956, the two poets began to build a life entirely around the mutual support of each other's writing, what their daughter has characterized as an "unsustainable idyll" and a "hermetically sealed bubble" ("Sylvia Plath's"). Two children were born, Frieda in 1960 and Nicholas in 1962. In the midst of writing and welcoming babies, Plath and Hughes moved to an old manor house in Devon, Court Green, and let their London flat to the poet David Wevill and his wife Assia. A few months after the birth of Nicholas in 1962, David and Assia Wevill came to Court Green for a weekend visit.

What happens next is up for dispute, and reveals the epistemological limitations of understanding intimate life, necessarily rendering intimate life writing a fraught endeavor. Multiple tellings of the commencing of an affair between Hughes and Assia Wevill exist, a point made by Tracy Brain in her comparison of the variegated accounts. Brain joins other scholars including Susan Van Dyne, Heather Clark, Jacqueline Rose, and Joanny Moulin in foregrounding the "problem of biography," and how the particular case of Plath and Hughes illuminates its challenges to knowledge, perspective, and narrative. In her writing on the dangers of reading confessional poetry autobiographically, Brain looks at Paul Alexander's telling in *Rough Magic*, wherein Assia Wevill is a "marriage-wrecking seductress"; Anne Stevenson's in *Bitter Fame*, wherein Plath herself is blamed for imagining sexual tension between Hughes and Wevill and then overreacting with jealousy, possessiveness, and rage that all but guaranteed Hughes would stray; and competing interpretations of the poems supposedly generated out of the experience ("Dangerous").

We might add to this tissue of uncertainty the narrative relayed by Assia Wevill's biographers Yehuda Koren and Eilat Negev (themselves a married couple). Here, Plath is "suspicious and resentful," her "emotional radar . . . extremely sensitive to the slightest perceived invasion of her conjugal space by other women" (90–91). Hughes is "captivated," "caught up in an inevitability as he fell in love with this exotic woman," and is already planning his "pursuit" of "his prey" as she catches a train back to London with her unassuming and unwitting husband (88, 94). David Wevill himself claims that Plath saw his wife and Hughes kissing, although this is nowhere else corroborated:

> I said to Assia, "What happened to Sylvia? She changed completely, she was so friendly before." And Assia answered, "Ted kissed me in the kitchen, and Sylvia saw it." David did not probe any further, and Assia did not elaborate as to whether Ted had merely lightly brushed her lips with his or had proffered a more sensuous kiss; nor did she indicate if she had reciprocated. "It was the first time that something like that had happened in our relationship, and it wasn't characteristic of her." (90)

In his biography of Ted Hughes, Jonathan Bate repeats this story, paraphrasing the quotations from David Wevill and citing Koren and Negev (185–86). This reiterative practice across Plath/Hughes intimate life writing generates a kind of echo chamber, where stories are told and retold, facts are refracted, but no greater certainty is reached.

Koren and Negev's lively, if irresponsibly titillating, narrative reads Hughes's poetry with the backward eye Brain, as well as Van Dyne, caution against. As Van Dyne writes, the "contradictory stories these biographies tell" of the Plath/Hughes marriage show nothing so much as how "what they communicate is uncertainty" ("Problem" 15–16). At issue here is that, as James Phelan has stated, narrative is one subject *telling* another subject, "for some purpose," that "something happened" (217). The problem is that the biographical narrator is not always overt in communicating that what is being told is, in fact, uncertainty. To do so has the potential to compromise the rhetorical purpose, to breach the rhetorical situation, of biography. This is, in practice, a species of unreliability, of both knowledge and judgment (Phelan 33). Furthermore, Koren and Negev scour the textual universe of Plath, Hughes, and their acquaintances for evidence of when, precisely, the affair with Wevill began, with the effect of something like the opposite of a hermeneutics of suspicion. Just because the evidence isn't there doesn't mean it didn't happen, and it doesn't mean we can't read what *is* there in light of what happened later. For instance, by suggesting that the kiss described above may have been a light brushing or "more sensuous," the biographers raise our compulsion to infer the latter. The speculation is baseless, but it does go further to dismantle the performance of objectivity ostensibly (but not always) part of the biographer's endeavor, allowing us to read them instead as the overt, aspectual, limited narrators they are. Furthermore, David Wevill's dismissing of the supposed kiss—"It wasn't characteristic of her"—insinuates that there must have been something overpowerfully stimulating about Hughes's presence: a schema perpetuated by numerous readers of the poet. Tracy Brain closes her consideration of the competing versions and reversionings of the Wevill weekend with the salient point that underlies much of my work here: "If the marriage hadn't gone wrong and ended, biographers wouldn't present the Wevills' visit as they primarily do, with a distorting hindsight" ("Dangerous" 15–17).

It seems that neither Plath nor Plath's readers can envision this moment unimbricated in genre. One of the scholars preoccupied with "the problem of biography" in Plath/Hughes studies, Joanny Moulin, suggests, "The love affair between Ted and Assia that developed from this visit was perhaps rather the consequence than the cause of the tensions in Sylvia's and Ted's marriage"; Moulin writes further that Wevill's ill-advised phone call to Court Green, intercepted by Plath, "gave rise to a melodramatic scene" wherein the betrayed wife throws the philandering husband out and then burns his papers. Moulin concludes, "Might Hughes have been 'more sinned against than sinning' in the events that led to this separation? Can a biographer narrate this story without implying a view on this?" (20). Several things are worth pointing out here, particularly regarding perspective. First, Moulin's characterization of the scene as "melodramatic." There seems to be an affective as well as aesthetic response implied in the situating of this scene within the formal context and reading framework of melodrama: readers will recognize the betrayed wife and philandering husband from countless other depictions of marital cheating, and the schema engendered in the reader will, supposedly, allow for gaps to be filled both in the narrative and in the reader's experience. But does Moulin's shorthand really do justice to the events? The term "melodrama," freighted with literary-cultural associations, gives away the critic's perspective. Moulin hints that taking a stance is inevitable, unavoidable: "Can a biographer narrate this story without implying a view on this?" Here the biographical narrator is clearly presented as another wrinkle. The biographer cannot be objective, and is thus, in the context of the expectations of the form, unreliable; the biographer was not there to *see*, and can therefore *show* only through a particular lens.

What is clear in the life writing responses to the Assia Wevill episode, and the stakes for thinking about couplehood and intimacy, is this: adultery turned into a crisis for Plath and Hughes because the story they constructed about themselves was one of fusion, and there they would find happiness. Their "we" could not accommodate difference, did not provide the equipment for a rupture in their unity, did not allow space for becoming. Adultery created what I have called elsewhere a "wound of doubt" that could not be gotten over; it laid bare to them the epistemological crisis at the core of intimacy, and the ontological crisis that comes with betrayal, one they were not able to renarrativize together. What I find to be fascinating about the case is that the necessarily contingent and incomplete work of renarrativization, of reinstantiating the world of the couple, was left to Hughes and to biographers—to Hughes's *Birthday Letters*, a poetic retelling of his marriage published just before his death in 1998, as well as to Janet Malcolm in *The Silent Woman* and Diane Middlebrook in *Her Husband*, among others—but in the final analysis few are able to move past that moment of rupture. The story did not have to end that way, but once it did envisioning an alternative possible world becomes *im*possible. Such an impossibility leads to a breakdown of the potential for the couple to be a site of ethical recognition—but it also leads to a problematic ethics of reading on the part of the biographer.

While Plath and Hughes scholars take the poets' biographers to task for the distortions they perpetrate by reading the poetry biographically, I am interested not in how such readings distort our understanding of the poems but in how such readings perpetuate a deterministic, teleological view of couplehood narrative. Adultery might be read as the breaking point, as the moment of fissure in the "we," but this does not necessarily mean that we look at that rupture and then read backward for signs. Moving forward, I take as my objects of analysis biographical writing about Plath and Hughes, as well as some of their own efforts to narrativize their couplehood, in order to show that the kinds of teleological and schematic readings made possible by these objects and efforts illuminate the limits of writing about intimacy, even in *understanding* intimate life and its tectonic shifts.

Heather Clark's impeccable scholarship on the intertextual relationship between Plath and Hughes uncovers the hitherto unrecognized ways the poets influenced each other. Her work allows us, further, to bear witness to the intersubjective nature of their archive, and, by extension, the intersubjective nature of the intimate archives of couples who rely on thick textuality, on polymorphous discursivity, to construct their couplehood. I would like to show how Clark's work can be extended toward theorizing not only the world the couple made to foster their own creativity and becoming but also the *storyworld* they found necessary to generate the narrative of their couplehood. Furthermore, we can examine how that story, and the storyworld it engenders, is transformed over the time of their marriage. To Clark's keyword of "hothouse" I add another word that recurs throughout Ted Hughes's letters: "mausoleum." We might consider the valence of this word in light of our earlier discussion of Leslie Stephen and Virginia Woolf. The "rainbow" of becoming that was part of the couplehood in its flourishing becomes the "granite" of fixity, stasis, entombment, once that shared world comes to be dismantled. In considering the glass bell jar that provided the self-contained space for their "hothouse" world of two, we consider, too, the cracks, to pick up Bate's metaphor in narrativizing the end of their marriage (197).

Perhaps the first thing to make clear is that I follow Clark's interpretation of the evidence provided by, among other texts, Hughes's letters, and their daughter Frieda Hughes's reading of her mother's letters ("Sylvia Plath's"), indicating that as Plath's husband and fellow poet, Hughes was supportive, dedicated to the prospect that their shared life together would benefit her writing career as much as his own. As Clark writes, "Since Hughes had come to see Plath's poetry as part of a project that belonged to 'we' rather than 'I,' his insistence on his 'version' of Plath grew out of his sense that she was his poetic partner and collaborator" (171). Here we get at a tension in the writing of couplehood, one that is simultaneously generative and potentially destructive. On the one hand, to construct a "we" that is mutually flourishing seems the ideal; on the other hand, the creation of that "we" radically alters the ontological state of each subject within the union. Should the "we" break apart, each "I" is transformed, ontologically speaking, and the being of each individual is forever caught up on the versions made as a result of being part of the "we." In other words, being in a "we" with and cocreated by Ted Hughes engendered a version of Sylvia Plath, and vice versa, that rendered them each different from who they had been. Realizing then they were different *from each other* was part of their trauma, even as they carried the previous versions of themselves around with them, each alone.

At this point we will consider the intertextual, intersubjective, and intermental nature of Plath's and Hughes's work not only to create a body of poetry but also to narrativize a couplehood—Clark's "hothouse." Further along, we will turn to Hughes's attempts to escape from the narrative created by Plath's death—the "mausoleum." Her suicide not only catalyzed the ontological shift for Hughes from husband to widower; it also generated a narrative which he played no role in creating, interpellating him in the position of reader rather than author or narrator.[2] For a pair for whom the entire work of coupling was to generate a shared narrative, the death of one had the dramatic effect of radically altering the story to be told for the other.

The process of cocreating a "we" began early in the relationship between Plath and Hughes, and from the beginning it had a public or visible nature. Perhaps this explains, in part, how it is that their couplehood has drawn such attention, despite the fact that, as Diane Middlebrook puts it so strikingly, "One of the most mutually productive literary marriages of the twentieth century . . . lasted only about twenty-three hundred days" (*Her* xv). In 1961, the pair gave an interview for the BBC with Owen Leeming, part of a program called *Two of a Kind: Poets in Partnership*. This interview has been mined extensively for evidence of the poets' collaboration, and the resulting readings bear just as many competing interpretations as the final line of Hughes's poem "Lovesong": "In the morning they wore each other's face" (*Collected* 256).[3] Middlebrook opens her couple biography *Her Husband* with the dialogue with Leeming, emphasizing the difference in their responses to the question of whether they are similar or different (*Her* xv–xvi). According to Hughes, he and Plath "drew on a shared mind for quite different purposes," while, according to Plath, she and Hughes "had very different backgrounds" but "she kept discovering unexpected likenesses" (xvi; see also Middlebrook, "Poetry" 163). A reader not necessarily open to interrogating the critical schema that has arisen around the marriage might see in this exchange the prefiguring of rupture: clearly, such a reader might say, the two poets do not see eye to eye on their very intimacy. What seems to be illuminated here on the part of the poets is an awareness that difference is the necessary condition for intimacy; indeed, to not read intimacy as inherently involving difference, and the recognition of alterity, may be in fact to read it unethically. Without difference, there is no reaching toward, no radical effort to be made toward shared knowledge or mutual recognition. Without difference, there is no weirdness to recognize and accept.

To depend not on difference but on *sameness* for an understanding of intimate life is unethical, to return to our conceptualization from the introduction to this book. To insist upon sameness is to fail to recognize the other. Yet this is precisely the danger of intimacy as well. For within difference lies a radical uncertainty and the potential for epistemological crisis. This is not to say that I find within Plath's and Hughes's contradictory responses the seed of rupture. What I do see is the two poets constructing and performing intimacy in a way that minds the gap. A further look at the interview might illuminate the self-consciousness of this endeavor, the importance of storymaking as part of the process of worlding, and the intermental activity between the two that leads to an attentiveness to becoming in the creation of the "we." It might also allow us to consider the comments about the couplehood separately from the comments about the poetry, a conflation I think at times leads to misreading. For all of the exemplary reading done by Heather Clark on the mutual conduits of influence between Plath and Hughes, for instance, the interpretation of the interview with Leeming suffers somewhat from this conflation of creating poetry and creating couplehood:

> When he asked whether there was anything in their collection "to" or "about" each other apart from the dedications, Plath responded with an unusually muddled answer—one that revealed her deep anxiety and ambivalence about the very nature of poetic "partnership" itself. . . . The two poets continued to send contradictory messages about their collaborative relationship throughout the interview. (Clark 1)

Clark describes Plath as "vague" as to how their poetic partnership came about, and ambivalent about whether it is mutually beneficial (1). With a closer look at the interview, I would like to suggest that both poets are responding to the uncertainty—even mystery—that comes with such intimacy, and, furthermore, while they respond to Leeming's invitation to tell the story of their couplehood, his coaxing, they also run up against their own inability—not to say unwillingness—to provide untrammeled access to their private life.

Leeming begins with an invitation to narrative, with coaxing: "Would you like to tell us how it happened?" This gesture is meant to prompt the autobiographical telling of how the two met, an analeptic return to the encounter. The response is interesting given the vast quantities of ink that have been spilled on the narrating of that very encounter. Diane Middlebrook recounts it at the start of *Her Husband*, in the chapter entitled "Meeeting (1956)," within the first two pages: at a drop party for the first (and only) issue of *St. Botolph's Review*, Plath and Hughes approached, pursued, one another. "They sparred a bit," Middlebrook writes, "Plath nervy and exhilarated. He suddenly kissed her, hard, and she retaliated—she bit him on the cheek until blood ran. He snatched off her hair band and silver earrings, and walked out" (*Her* 3). Plath famously proclaimed in her journal with vigorous language that this "hunky" poet would be the only man who could match her poetic energies and her erotic desires (*Her* 18–19; Plath 205). While the telling of sex and erotic experience is, I claim, a narrative regularity across the corpus of the couples studied here, I do spend less time on it in this chapter in favor of other regularities, particularly intermentality, perspective, and gaps. Nevertheless, it is powerfully present in the Plath/Hughes intimate life writing, told in detail by Plath in letters and journals, and re-narrativized across biographical texts, such as *Her Husband* and the gallery exhibitions devoted to the couple, two of which are examined in this chapter. What is interesting here is that for all of the attention paid to the first encounters between Plath and Hughes, especially their sexual dynamic, in their own telling of the encounter the couple has it go *untold*. None of this "blasting," this "bang smashing" is to be found in the decorous interview with Leeming. Rather, Plath says they met at a party, and then, "didn't we somehow after this . . . suddenly we found ourselves getting married." The privately told version differs from the publicly performed version; this is expected enough, given at the least the fact that one might not wish to transgress the Editorial Practices of the BBC. Yet the deliberately vague way in which Plath constructs the meeting is presented almost as though the marriage occurred separately from any will or agency exerted on the part of the two.

This vague, almost wondering tone continues as Plath attempts to account for their writing together, each turning to different subjects once they married.

She says to Leeming, in response to his observation that their poetry does not seem to directly engage their relationship, "Something happened, I don't know what it was. . . . We began to free each other for other subjects." Again, Plath articulates a kind of uncertainty. To return to the metaphors of the "hothouse" and the "bell jar," the world created in that "something happened" is both containing and freeing. A bit further on, Hughes attempts to account for the "something" by suggesting, in response to Leeming's prompts, that a kind of intersubjectivity is at work. In fact, it seems that Leeming is deliberately engaging with the possibility; he asks whether "your temperaments are parallel or do you think they're in conflict . . . a marriage of opposites." Hughes's response speaks to the effort not only of creating poetry but also of creating a narrative of fusion, or "fusion texts," to use a term from Peter Rabinowitz (96). Margaret Uroff, in her early study of the mutual influences exerted by Plath and Hughes on each other, picks up very explicitly on this language of fusion, writing that the two poets sought to "forge a new kind of love poetry," predicated on fusion and "passionate union" (70–71). This occurs through shared intersubjective effort:

> [Our temperaments] lead secret lives . . . *they content themselves in an imaginative world*. . . . I also have in a way Sylvia's experiences of [her life] and all the experiences she's had in the past. . . . Two people who are sympathetic to each other . . . in fact make up one person, one source of power which you can both use. . . . *You know more about something* than you from your own life have ever really learned; I'm drawing on my wife's knowledge. (emphasis mine)

Whereas Plath's responses suggest a kind of uncertainty—something has happened that she cannot fully explain or account for, something unknowable—Hughes's responses detail the epistemological stakes of couplehood, the mental work involved in the making of the "we."

For Hughes, the coming together of husband and wife means a fusing of experiences and knowledge. According to Rabinowitz, fusion texts evince particular cognitive features and patterns as emblematic, and they can provide especially heated moments for readers (96). These include emotional valence, depth, reciprocity, multiplicity, angle, occlusion, sincerity, and consistency (89–92). It is easy for some critics, I think, to read Hughes's words and find a kind of effacing of Plath; they might see not just mutual influence but a kind of appropriation of her experiences for the work of a seemingly more dominant partner. I wonder if what we are actually doing when we read suchly is to reify a schema of victimhood, or injury, that somewhat distorts the story being told. Hughes's description of the process of "making up one person, one source of power which you can both use" strikes me as the work of a "we," something revealed via a cognitive approach to the narrating of intermental activity that is part of his attempt to narrativize what happens between himself and his wife. For Hughes, the mental, epistemological, phenomenological, affective, even dispositional exchanges he shares with Plath carry "emotional charge" (Rabinowitz 89). This becomes especially significant when we consider the affective import of Hughes's letters, particularly with regard to happiness. We might see depth as well, in Hughes's attempts to account for the "secret life" of their temperaments: not only is he acknowledging their moods, affects, dispositions, and sensibilities, he is also suggesting that these aspects of their inner life have *their own* inner life. Depth is further evinced by the embedding of multiple metarepresentations of mental activity. Hughes is telling of experiencing his wife's experiences; he is knowing more about his own life and the world by knowing what she knows. His speaking about "sympathetic" persons suggests the significance of reciprocity and mutuality in his imagining of intermental activity, as well as sincerity and consistency. If it sounds somewhat like I am idealizing this moment, perhaps I am. If I am, perhaps I am following the lead of the poets themselves and their own imaginative and creative processes. And if I am, and if they are, then the failure of intersubjectivity, and thus of the narrative of couplehood the two have built to sustain themselves, will prove to be seen as the traumatic rupture and loss it indeed was.

In her own narrativizing of the Plath/Hughes marriage, Diane Middlebrook makes use of a similar conceptualization, that of the "we," and that of its failure. At the start of the chapter she entitles "Struggling (1956–1963)," she does more than any previous biographer to tell the process of worldbuilding undertaken by the couple. Attention to temporality in the structure of Middlebrook's biography reveals that the subsequent chapter, "Prospering (1957–1963)," overlaps almost completely with "Struggling," and that the last two chapters that address Plath's suicide before turning entirely to the years 1963–98—"Separating (1962–)" and "Parting (1962–1963)"—are both macro- and micro-temporalities, telescoped and concentrated instances of time and event, within that span. Thus, "Struggling" and "Prospering" narrate metaleptically the crucial years of the marriage from two different perspectives, telling tensions and successes and, above all, ambivalences. "Separating" not only narrates Hughes's adultery but, in its open-ended duration, even beyond the death of Hughes himself, it suggests that the story is never ending as we, readers and critics and biographers, continue to attempt to make sense of this rupture, a rupture that has resulted in a story with neither narrative nor emotional closure. In this, Middlebrook rejects a teleological telling. "Parting," in the circumscribed temporality of one year, highlights and concentrates the singular trauma of Plath's suicide. Overall, Middlebrook in her structure and manipulation of chronology is sensitive to the nonlinearity of modern intimate life narratives, as she, the biographer/arranger, renders the complexities of their arcs. Middlebrook even enacts the coming together of parallel lives into a "we" signified by three chapters all dated 1956, the year the two met: "Meeting," "Romance," "His Family." The moment of encounter—1956—is rendered a kernel of the narrative, and told from multiple perspectives and multiple positionalities.

And so the telling of the "we" performed by Middlebrook offers an opportunity to rethink the story of Plath and Hughes, and to theorize the nature of couplehood and intimate life writing. She positions these comments at the start of her narrating the newlywed couple's honeymoon:

> How mock-heroic is the war between the sexes—the mere, embarrassing grating of his "I" on her "I" behind the little pickets of that pronoun "we" is almost always the active provocation. It's a real war, though, which is why the marriage of Hughes and Plath is of enduring interest. They were so passionately in love, at the outset; they were so attuned to one another, during the years they were struggling to turn themselves into artists. Yet their differences finally became irreconcilable, and their marriage had the most catastrophic ending that could possibly be self-inflicted. When relationships break down, the fault lines can usually be glimpsed by the way the pieces fall. From the elevation of retrospect we can watch the fissures shape in the marriage of Hughes and Plath from the earliest weeks of their life together as Mr and Mrs: a man and a woman with little money and large ambitions living out of the same suitcases, inhabiting the same kitchens, bathrooms, bedrooms; eating at the same table, working at separate desks. . . . Nothing sensational, the conflicts arose because, to oversimplify, marriage opens

> a joint account in the language bank, with "we" as the currency, and that pronoun yokes two individual identities with different stakes in marriage. (*Her* 82–83)

Sustained attention to this substantial passage reveals ways of thinking about intimate life writing beyond the individual case of Plath and Hughes and their corpus, as well as the interpretive potential of biographical narrative writing. The decision to place this passage at the start of the marriage, as the couple steps off into the liminal and transformative space of the honeymoon, highlights the ways entering into a couple can be read as an alteration of ontological status.[4] It is also an interesting narrative choice: before we can tell the story of the couple, we must engage with the stakes of that pairing. The shifts in ontological status are revealed as Middlebrook links the creation of the couplehood with the creation of the artistic subject, attending to the processes of becoming: "struggling to turn themselves into artists," "the marriage of Hughes and Plath from the earliest weeks of their life together as Mr and Mrs." Their marriage was an essential part of who they would become, even as, in Middlebrook's view, their transformation into "Mr and Mrs" sowed the seeds of their destruction.

In laying out the stakes of this ontological transformation, Middlebrook uses the very language the couple has itself established for narrativizing itself: "They were so passionately in love, at the outset; they were so attuned to one another." Here we find echoes of the interview with Owen Leeming, and an acknowledgment of the depth of intermental activity and mutual affects leading to what they perceived, from their situatedness within that couple, to be fusion. That situatedness, the phenomenological experience of intimacy and the aspectual nature of narrating it and its creation, is revealed in Middlebrook's declaration that, "when relationships break down, the fault lines can usually be glimpsed by the way the pieces fall. From the elevation of retrospect . . . ." An essential tension in intimate life writing is here acknowledged, with implications for the narrative regularity of perspective; what we know and what we tell, and how, depends entirely on where we stand, and it must always be incomplete. The biographer approaches the subject from a position that is necessarily aspectual, and must needs be different from whatever might be known from within. Moreover, it is this tension which leads to the danger of schematic and deterministic reading, for which, despite my overall delight with this passage, I must criticize Middlebrook. Our retrospective perspective reveals "fissures" in that "fusion text," in that unity, in that "we." However, this is only a perspective on one of several possible worlds. The work of any biographer, particularly those tangling with Plath and Hughes, must find that the imaginative worlds of the poets, their experiences and their creative work of becoming, might have led to wholly different outcomes.

A number of critics have argued, rightly so, that to fail to acknowledge the writtenness of the lives of the poets, especially that of Plath's, is to be unable to grapple with the ambivalences performed across her work and life. As Janet Malcolm writes, "It wasn't that she [Plath] was more divided than the rest of us but only that she left such a full record of her ambivalences—which is why the study of her life is both so alluring and so disturbing" (*Silent* 88).

It is my contention that couples deploy narrative, discursive, and textual practices as part of constructing their "we"; and as Plath uses these practices to generate "proliferating personae" (Van Dyne, "Problem" 6), there is great potential to craft alternative couple emplotments, as well as to represent ambivalence about the entire intersubjective project. Even as Plath is writing what Middlebrook, channeling the perspective of Hughes, characterizes as "conventional plots in which people got born, married, or killed" (xvi), Plath, along with Hughes, seeks an alternative to just such a conventional emplotment when it comes to being husband and wife, looking for "a script she could live with" (Van Dyne, "Problem" 6). At the same time she also searches for ways of being singular, even within a "we."

Yet, as we have already noted via Moulin's use of the term "melodramatic," such emplotments are not easy to escape, especially when one is enacting that most clichéd story of marital infidelity. Middlebrook resorts to the language of emplotment in her proleptic anticipation of the end of the marriage here on the eve of the honeymoon: "Their marriage had the most catastrophic ending that could possibly be self-inflicted." Middlebrook herself has attempted an undoing of the conventional plot, as might be witnessed by her manipulation of chronology and temporality. Still, the efforts of this unconventional couple are still subject to the conventionalities of plot, illustrating just how difficult it is to heed the call put forth by Lauren Berlant to imagine new emplotments for intimate life. No matter what they try to do, their catastrophe has to be the wronged woman and the cheating man, and their biographers struggle to emerge from the constraints of that plot. Thus the "we" of Plath and Hughes was in some ways the victim of plot. At the same time, the "we" is always imperiled by the "I," as Middlebrook points out: "Marriage opens a joint account in the language bank, with 'we' as the currency, and that pronoun yokes two individual identities with different stakes in marriage."

More private documents from both Hughes and Plath, their letters and journals, provide evidence for the intermental and affective work of creating their "we." One of Hughes's letters, to his older brother Gerald dated May 1957, offers some insight into this process.[5] This is the letter that contains the line "Marriage is my medium," a line taken up by many Hughes critics and biographers, including Heather Clark and Jonathan Bate. Clark, in particular, considers it in light of substantial evidence that the two writers were involved in a mutually productive and supportive collaboration (a "working partnership," not a relation of "master and acolyte") (49–50). To proceed:

> Well, my life lately is splendid, wonderfully repaired from what it was. Marriage is my medium. Also my luck thrives on it, and my productions. You have no idea what a happy life Sylvia and I lead or perhaps you have. We work and walk about, and repair each other's writings. She is one of the best critics I ever met and understands my imagination perfectly, and I think I understand hers. It's amazing how we strike sparks. (*Letters* 97)

Not all of Hughes's letters speak this explicitly of happiness. A letter a month later to his sister Olwyn Hughes refers to tension during a visit to Hughes's parents in Yorkshire, and another to Gerald refers to having to meet Plath's friends and relations during their time in America as "wearing" (*Letters* 99, 103). Nevertheless, I pause on this letter specifically for two reasons. First, its significance arises not because of its singular nature but because of the explicit connection drawn by Hughes between the intersubjective endeavor shared by himself and Plath—or, at least, his *perception* of that sharing—and his happiness; and, because of the very fact of its telling, the telling of a version of the couple to an interlocutor for a particular purpose.

Hughes suggests that being married suits him, and the ambiguity of the word "medium" is striking. It could be that it is via marriage that the inspiration needed for his work comes, and we are meant to read the supernatural associations that come with it. It could also be that, like a medium used to grow cultures, Hughes himself grows and becomes. It could also be that marriage itself is the means of making the art he strives to create. Marriage is the material of art. He also situates this moment within the perceived arc of his own life narrative: "My life lately is splendid, wonderfully repaired from what it was." In beginning the story of the marriage, in situating himself within that "we," he is moved to think about the story his life has taken thus far, in time. Telling Gerald Hughes of the "happy life" Hughes leads with Plath, one finds three embedded metarepresentations of cognitive activity: Hughes reflects on his own "happy life," and, in suggesting "you have no idea . . . or perhaps you have," he thinks about whether Gerald Hughes can enter into the intimate world he has created, and then ponders the possibility that such happiness, such understanding, might be accessible to one outside his own intimate experience. Additional metarepresentations are present in Hughes's thinking through his mutual understanding with Plath, including her "understanding" his "imagination" and his "thinking" he "understands."

A journal entry by Plath about a year before, July 22, 1956, echoes the creative and cognitive connection Hughes describes. She writes, "Living with him [Ted] is like being told a perpetual story: his mind is the biggest, most imaginative, I have ever met. I could live in its growing countries forever" (239). What this seems to reveal, to me, is the mental activity essential to love, *and* the telling to others of that mental activity, along with the telling to oneself (an important activity in its own right, as observed by Peter Goldie). Finally, Hughes depicts himself in his letter to his brother as "amazed." This letter provides the germ of the language we find several years later in the interview with Owen Leeming. While the interview for the BBC was a kind of public performance, honed through years of reflecting on the work and value of their connection and collaboration, the letter to Gerald Hughes offers some insight into the early thinking-through of what it means to make and find happiness in another. Likewise Plath finds a home in the "growing countries" of Hughes's mind, and she finds story. Again, in the discovery of an "imaginative world," in the "mak[ing] up of one person," we discern reverberations from the BBC interview in Plath's journal writing.

This "mak[ing] up of one person" is commented upon by Plath in her journals, and an entry from March 4, 1957, testifies to participation in the discursive making of fusion. She writes, "I get quite appalled when I realize my whole being . . . has grown and interwound so completely with Ted's that if anything were to happen to him, I do not see how I could live. . . . There is just no one like him. Who fits" (268). A schematic reading of this passage might emphasize the phrase "I do not see how I could live," looking ahead to the catastrophe of the end of their marriage. I, however, would like to focus on "has grown and interwound so completely," and the assertion of Hughes's singularity and "fit." The valence of organicism raises to my mind a perception that Plath sees this as generative. Furthermore, Hughes may be singular and she "interwound," but her preoccupation is whether *he* fits with *her.* Her feeling of being "appalled" could come just as much from her realization that her understanding of herself as autonomous is being undermined as it could from a proleptic apprehension that the relationship is destructive. Plath's language evokes a kind of symbiosis, and affirms *his* singularity, even as it calls her own into question. It is that tension between autonomy and the desire for singularity, and the generative power of the "we," to which we now turn.

Even as the "hothouse" was generative for Plath too, another metaphor of confinement makes its way into her language, as we see from this entry of February 19, 1959:

> I, sitting here as if brainless wanting both a baby and a career but god knows what if it isn't writing. What inner decision, what inner murder or prison break must I commit if I want to speak from my true deep voice in writing (which I somehow boggle at spelling) and not feel this jam-up of feeling behind a glass-dam fancy-facade of numb dumb wordage. Somewhat cheered by *The Spectator* printing my two small poems. I think success would be heartening now. But, most heartening, the feeling [as if] I were breaking out of my glass caul. What am I afraid of? Growing old and dying without being Somebody? (*Journals* 463)

Erica Wagner makes a connection between the "glass caul" in this entry and Plath's "bell jar" (156); while I take issue with her removal of the phrase from its context in order to suggest a deeper mental instability rather than the crisis of confidence this passage seems to enact, she points out a metaphor equally as resonant as "hothouse" and "mausoleum."

Anne Stevenson picks up on this troping as well when she writes, at the time of the start of the composition of the *Ariel* poems, that "Ted Hughes must have begun to feel himself trapped under the same doomed bell jar" (239). A brief interrogation of this line reveals all of the concerns critics have with "the problem of biography." "Must have" is never a propitious turn of phrase in biography: how do we know? What point of view is the biographer attempting to promulgate from behind a stance of objectivity? Middlebrook acknowledges the overwhelming difficulty of escaping from the arc the story seems to have laid before it. She writes, "The knowledge that Ted Hughes had, and that we have, of February 1963—knowledge of Hughes's infidelity and Plath's suicide—always exerts a strong gravitational pull on efforts to understand them as a married couple. Their story is forever simplifying itself into a tragedy and rushing toward its horrible ending" (*Her* 86). We do have the knowledge, and it does have a pull on our understanding; but our knowledge is always incomplete, as are our efforts at acknowledging the multiple versionings of this narrative and its tellers in all their complexity.

To return to Plath herself: the "I" dominates in this passage from the journals, as well as a focus on her own "inner" and "deep" self. The "breaking out" she seeks seems to be not only a breaking out of the self but a breaking out of the unit she has made with Hughes: her references to "success," to being "Somebody," are external facing, not necessarily looking inward to the world she has made with her husband. Susan Van Dyne writes, "Had Plath not insisted so hyperbolically throughout the 1950s and early 60s to herself and others that Hughes was the vital engendering force of her poetic voice . . . her poetic repudiation of this myth and these roles might not have been so extreme" ("Your" 89). It is clear throughout Plath's writing, and writing about Plath, that the "myth" created by herself about Hughes held both creative and destructive power; it is also clear that Hughes contributed to the creation of that narrative, and that he similarly mythologized Plath. ("It's amazing how we strike sparks.") Yet here we see a singular attempt by Plath as a singularity—as an "I"—to work out her own story, her own metaphors. Her sense of "breaking out" is self-generated, separate from the "we."

In a journal entry from February 9, 1958, Plath writes, "How did I get to be this big, complete self?" (322). A multimodal biographical intervention into telling the life of Plath highlights her singularity within her "we" with Hughes, her envisioning of an autonomous, "complete" subject, and uses the private language created by herself, her private metaphors. In the 2017–18 exhibition *One Life*, held at the National Portrait Gallery of the Smithsonian in Washington, DC, curators Dorothy Moss and Karen V. Kukil signal their emphasis on the oneness of Plath. Her relationship with Hughes, represented by journal entries about their meeting and marriage as well as by the famous elm plank desk Hughes made for her at Court Green, is not the central focus, but a chapter in a life given an arc in the space of a room. This is in contrast to a 2005 exhibition at the Grolier Club in New York, *"No Other Appetite": Sylvia Plath, Ted Hughes, and the Blood Jet of Poetry*, curated by Stephen C. Enniss and Karen V. Kukil. That exhibition led viewers through the story of the Hughes/Plath marriage, narrativizing their couplehood through letters, journal entries, photographs, and poems, many of which also appeared in *One Life*, illustrating the difficulty of separating the one from the "we."

At the center of the gallery dedicated to *One Life*, the curators placed an installation of glass bell jars, created by sound and sculpture artist Jenny Olivia Johnson and entitled *Glass Heart (Bells for Sylvia Plath)* (Figure 5.1). In order to walk around the room to view the pages, photographs, and artifacts on the walls and in the vitrines, visitors had to circle the low platform on which the bell jars were set.

Figure 5.1 Photograph of *Glass Heart (Bells for Sylvia Plath)*, art installation by Jenny Olivia Johnson featured in *One Life*. Photograph taken by the author; permission to publish granted by the artist.

Contained within the bell jars are strings of flickering red and blue lights, and when one taps the jars, cello and piano music accompanied by an ethereal vocal singing quotations from "Ariel," "I Thought I Could Not Be Hurt," "Poppies in July," and Hughes's "Last Letter" arise. Among the other resonances Johnson hopes to suggest she includes "fragile enclosures of memory" (qtd. in Moss). This sculpture combining the aural and the visual is simultaneously ghostly and wholly tangible, spectral and present. It also renders entirely central this key metaphor for Plath's thinking about her subjectivity and autonomy in relation to others. At the same time, the co-mingling of Plath's and Hughes's texts in song bring them together at the hands—literally, physically—of those outside their union, those reading their life as they move through the room.

To what extent is the curator of an exhibit such as *One Life*, focusing on telling and showing a life, performing the same work as a biographer, even an editor or an archivist? And to what extent is the same possibility for distortion, for epistemological failure in the face of material reality, (ever-)present? Karen V. Kukil, who, in addition to serving as a cocurator for both exhibitions is also the archivist of Plath's papers at Smith College and her editor (of the unabridged *Journals* and the complete letters), reflects on what bringing the unabridged journals out into the world means for our understanding of Plath: it is "like reading a full-blown novel after a true confession story. The essence of Sylvia and Ted's life together is more romantic and more tragic than the plot of any invented piece of fiction" ("Reviving"). Notably, Kukil casts her thinking about the implications of her editorial work in terms of emplotment. She also suggests, a thought echoed by reviewers of her edition of the complete collected letters (of which one volume has been published as of this writing), that access to the "real Plath" allows us to revise an understanding of her as pathological; the headline to the review in the *Irish Times* even trumpets that the new edition "rescues" Plath from "the bell jar" ("Reviving"; O'Brien). The work of selecting as well as framing seems essential to managing the epistemological and phenomenological demands of the life as well as the demands of those who would read it (or view it).

Moreover, in selecting and framing, the curator as well as the biographer (even the editor and the archivist) tells a story. As Crowther and Steinberg put it in their discussion of the "living" archive (note that Steinberg also worked with Kukil in the editing of the complete letters),

> Even if there was a complete archive . . . it would [not] be possible to access either an "authentic" or a "complete" Sylvia Plath. . . . This then further throws into question the notion of objectivity, both in the representation of Plath herself and the meaning attached to this figure by researchers working in her archive. . . . But what we can trace is a creative process, a fascinating glimpse into the intersection of the professional and the personal. (16)

The "throwing into question" the "notion of objectivity" holds for both the biographer and curator. For the work of selection, it seems, must be considered highly personal, and the personal process of selection uncovers intersections and interpretations meaningful for the individual doing the work of intervening in that story of the subject's becoming, of her own process. As perhaps is clear from this chapter, the work of making that story for those studying Plath and Hughes prompts its own set of cognitive metarepresentations on the nature of telling a life. Or, as Jacqueline Rose states in an extensive and important discussion of the Plath archive, wherein she writes of the "coercive nature of biography as a form of writing" and "the fantasy of omnipotence" which supports it: "We are in fact in no position to know what happened, concretely, between Plath and Hughes. All we have is the texts of its endless rewriting ('endless' because of the way commentary finds itself drawn into, repeating, their drama)" (93, 125).

Rose speaks aptly of "the fantasy of omnipotence"; how can biographers know what has occurred in the intimate life of two people, when it might be evident that the people involved themselves are not sure what's happened? When the other remains unknowable, ever more inaccessible? While Plath was forced to confront the unresolvable doubt at the core of her marriage in the adultery of her husband, in her death Hughes was left with an insurmountable uncertainty. The failure of intersubjectivity and the collapse of a shared intermental narrative had the effect of radical ontological shift for "her husband," something made evident in "The Offers," published in *Howls and Whispers*, a short collection of privately printed autobiographical poems about Plath that preceded *Birthday Letters* in 1998. The poem casts Hughes as Orpheus being called down to the underworld to rescue Eurydice. In "The Offers" the dead wife becomes an unknowable, ungraspable figure. He first sees her: "Your part in the dream was to ignore me. / Mine was to be invisible — helplessly / Unable to manifest myself" (*Collected* 1181). The speaker of the poem seems to slide away from being when confronted with this figure of death. Her transformation is recorded: "You seemed older—death had aged you a little"; "To see you you and yet / So brazenly continuing to be other"; "You were there. / Younger than I had ever known you. You / as if new made, half a wild roe, half / A flawless thing" (*Collected* 1181–82). The interpellation of "you," and its repetition, particularly as in "To see you you" and "ever known you. You," has the speaker hailing this figure from beyond while also seeming to want to insist on the "youness" of her; this reads as an attempt to identify the "you" as the person lost, even as the speaker cannot be sure in her difference. She is "other," inaccessible and unrecognizable and yet prompting profound obligation. Recall the language of "similarity" and "difference" from the poets' 1961 BBC interview. In death, the wife is the same but different, and the difference of death is insurmountable. The lines "You / as if new made, half a wild roe, half / A flawless thing" echo the text of William Wordsworth's "Lines Written a Few Miles Above Tintern Abbey": "These hedge-rows, hardly hedge-rows"; "when like a roe / I bounded o'er the mountains"; "Therefore am I still / A lover . . . of all the mighty world / Of eye, and ear,—both what they half create, / And what perceive." The new being replacing the previous version of that being, the phenomenological force of perception, the qualifying uncertainty of "hardly" and "half," the rejection of ontological and epistemological fixity, and the living animal spirit signifying youth and newness: these Hughes's poem shares with his poetic precursor, and draws on those rhythms and images to write of becoming. Not of youth into maturity, but of death into another form of becoming.

"The Offers" presents the radical unknowability of the other in love and in death, as well as the ways one becomes unknowable to oneself, in some ways, as a result of such a transformative and catastrophic event. The language of "we" continues to recur throughout Hughes's private writing regarding Plath, often in the context of responding to those who would appropriate and intervene in that "we." For instance, he writes to A. Alvarez in 1971, after Alvarez published his memoir of Plath in the *Observer* (in advance of the appearance of his book *The Savage God*), "It is infuriating for me to see my private experience & feelings reinvented for me. . . . Please stop toting us around like a flea circus" (*Letters* 325). This language echoes other statements by Hughes wherein he seeks to regain control of his story, such as a November 1989 letter to *Bitter Fame* author Anne Stevenson: "My simple wish [is] to recapture for myself, if I can, the privacy of my own feelings and conclusions about Sylvia, and to remove them from contamination by anybody else's" (qtd. in Malcolm, *Silent* 142; this letter does not appear in the *Collected Letters*). More positively, he writes to Seamus Heaney after the publication of *Birthday Letters*:

> I'd come to the point where there seemed no alternative. Given the funny old physical corner I've got myself into [presumably the cancer that would end Hughes's life shortly after the publication of *Birthday Letters*] and the mysterious rôle in my life that SP's posthumous life has played—and that our posthumous marriage has played—publication came to seem not altogether a literary matter, more a physical operation that just might change the psychic odds crucially for me. (*Letters* 703)

He describes the struggle with and within his "posthumous marriage" with Plath, a union that seems to not have ended after all (as gestured toward by Middlebrook in the chapter title "Separating (1962–)")—just taken a different form, as its members have taken different forms. The process of bringing out *Birthday Letters*, for Hughes, transcends the literary, and we might be reminded again of the language of mystery Hughes used to describe his union with Plath: "mysterious," "psychic," the work needing to be done even beyond any agency or will he might exert as an individual, the power of the two taking over.

Within the "we" of a couple, the relationality of subject to other presents ethical and epistemological challenges; or perhaps, more accurately, it is precisely within the "we" that those challenges are laid bare, made visible, their stakes painfully clear. The failure that came with betrayal of the intermental fusion narrative created by Hughes and Plath meant the end of the "hothouse" that had been a source of frustration, yes, but also a source of creative energy and, even, happiness. As Hughes writes in a letter to Gerald Hughes from December 1962, "The main grief for me is that a life that had all the circumstances for perfection, should have been so intolerable" (*Letters* 209). If we recall Diane Middlebrook's comment—"Their marriage had the most catastrophic ending that could possibly be self-inflicted" (*Her* 82)—we find Hughes's sentence to be poignant: the grief he feels at this point, where the marriage is falling apart, cannot begin to anticipate the grief to come. We should also hearken back to the earlier letter to Gerald Hughes in the course of our discussion of happiness, and note the affective shift.

Hughes's chronicling of the last days of their marriage, and Plath's life, offers a reporting of his mental activity, and what he perceived to be the breakdown not only of their relationship but of their intersubjective connection and intermental narrative:

> Only in the last month suddenly we became friends, closer than we've been for two years or so. Everything seemed to be prospering for her, and we began to have happy times together. . . . We were utterly blind, we were both desperate, stupid, and proud—and the pride made us oblique, she especially so. . . . I don't ever want to be forgiven. I don't mean that I shall become a public shrine of mourning and remorse, I would sooner become the opposite. But if there is an eternity, I am damned in it. (*Letters* 215)

Note again the word "happy." One aspect of Hughes's mourning is the aspectual nature of his telling; from his perspective, from where he was situated in these weeks with Plath, his affective experience was one of happiness, and of shared happiness. At the same time, part of their "we" has become a shared desperation, stupidity, and pride. Infidelity led to a collapse of the union they imagined they had. Hughes came to imagine a reconciliation, and a rejuvenation of that shared mental life. His grief is not only for his dead wife but for the last catastrophe of the loss of connection.

Hughes's attempts to renarrativize his relationship to Plath have him envisioning possible worlds, or reimagining new ontological boundaries wherein other plots would be available (Ryan 175). This very act seems a form of resistance to those, including biographers, who would tell the couple's story through schema. He writes to Lucas Myers in 1984:

> I wonder sometimes if things might have gone differently without the events of 63 & 69. I have an idea of those two episodes as giant steel doors shutting down over great parts of myself, leaving me that much less, just what was left, to live on. No doubt a more resolute artist would have penetrated the steel doors—but I believe big physical changes happen at those times, big self-anaesthesias. (*Letters* 489)

The "events" of 1963 and 1969—the suicides of Plath and Assia Wevill, respectively—are kernels in Hughes's story, but the suggestion that "things might have gone differently" provides insight into a kind of mental activity—wondering—that leads to alternative plots. At the same time, however, Hughes cannot go further, and those plots remain riddled with gaps that cannot be filled.

The truth value of those possible worlds beyond 1963 and 1969 bear no weight compared to the "giant steel doors" closing off the imagining of alternatives, and the subject left after the alterations wrought by those events—"big physical changes . . . anaesthesias"—cannot after all be imagined differently. Elsewhere, Hughes is able to acknowledge that a parallel narrative has run alongside the narrative created with Plath. He writes to W. S. Merwin in 1988: "I've had a double sort of existence—one as typecast in the Plath drama, one trying to ghost along somewhere close to the life I might have had. . . . This other life has been satisfactory more than enough" (*Letters* 545). Here the possible worlds emerge as spectral alternate stories, "close to the life I might have had."

With Plath's suicide, Hughes believes "the rest is posthumous" (qtd. in Enniss and Kukil 56; the letter which is the source of these words does not appear in the *Collected Letters*). He describes himself and his children living in a "mausoleum"; the word appears in letters many years after Plath's death. Hughes writes in "The Offers":

> It seemed you had finessed your return to the living
> By leaving me as your bail, a hostage stopped
> In the land of the dead.
> Less and less
> Did I think of escape.
> Even in my dreams, our house was in ruins. (*Collected* 1183)

It seems the idea made its way into "The Offers" via the line "Even in my dreams, our house was in ruins." (We might here recall Leslie Stephen's own creation of the *Mausoleum Book* upon the death of his wife.) Furthermore, his very sense of himself as a husband was altered by the notion of living in a "mausoleum," not subject to the futurity of coupling but rather caught in the posthumous. He writes to Aurelia Plath, Plath's mother, in 1975, on the occasion of preparing *Letters Home* for publication:

> Frieda & Nick are already living in a mausoleum—I just want to cut down the furnishings & the tourist visitors & the general mess of publicity. I certainly don't want my private life with Sylvia exposed. Carol [Hughes, the poet's second wife] feels enough like an also-ran, & I feel quite enough of a second-hand relic husband, as it is. (*Letters* 364)

In a later letter, to Anne Stevenson, he places Carol Hughes in the "mausoleum" of Plath's posthumous existence: "You'll be able to imagine, Anne, my wife's role as shadow curator (and prisoner) of Sylvia's mausoleum—besieged in what she regards as her own home" (*Letters* 516). Hughes's characterization of himself as a "relic" suggests he is left over from the time with Plath, an artifact from a disappeared and distant past; yet it also bears the suggestion of a religious artifact, reminding one that Middlebrook did title one of the chapters of *Her Husband* "Husbandry," one who tends, who stewards something valuable. Nevertheless, in raising the specter of "mausoleum," Hughes positions himself in a state of never-ending mourning; indeed, he seems to bury himself along with his children and the unfortunate second wife. The relic is buried in the tomb, part of the monument. One should recall here the story of Plath's grave vandalized by readers believing that Hughes indeed compromised the "husbandry" of Plath's work and memory (not least in identifying her on the stone as "Sylvia Plath Hughes"). This story played out in the pages of the *Guardian* and the *Independent* in April 1989 (*Letters* 552–61). In conjuring himself and his life as a mausoleum for Plath, is Hughes creating a more effective, more lasting—because more private—monument than the one that literally marks her passing in and from the world? Is mourning not "granite" but "rainbow," not fixing in the tomb but part of that ongoing process of becoming via creative and affective force?

In another section of the very long letter to Alvarez quoted earlier, Hughes writes with the well-being of his children in mind:

> They had enough of the facts & the truths, living in the mausoleum Sylvia left for them. What your memoir supplies is not just facts (so few of the facts—so many fictions & mere speculations trying to be facts) but poison. Poison is no less poison for being a fact. . . . And these are poisons that you alone have brought into existence, in this memoir. (*Letters* 324)

Here, Hughes acknowledges that facts and truths might be the realm of the biographer, but it is too easy for such work to slither into speculation and fiction. What is telling is that Alvarez makes story through his memoir, and that Hughes grants him that power over Plath's, and by extension, his, life. As memoirs such as Alvarez's come into circulation, Hughes is interpellated not as storyteller but as reader. Even as he was laboring to become an effective reader of his wife's posthumous work—reclaiming their collaboration as described by Diane Middlebrook (*Her* 263–64; "Call and Response") and transcending mere "uxorial fatuity," as he wrote to Robert Lowell in 1966 (*Letters* 264)—he was compelled to manage his own affects by managing those who would appropriate their narrative. In the words of Janet Malcolm, "It is Hughes's bitter fate to be perpetually struggling with Plath over the ownership of his life" (*Silent* 140). The one who played a key role in that narrative of "we" is also the one who ultimately appropriated Hughes's "I"—Plath.

In her many conversations with Plath biographers captured in *The Silent Woman*, Malcolm enacts Liz Stanley's call for biographers to recognize and make transparent the ways their work is intertextual, and how multiple voices speak back to each other in polyvocality (15). Malcolm's purpose in doing so is to render the epistemological gaps in the project of biographical narrative. One of her key interlocutors is Jacqueline Rose, who speaks eloquently to Malcolm's position: that accepting the pretense of performing a position of objectivity and certitude is to efface the fundamental issue of life writing, and relational life writing in particular. That fundamental issue is, as Rose writes in *The Haunting of Sylvia Plath*, "the impossibility of objectivity, the limits of knowledge as such" (97). Of the impossibility of knowing engendered by biography, Rose says to Malcolm, "You have to live with the anxiety that such uncertainty generates" (*Silent* 175). To accept such uncertainty about our own lives and the lives of others would be radical indeed. It would mean acknowledging that gaps go unfilled, that closure is impossible; and it would tend us further toward an ethics of reading through the recognition of unknowability.

Coda

Such an acknowledgment may be beyond our reach because of the appeal of those aspects of relational life narrative that suggest coherence and closure are available. This book has put forth claims and analysis made possible by a reparative stance which informs an ethics of reading intersubjectivity and intertextuality (Sedgwick 149). We have borne witness to such enactments of intertextuality and intersubjectivity—and of their failure. We have found what Sara Ahmed might characterize as "strange and perverse mixtures of hope and despair, optimism and pessimism" (163). These entangled and extravagant affects are narrativized through time and minds, through encounter and loss, through worlds made by subjects with and through others.

The literary subjects in this book sought, and often found, happiness with and through an other, even if only briefly, but often for an entire life. Some of the most powerful writing discussed in this book emerged from *unhappiness*, from having to grapple with an array of miseries through creativity, managing an assortment of bad affects in the form of jealousy, shame, betrayal, fear, resentment. Ahmed, in appreciating but questioning Rosi Braidotti's "affirmative ethics," asserts, "When we are estranged from happiness, things happen. Hap happens" (218). The negative encounter can be a site for ethics, too, not only that transformative encounter of love. Yet of queer theory, Elizabeth Freeman asks why it is that "only pain seems so socially and theoretically generative?" (12). I will not suggest that the answer resides in the normative emplotment of "happily ever after." Such a move forecloses possibility and replicates the problems with the understandings of intimacy this book has sought to dismantle.

But might not the possibilities allowed by openness to "hap," rather than happiness, position us as available to Braidotti's "joyful affirmation"? Braidotti writes, "The moment of negative passion . . . is the prelude to the ethical gesture that involves transcending the negativity and accepting the displacement of the self through the impact of an other that is so very close" (198). Relational life writing narrativizes these moments, creating a space for the radical recognition of the other and the flourishing of becoming. This is the power, the force, the *potentia* of intimacy. It is the art of living intensely, with others.

Notes

Introduction: Reading Intimate Life Writing: Act, Practice, Process

1 To start, I am indebted to Heather Clark for directing me to the McGann quotation that provides the opening for this introduction.

Noted biographer Hermione Lee also takes up the definition of "life writing": "Different ways of telling a life-story—memoir, autobiography, biography, diary, letters, autobiographical fiction." She also notes that the term can be used "when the distinction between biography and autobiography is being deliberately blurred" (qtd. in Saunders 4). I will be using the term mostly in the first sense, occasionally in the second. The more open definition of "life writing" also emerges from feminist concerns and practice in auto/biographical discourse, as a way to include forms of self-referential texts not accounted for by narratives privileging a notion of the "autonomous, universal, solitary, transcendent" self (see Smith and Watson, *Reading* 215–218). Marlene Kadar articulates how a reenvisioning of auto/biography through "life writing" is shaped by feminist theory (3–7, 10, 12); this is picked up as well by Laura Marcus, who asserts that the use of the term "life writing" makes an "argument against hierarchization . . . paralleled by a widespread growth of interest in forms of personal writing, such as diaries, letters, and journals . . . as texts in their own right" (*Auto/Biographical* 231).

Intimate life writing *as a practice* of course has gone on well before the literary historical starting point of this study, and beyond the Anglo-American individuals I take as my corpus. Consider the letters of Héloïse and Abelard, or William Godwin's *Memoirs of the Author of a Vindication of the Rights of Woman*, written after the death of Mary Wollstonecraft, just to cite two examples that had an influence on early stages of this project. Peter Gay's *The Education of the Senses*, part of his five-volume *The Bourgeois Experience*, documents nineteenth-century private intimate writing, including some very powerful letters. I do think that as life writing took on new forms over the first half of the twentieth century, drawing on new epistemes and new energies (some of which are precisely the focus of Gay's work), intimate life writing of the types I am analyzing here emerged with a distinct set of world- and subject-making priorities.

2 See Elizabeth Bruss on the work of defining autobiography as a genre, which she seeks to do through speech-act theory. In formulating (and tempering) my claims, I have found Julia Watson's "Is Relationality a Genre?" to be most helpful.

3 See also Liz Stanley, *The Auto/Biographical I*, for an explicitly feminist critique, informed by Stanley's positionality as a working-class lesbian and biographer.

4 Theoretical investigations of the concept of storyworld I have found particularly useful include Herman's *Story Logic* and Ryan's *Possible Worlds, Artificial Intelligence, and Narrative Theory*. I discuss Breger at several points in this introduction, as part of defining my intervention in narrative and affects. See also Smith ("Performativity" 18).

5 Biographical texts that were important in shaping my thinking on this project over its many years of development (including through several papers given at conferences), and which do much of what I suggest couple biographies do, but which I ultimately decided against including, are: Rosemary Ashton, *Thomas & Jane Carlyle: Portrait of a Marriage*; Hazel Rowley, *Tête à Tête: The Tumultuous Lives & Loves of Simone de Beauvoir & Jean-Paul Sartre*; Edith Gelles, *Abigail and John: Portrait of a Marriage*; Doris Kearns Goodwin, *No Ordinary Time: Franklin & Eleanor Roosevelt*; Brenda Maddox, *D. H. Lawrence: The Story of a Marriage*; Mary S. Lovell, *A Rage to Live: A Biography of Richard and Isabel Burton*; Sydney Janet Kaplan, *Circulating Genius: John Middleton Murry, Katherine Mansfield, and D. H. Lawrence*. A number of studies, both biographical and theoretical, have considered creative and collaborative relationships between couples; these include collections edited by Perry and Brownley, Chadwick and de Courtivron, and Stone and Thompson. Finally, several prosopographies on couples were also formative: Phyllis Rose, *Parallel Lives*; Katie Roiphe, *Uncommon Arrangements*; Lesley McDowell *Between the Sheets*. I decided to limit my investigations to Anglo-American literary couples of the early to mid-twentieth century; to eschew sustained engagement with the study of creativity; and to focus on individuals rather than groups. As should also be clear, this is not itself a work of biographical writing, though biographical information is provided where necessary to help make sense of the texts under consideration.

6 I use the words "making" and "creating" throughout this book. I am inspired by Rosi Braidotti to do so, in her assertion that thinking "is the skill that consists in developing a compass of the cognitive, affective, and ethical kind . . . *Homo faber* is better suited for this task than good old *homo sapiens*" (177). What does this cognitive, affective, and ethical sense provide? No more or less than a sense of

who we are. Readers are also encouraged to consult Braidotti's entry on the ethics of joy in *Posthuman Glossary* (221–24).

7 I leave it to readers to consider further the political implications of "minor" with regard to Deleuze and Guattari's theorization of the category. I will say that thinking of some of the writers here as "minor" in relation to their more well-known partner—even if the "minor" figure came to somewhat greater renown over time—through Deleuze and Guattari, even in thinking of the more well-known figures themselves who are often read as marginalized, often due to their sexuality, allows us to suggest a response to Lauren Berlant's call to rethink intimacy for those who cannot, do not, or will not participate in dominant or hegemonic frameworks (5–6). We might read the pairings of these "minor" and less "minor" writers, or those writers imagined to be "minor" due to their marginalized position, as deploying the "political" and "collective" force necessary to reimagine intimacy (Deleuze and Guattari 59–60), in addition to the suggestion that their inclusion here on the terms delineated might perform the work of dehierarchization in auto/biography. What might this work add to readings of biographies—those "portraits of a marriage"—that hierarchize and thus reify the imbalance between dominant and nondominant partners (such as, for instance, *Carol and John Steinbeck: Portrait of a Marriage* by Susan Shillinglaw), or which make the attempt to overturn that imbalance by showing the significance of the seemingly "minor" or "marginalized" ("marginalized" by gender, political position, etc.) partner (such as, for instance, *Abigail and John: Portrait of a Marriage* by Edith Gelles). I would like to here acknowledge my debt to Brenda Maddox on this and so many other aspects of this work.

A related point relevant throughout is: biographical writing about couples sometimes relies on emplotting one member of the couple as an "injured part[y]" (Linzie 5); this person is often read as having toiled in semi-obscurity, subjugating their own desires or ambitions (sexual or otherwise) to the other "genius" half. I would like to suggest that such an emplotment in these seemingly "asymmetrical relationship[s]" becomes problematic if we read the "supposedly injured party" as "both coauthoring and helping to enforce it" (Linzie 5).

8 In this book, I do focus on sexual relationships, following my authors' own prioritizing of the sexual and generally embodied aspects of their intimate lives and experiences, and the ways they saw these as a constituent aspect of their subjectivity, their subject positions, and their relationships. In other words, I do not at all wish to suggest that sex is required for intimacy; I do wish to acknowledge that for the writers under consideration here, in the couplehoods they created, sex is a significant element of what constitutes intimacy in the

manner they are imagining it. As we shall see, it is very much constitutive of the processes of worldmaking taken on by these figures. I would recall us to Smith and Watson's reminder that embodiment is a key component of life writing, and that sex and sexuality feature as key themes in its practice (*Reading* 278–79).

9 For Lauren Berlant, contemporary notions of intimacy do not allow for those—"the queers, the single, the something else"—"who don't or can't find their way" in the plots deemed acceptable for life narrative (6). As a result, she calls for a rethinking of intimacy that would transform such hegemonic plots and ideological institutions; further, it is the very instantiation of intimacy, desire, that might be deployed for such work, as desire itself is "destabilizing" (6). A number of readers may look at my approach and note that, indeed, the writers under consideration—those couples and their biographers—participate in the emplotments that come in for Berlant's critique; some of them, more so, are entangled, caught up. I would ask why it is that these emplotments have such resonances for these figures' attempts at intimate life writing, and why these emplotments find such sustaining power in relational narratives. When these literary couples seek to fulfill their "aspiration for a narrative about something shared," why do these narratives come with such identifiable regularities?

Chapter 1

1 See Claire Tomalin's *The Invisible Woman: The Story of Nelly Ternan and Charles Dickens.*

2 In this first chapter, the couples discussed were married in the traditional sense, and words like "spouse" and "couple" might be read in this context. In the rest of this book, only the subjects in the final chapter—Sylvia Plath and Ted Hughes—were married in a conventional sense (carried out via the institutional and structural mechanisms of sanction by church or state), but the others either spoke explicitly of themselves as living in versions of marriage and/or were perceived by outsiders to be doing so, for at least part of the duration of their couplehood. I have tried to be attentive throughout to context, generally avoiding the use of the word "marriage"; using the words "spouse," "husband," or "wife" only when called upon to do so by the authors themselves; and using more general words such as "couple" or "union." This is also my reasoning for relying heavily on "we." While I understand that "couple" denotes "two," and for some connotes exclusivity as part of that arrangement, and that this might present challenges for those wishing to apply my work to intimate relationships beyond two, in

these very particular cases, in the corpus generated by these subjects, "couple" means two, and does connote some form of exclusivity (even when there are understandings within the pair of a more semi-open nature). It is my hope that for those wishing to broaden the inquiry here to other forms of intimate life and life writing, "couple" or "union" will not prove limiting, as "couples" and "unions" can function within a wider range of intimate networks with varying understandings of what this means for the individuals involved. It is also for this reason that throughout this book I have eschewed the use of the word "dyad" when speaking generally about intimates.

3 Both Woolf and Nicolson address Sir Sidney Lee's "Principles of Biography," delivered as the Leslie Stephen Lecture at Cambridge in 1911. Lee was Stephen's colleague on the *Dictionary of National Biography*. Derek Ryan has gone a long way toward dismantling the critical assumptions underlying readers' continual return to the binary of "granite" and "rainbow" to explain Woolf's work in life writing. Ryan argues convincingly that we must situate Woolf's use of the granite/rainbow analogy within other ways of making meaning in the "relationship between nature and culture," and that her use of "granite" in particular is more multivalenced across her *oeuvre* than many critics have accounted for (28). This point about "granite" has informed my discussion of Sylvia Plath and Ted Hughes in Chapter 5, in the context of Hughes's use of the word "mausoleum" to refer to his position as widower and all it entails after Plath's suicide. I am also indebted to Ryan for directing me to Braidotti's work.

4 See also Heike Bauer, *English Literary Sexology*; and Liz Stanley's biographical attention to Edward Carpenter, Havelock Ellis, and Ellis's wife Edith Lees (225–33). For scholarship on Bloomsbury ideas of intimacy, private life, and personal relationships, see Jesse Wolfe's indispensable *Bloomsbury, Modernism, and the Reinvention of Intimacy*.

5 When talking about Bloomsbury and ethics, the starting point for a number of critics is G. E. Moore and his *Principia Ethica* of 1903, and Woolf's reading of Moore in 1908; see Ann Banfield, Lee Oser, Tom Regan, and Jesse Wolfe. I do think Moore's work is important contextually to the core of Bloomsbury members drawn from the Apostle group at Cambridge, of which Moore was a member. However, I also think that the significance of Moore tends to be overstated, which occludes other possible conceptualizations of ethics in thinking about Bloomsbury, including readings that might emerge from engaging thinkers as diverse as Emmanuel Levinas, Rosi Braidotti, and Sara Ahmed, all of whom inform my writing here and elsewhere. See my essay on Woolf and narrative ethics forthcoming in the *Oxford Handbook of Virginia Woolf*, edited by Anne Fernald.

6 Virginia and Leonard Woolf's Hogarth Press published numerous texts related to life writing in the 1920s and 1930s. As Claire Battershill's exciting and original archival research into the Press has shown, the Woolfs made significant interventions into the life writing marketplace via their lists, their reviews, their purchases, and their own writing. While Virginia Woolf never published her own memoirs or autobiography (*Moments of Being*, a collection of memoir fragments and sketches, was published posthumously), one of Leonard Woolf's major achievements is his multivolume memoir. The Woolfs published life writing by all the authors under consideration in this chapter: Leslie Stephen, *Some Early Impressions*, published by the Hogarth Press in 1924; Vita Sackville-West, *Joan of Arc* and *Pepita* (about her grandmother) in 1937; Harold Nicolson, *Jeanne de Hénaut* in 1924 and *The Development of English Biography* in 1927 (see Appendix A, Battershill 179–88). Another significant site of Bloomsbury auto/biographical writing was the Memoir Club, started in 1920 by Molly MacCarthy; see S. P. Rosenbaum, Ruth Hoberman, and Hugh and Mirabel Cecil.

7 There are numerous examples of such writing, along with memoirs of widow(er)hood, that may be drawn from our very moment. See, for instance, *American Widow* by Alissa Torres and Sungyoon Choi, *The Year of Magical Thinking* by Joan Didion, and *A Widow's Story* by Joyce Carol Oates, to name just a few recent examples. Liz Stanley takes up Victorian biographical writing by widows and widowers, especially James Anthony Froude on Thomas Carlyle; she characterizes Froude's work as "loving" (130, 181–82).

8 In addition to Zwerdling, see Katherine C. Hill.

9 Also worth noting: in her polemic on adultery *Against Love*, Laura Kipnis argues that infidelity alters the participants' relationship to time, demanding as it does that they exist outside conventional social restraints and obligations. (I mention this again in my discussion of Isherwood and Bachardy.)

10 I do not take up the Sackville-West/Nicolson letters on their own here, as my attention is on the narrativity of *Portrait of a Marriage* and the function of the letters as deployed within that text by Sackville-West's narrator-arranger, her son. However, those interested in further examination of the intimate life writing of this pair are encouraged to consult them; many of them were written during Harold Nicolson's career with the Diplomatic Service when the two were separated for extended periods of time. The conversation for the BBC, "Marriage: A Discussion between Victoria Sackville-West and Harold Nicolson," may be found in the June 26, 1929, issue of *Listener* (the inaugural issue).

11 At this point Sackville-West also discusses her reasons for writing, already gestured toward in our noting of Nigel Nicolson's preface: namely, that she wishes

to provide a "truthful record" of a lesbian "connection," and that, in the future, such "connections" will no longer be "regarded as merely unnatural, and will be understood far better" (105). She continues, "I believe that then the psychology of people like myself will be a matter of interest" (106). Incidentally, the novel Sackville-West wrote about the Trefusis affair, *Challenge*, was not published in the United Kingdom until 1974. I offer that we might read this aspect of Sackville-West's purpose via Melanie Micir's concept of the queer intimate archive, discussed in more detail in Chapter 3. It might also be worth comparing *Portrait of a Marriage* with Valentine Ackland's *For Sylvia*, considered in that chapter.

12 In addition to Rosenfeld, see George Spater and Ian Parsons. One might also look at Leonard Woolf's memoirs and his "autobiografiction" on his engagement and marriage to Virginia Woolf, the novel *The Wise Virgins*. It should be noted here that Virginia Woolf had a brief affair with Vita Sackville-West, in the midst of their ongoing friendship; by all accounts, this was not perceived as a threat to either marriage, and resulted, of course, in Virginia Woolf's writing of *Orlando* (1928). In addition to Suzanne Raitt, see Karyn Z. Sproles and Louise DeSalvo.

13 Ruth Hoberman reads *Flush* as Woolf's intervention in the patriarchal discourse of biography. Ruth Vanita and David Eberly both connect the writing of *Flush* to the writing of *Orlando* via desire and lesbian longing. Jeanne Dubino reads *Flush* through animal studies and the anthropocene. Anna Snaith argues that "in *Flush*, Woolf explores the politics of relegation and hierarchy, linking systems of value along literary (canonical and generic), class, gender, species, and racial lines" (615); she situates this within the context of the rise of fascism in the 1930s, but it also seems that Snaith's argument resonates with much of what we have been saying about life writing, making *Flush* a particularly apt exemplar of the ways in which auto/biographical texts can destabilize hierarchy and power relations among subjects. See Battershill for a very helpful account of the shifting critical fortunes of *Flush*, its reception and subsequent marginalization in Woolf scholarship, and its position in the life writing ecosystem of which Hogarth Press was a part (98–107).

Chapter 2

1 It is often said that Stein wrote the *Autobiography* as a way to achieve greater celebrity, to write something that would be considered more "popular," and perhaps to generate income. Diane Souhami makes reference to the May Bookstaver incident and Toklas's jealous response to this previous affair of

Stein's, as well as to Stein's distaste for writing in a "money-making style" even while she suspected the book would be "commercially successful" (187, 189, 190). While the book did prove to be popular, I follow Cope as well as Janet Malcolm (also discussed in this chapter) in reading the affects of the situation as significant.

2 A pause to note that the making of Stein's and Toklas's world of two did involve the expelling from that world, including the salon itself, of individuals perceived as not willing to participate. These included Leo Stein, Gertrude Stein's brother, and Ernest Hemingway, who is taken up later in this chapter. Souhami refers to this development as "ousting the others" in a chapter of that name in *Gertrude and Alice.*

3 See Catharine R. Stimpson on the significance of embodiment and sex in Stein's work ("Somagrams"). Stimpson also says that to "oversimplify the Stein/Toklas marriage . . . is stupid" ("Gertrice/Altrude" 130). Sandra Gilbert and Susan Gubar see Stein and Toklas replicating heterosexist and patriarchal structures as a way for Stein to "appropriate male authority" (qtd. in Linzie 96). Sidonie Smith, however, regards Stein, particularly in the *Autobiography*, as "undoing" gender identity through the "performance" of heterosexual "norms" ("Performativity" 29). Leigh Gilmore interprets their performance of these subject positions within a kind of lesbian "playfulness," enacting a version of "butch-femme relations" as "Gertrice/Altrude" (a doodle found in Stein's papers), rather than something "grimly essentialist" (64); Gilmore, in that context, puts forth a really interesting reading of the *Autobiography* as a lesbian gift of exchanging "*I*'s" (65–66). (Stimpson notes "Gertrice/Altrude" in her essay for Perry and Brownley's *Mothering the Mind*, too.) In a very persuasive essay, Chris Coffman extends Gilmore's work, reading Stein's masculinity as bearing a "heterogendered desire" for Toklas and a "homosocial desire" for men (65). Souhami's 1991 *Gertrude and Alice* was published before the availability of the Stein/Toklas love notes collected in *Baby Precious Always Shines*; as editor Kay Turner points out, these were not catalogued at Yale until 1995, although they were first made available to researchers in 1981 (7).

4 In reading *As a Wife Has a Cow*, Ulla Dydo points out that the rest of the text, *A Book* (as in, *A Book Concluding With As a Wife Has a Cow*) should also be considered. It is the book itself that is the gift, and the fruits of sexual fulfillment. Because Stein is able to give Toklas "cows," here orgasms, she is then able to give her "babies," or books, so the two go together, again, in the kind of circularity and continuity that is part of Stein's thinking about narrative (*Gertrude* 74). In general, Dydo's scholarship has been essential to my work in this chapter.

5 This domestic and emotional labor—including managing Stein's writing, cooking and cleaning, serving as secretary and housekeeper—is one of the reasons some have put forward the critiques of the Stein/Toklas "marriage" and its reinscribing of patriarchal and heterosexist norms as noted earlier. The critical consensus has shifted significantly, thanks to work along the lines of that cited previously (n. 3).

6 The *Cook Book* as memoir is a life writing narrative, but I will also be arguing that the recipes themselves embedded within the memoir may also be construed as narrative. Part of what generates the high degree of narrativity in food memoir (gastrography), I claim here and elsewhere, is the interpolation of recipes which serve, themselves, as micronarratives, depending on duration, order, time, and event as regularities (Utell, *Engagements* 100–2).

7 I am particularly grateful to Melissa Bradshaw for the observations that made this line of thought possible. Bradshaw is, of this writing, undertaking investigation of Stein's cultural afterlives.

8 Sarah Garland points this out (44), also citing Linda Simon's *The Biography of Alice B. Toklas*; as does malcolm (*Two* 5).

9 The other text by Janet Malcolm under consideration in this book, *The Silent Woman*, addresses itself similarly to the epistemological and ethical challenges inherent to the work of the biographer; there, her focus is on Sylvia Plath and Ted Hughes, and we will engage that text in Chapter 5.

10 See the chapter in Ernest Hemingway's *A Moveable Feast* entitled "A Strange Enough Ending" (91–93). See also Linzie's treatment of the episode (10–11).

Chapter 3

1 In his study of James Joyce and betrayal, James Alexander Fraser argues persuasively that an understanding of betrayal is essential to grappling with relationality: all relationships hold within them the potential for betrayal, and the state of being betrayed necessitates the managing of an ontological shift. Betrayal forces us to ask not *how can I truly know another person*, but rather *who am I really, now, in relation to this other person.*

Warner's grief was doubled with the death of Ackland from cancer more than ten years before her own. *I'll Stand By You* was the product of Warner's last years, and a textual manifestation of her profound mourning over the loss of her lover, considered by her to be wife. Ackland and Warner saw themselves as married, and were seen by many of their friends and acquaintances to be so; scholars who have studied the pair follow their lead on this, such as Janet Montefiore who characterizes the relationship as "happily married" ("Authority" 125), and Melanie Micir, who catalogs references between the two women to their marriage as they appear in the letters (127). One friend and frequent correspondent and confidant of Warner's, Alyse Gregory, wrote in her journal, "Sylvia and Valentine have built their life much as married people build theirs, only it is more sensitively poised" (qtd. in Harman, *Sylvia* 127).

2 See Montefiore's comprehensive (as of this writing) bibliography of Warner's work and commentary thereon. This bibliography includes Micir's article, which comes from her forthcoming (again, as of this writing) book *The Passion Projects: Modernist Women, Intimate Archives, Unfinished Lives* (Princeton UP). Micir's scholarship will prove essential to the field and to our understanding of life writings and their archives, and I here acknowledge with gratitude conversations and email exchanges with her over the years that have been fruitful to my own thinking. This article of hers in particular prompted me to look more closely at the letters Warner exchanged with William Maxwell, and I do attend to some of the same letters Micir does in my own writing here, focusing on Maxwell as a reader/narratee of Warner's intimate life writing granted a form of access to her worlding with Ackland, which in turn facilitated Maxwell's own creation of a storyworld in apprehending their narrative.

3 Critics have attended to Warner as a biographer, considering her *T. H. White*, which Janet Montefiore has deemed a "classic." For Montefiore, Warner's "moral sense," her "detached sympathy," and her refusal to make White's homosexuality his most important feature make the life a superior rendering ("Authority" 124, 128). Warner disliked Michael Holroyd's groundbreaking biography of Lytton Strachey for all the ways she saw Holroyd doing the opposite, calling it a "drudging performance"; see Micir's reading of Warner's correspondence with David Garnett (125–26). In one letter, dated October 2, 1970, she writes to Garnett, "Please, if only for my peace of mind, outlive Michael Holroyd. For my pleasure, too, come to that" (*Sylvia and David* 156).

4 I was drawn to Heather Love's *Feeling Backward* for its chapter on Warner's novel *Summer Will Show*, and found the theorization of failure, feeling, and the past to illuminate the life writing as well, particularly Ackland's *For Sylvia*. More broadly, Love's work is integral to some of what I am trying to do here because, as Love articulates in an interview with Sarah E. Chinn, "fine-grained accounts of affect are really important for addressing a whole host of non-normative and minoritarian experiences, queer, trans, and otherwise" (Chinn 125).

5 Ackland was Warner's first and only lesbian lover. Prior to her involvement with Ackland, Warner had had relationships with men, including a long affair with a married man that was dissolved upon her partnering with Ackland. Mulford writes of the two women's differing attitudes toward fidelity thusly: "[Ackland] sought release in her drinking, and in relationships with other women. Sylvia, however, remained faithful to Valentine. When asked later why she did so, she replied simply that Valentine was the best lover she ever had" (152). A poem on "lesbian love," "Never love unless you can—," was found in Warner's unpublished work and collected after her death (*New* 254). She writes, in part:

> sometimes they [lesbians] will fall to musing,
> all delight and love refusing;
> sometimes meek and sometimes grand,
> sometimes bite the generous hand,
> yet, take all in all, improving
> with the years at loved and loving—

6 See Michel Chion on the figure of the *acousmêtre*.

7 I am reading Mulford's book as a couple biography, but the author herself takes as her purpose a study of Warner's and Ackland's politics that places their leftist position and active role in the Communist Party as central to their lives and their writing (hence their presence in recently opened MI5 files). I in no way mean to diminish the significance of Warner's and Ackland's politics, or Mulford's work, with my focus more so on their intimate life writing, and am cognizant of the ways in which some critics believe that it is Warner's and Ackland's left-wing stance (along with their gender) that has led to their neglect in the scholarship of literature of the period.

8 See my *James Joyce and the Revolt of Love: Marriage, Adultery, Desire*; and see James Alexander Fraser's insightful response to my work in his *Joyce and Betrayal*. My rethinking of the implications of erotic betrayal for an ethics of alterity is indebted to Fraser.

9 Judd self-published the collection; a new edition is being undertaken as of this writing by Handheld Press. The volume also includes letters among the women and White's romantic partner, Evelyn Holahan. Holahan saw her relationship with White as a marriage, and the affair with Ackland had just as deleterious effect on Holahan as it had had on Warner, if not more so (Judd x). When Ackland found out that Holahan had fallen in love with White, she was rattled and wrote to White, "I will give you constancy of care and of protection. I will not leave you—nor will I ever fail you as lover, as husband, as companion"

(*Akeing* 253). For her part, by 1940 Warner had let White know that she did not wish to see her, but regretted their lost friendship and continued to write (*Akeing* 257).

10 See Ashley T. Shelden's critique drawn from queer theorizations of negativity, as well as Lee Edelman, Elizabeth Freeman, and Judith Roof.

11 Judd reads *I'll Stand By You* as "retaliation," emerging from Warner's "brooding" over the White affair after Ackland's death, and an unequivocal statement of her "vehement rejection of co-existence" (349). The difficult feelings expressed in the diary might lend some credence to this reading, but for the most part Warner speaks throughout her private writing of the project as one of reclamation and restoration—including restoring Ackland to herself—rather than as a form of retaliation. Warner reads Ackland reparatively in the course of making this project.

12 A sample of poems found in *I'll Stand By You* and their attributions: "This is the world exactly as Adam had it" (Ackland 5–6); "As it cries out from under the cover" (Ackland 8–9); "Space is invisible waves" (Ackland 12); "Here, where my wishes were, the leaves are lying" (Warner 116); "Because it is a fine Easter bank-holiday" (Warner 167–68); "And past the quay the river flowing" (Warner 229). The text of each individual poem appearing in *I'll Stand By You* may also be found in the respective collected poems of each writer; the page numbers here refer to their appearance in *I'll.*

Chapter 4

1 I would like to begin by acknowledging particularly the work of Jim Berg and Chris Freeman, and of Katherine Bucknell, which was integral to the writing of this chapter.

Auden and Isherwood had a brief sexual liaison as young men, in the midst of their longtime friendship. They traveled to Berlin together and to China (the latter of which resulted in the collaboration *Journey to a War*), and coauthored several plays in the 1930s (*The Dog Beneath the Skin, The Ascent of F6, On the Frontier*).

2 Isherwood's diaries are an invaluable record of the writing life, both in terms of material in process and in terms of the subject in process (Lejeune, *On Diary* 173).

Some of Bachardy's diaries are excerpted in his collection of deathbed portraits of Isherwood, *Last Drawings*, to be considered later in this chapter. Some have been excerpted and published alongside interviews Bachardy has given since Isherwood's death (see Mendez). However, they remain under seal and unavailable to researchers.

3 It was not uncommon for sitters to complain about how Bachardy's portraits could be taken as unflattering. See Whelan, and Bachardy himself (the remarkable "On Drawing Faces"), for Bachardy's artistic process.

4 This is a signature of Bachardy's work; see "Intimate without Excuses," a portfolio of Bachardy nudes published in *Christopher Street*, as well as his book *Drawings of the Male Nude*.

5 For a sample of the extensive writing on the Isherwood-narrator, see Geherin, Kamel, Thomas. In this chapter I follow Isherwood's lead and read him and Bachardy as both coauthors and co-narrators of their couplehood, and Bachardy as reader and narratee.

6 There also exists an "Animals" notebook held in the Isherwood papers at the Huntington, but this is not available to the public. Peter Parker mentions John Osborne's 1956 play *Look Back in Anger* in the context of his discussion of The Animals. In that play, a husband and wife in a tumultuous marriage refer to each other as Bear and Squirrel as a way to manage their strife. Isherwood and Bachardy knew Osborne well from their work in the theatre, and Isherwood stayed relatively close to him for years.

7 Here is the list of episodes:

Episode One: Introduction to the Animals
Episode Two: Something Bad Has Happened
Episode Three: I Want to Talk Cat-Horse Again
Episode Four: New Friends
Episode Five: Pandora's Box
Episode Six: David Hockney's "Giant Portrait"
Episode Seven: Unfinished Work and Unfulfilled Duties
Episode Eight: Our Play
Episodes Nine and Ten: *A Meeting by the River*, directed by Anthony Page, Acts I and II
Coda: Don Bachardy at Eighty-Two

8 In defining seriality here, I draw more on the thinking about serial narratives found in the study of prose fiction or graphic narrative/comics than I do on theorizations from game studies or work in film and television and other multimodal narrative forms (for the latter see Frank Kelleter). This podcast is not driven by the open-ended, consumer-centric, interactive production model we might find in serialized television narratives or in the multiverses of film cycles/sequels. It is likewise not really responsive to audience demand or interest; it is a closed system. I am more interested in the case of the serial podcast here insofar

as the adaptation into serial form generates narrativity that might not have been present in the original form of the letters.

9 Santi and Mascara saw their own couplehood as integral to the work they were doing on the film. In their essay on the making of the film, they say, "The film was four years in the making and solidified our partnership as filmmakers and our relationship as a couple. We met a few months prior to beginning this project, so in a sense, we adopted Chris and Don as role models, and we were inspired by their commitment to each other and, above all, to their work and creativity" (26).

Chapter 5

1 Special acknowledgment is due to Amanda Golden, Susan Van Dyne, Heather Clark, Jacqueline Rose, Janet Malcolm, Diane Middlebrook, and Karen V. Kukil for the work of this chapter.

Malcolm's *The Silent Woman* is a central text in the discussion of this chapter. Bate's biography less so, but it is worth pausing for a moment to provide a sense of how even an experienced and respected biographer and critic can find himself tangled in the nets of Plath/Hughes life writing. As with almost every other attempt to write the life of either poet, reviews of Bate's biography of Hughes were, to put it mildly, mixed. In the *New York Review of Books*, Malcolm calls Bate's book "incoherent" and accuses him of "blowing [Hughes] up into a kind of extra-large sex maniac." On the other hand, Christopher Benfey in *The Atlantic* characterizes Bate's work as "magisterial," and offers praise for Bate's proceeding even as the estate withdrew its support for the book: "Evidence that an uncompromising biographer hasn't been swayed by interested parties (read: Olwyn Hughes)." Interestingly, in a footnote to the chapter dedicated to the Plath/Hughes marriage, Bate describes Anne Stevenson's *Bitter Fame* as the "most accurate" (580), even as Stevenson's book has been criticized by others, such as Jacqueline Rose, for, indeed, being "swayed by interested parties," that is, Olwyn Hughes, whom Stevenson credits with something nearing a "dual authorship" role (ix), the result being, in Rose's words, an "assault" on Plath (93).

2 For additional scholarship on the intertextual nature of the Plath/Hughes relationship, see Uroff, Van Dyne ("Your"), Middlebrook ("Poetry"), Gill. I consider here Hughes as coauthor of a couplehood with Plath—coauthor of their intimate life—as well as reader of the story she went on to create without him. I do not take up the issue of Hughes as editor (of the first edition of *Ariel* and of

Plath's *Collected Poems*, as well as his involvement in the first edition of Plath's journals and her mother Aurelia Plath's work on *Letters Home*) which has been the subject of much fine scholarship as well as controversy. See Perloff, Rose, Van Dyne (*Revising*), Brain ("Sylvia"). I should also point out that the second volume of Plath's complete letters, those written during the marriage to Hughes, are still forthcoming as of this writing. Some excerpts have been published in the *Daily Mail* by Frieda Hughes, part of an edited version of her foreword to appear in that collection. Frieda Hughes claims that the letters do not substantially change her understanding of her parents' marriage: "While my father does not come out of them [Plath's letters from their period of tumult and separation] a saint, neither does my mother. . . . They both suffered, they both made mistakes. . . . Yet, in the beginning, there was great goodness and generosity and the kind of love that some of us never find in our lifetimes" ("Sylvia Plath's"; thank you to Amanda Golden for sharing this piece).

3 A number of critics and biographers have examined the BBC interview with Owen Leeming and the poets' relations with the BBC more broadly; in addition to Middlebrook, see Gill, Clark, Crowther, and Steinberg. Crowther makes much of Plath "remain[ing] very much in the shadow of her more famous and celebrated husband" at the time of the 1961 interview, citing particularly a question penciled on Hughes's letter accepting the invitation on behalf of himself and Plath: "What do we have on his wife?" (36). I have already pointed out, from a stance of critique, the propensity of biographers telling of couples to identify one member of a couple as "minor," or "silenced," or "injured" (to use Anna Linzie's word), not just in this case but elsewhere, and the ways that judgment reifies certain kinds of narratives, certain schema, certain ways of reading. Given the thoughtfulness of Leeming's questions and his apparent familiarity with Plath's work, it seems entirely likely that this question is more in line with the advance research required on the part of a producer in order to conduct a meaningful, intelligent interview. Once accessible only at the British Library or through the BBC archives, a recording of the interview has been made available online. Hughes's work for the BBC is well-documented; see Bate. Stevenson documents Plath's work for the BBC, and Crowther and Steinberg have revealed through their archival studies the extent of Plath's work for the BBC as well.

4 We considered this possibility in our discussion of *Flush*. See Helena Michie on the ontological transformation wrought by the liminal space of the honeymoon. While not all of the couples under study were "married," in the civil or religious sense, as has already been pointed out, they have still marked their ontological transformation via some transitional or liminal gesture; recall Warner's language

regarding her "bridal" night with Ackland. For those who have examined the Grolier exhibit, which I consider briefly here, see Gill.

5 I am inclined to more or less trust the positive feelings expressed by Hughes to his brother in this letter from early in the marriage; Hughes is similarly authentic-seeming later on when he writes about the troubles he is experiencing with Plath, and I am interested in the moves made by telling. By all accounts, the relationship between the brothers was solid and one of openness and respect; see Gerald Hughes's memoir.

Works Cited

Abbott, H. Porter. *The Cambridge Introduction to Narrative*, 2nd ed. Cambridge UP, 2008.

Abelard, Peter and Héloïse. *The Letters of Abelard and Héloïse*. Penguin, 2004.

Ackland, Valentine. *For Sylvia: An Honest Account*. Norton, 1985.

Ackland, Valentine. *Journey from Winter: Selected Poems*, edited by Frances Bingham, Carcanet, 2008.

Ackland, Valentine and Sylvia Townsend Warner. *Whether a Dove or a Seagull*. Viking, 1933.

Adamson, Judith. Introduction. In *Love Letters: Leonard Woolf and Trekkie Ritchie Parsons*, edited by Judith Adamson, Chatto and Windus, 2001, pp. xi–xxiii.

Ahmed, Sara. *The Promise of Happiness*. Duke UP, 2010.

The Animals Podcast, created by Katherine Bucknell, performances by Simon Callow and Alan Cumming, 11 episodes, 2017.

Ashton, Rosemary. *Thomas & Jane Carlyle: Portrait of a Marriage*. Random House, 2003.

Bachardy, Don. *Drawings of the male nude*, Twelvetrees Press, 1986.

Bachardy, Don. "Intimate Without Excuses." *Christopher Street*, vol. 9, no. 4, 1985, pp. 30–36.

Bachardy, Don. *Last Drawings of Christopher Isherwood*. Faber and Faber, 1990.

Bachardy, Don. "On Drawing Faces." *Michigan Quarterly Review*, vol. 19, no. 1, 1980, pp. 57–66.

Backscheider, Paula R. *Reflections on Biography*. Oxford UP, 2001.

Banfield, Ann. "Cambridge Bloomsbury." In *The Cambridge Companion to Bloomsbury*, edited by Victoria Rosner, Cambridge UP, 2014, pp. 33–53.

Barros, Carolyn A. "Getting Modern: *The Autobiography of Alice B. Toklas*." *Biography*, vol. 22, no. 2, 1999, pp. 176–208.

Barthes, Roland. "Interview: A Conversation with Roland Barthes," conducted by Stephen Heath. *The Grain of the Voice: Interviews 1962–1980*. Translated by Linda Coverdale, Northwestern UP, 2009.

Barthes, Roland. *A Lover's Discourse: Fragments*. Translated by Richard Howard, Hill and Wang, 1977.

Bate, Jonathan. *Ted Hughes: The Unauthorised Life*. Harper, 2015.

Battershill, Claire. *Modernist Lives: Biography and Autobiography at Leonard and Virginia Woolf's Hogarth Press*. Bloomsbury Academic, 2018.

Bauer, Heike. *English Literary Sexology*. Palgrave Macmillan, 2009.

Benfey, Christopher. "Getting Over Sylvia Plath." *The Atlantic*, January/February 2016 (accessed August 28, 2018).

Benjamin, Jessica. *The Bonds of Love*. Pantheon, 1988.

Benstock, Shari. "Authorizing the Autobiographical." Benstock, pp. 10–33.

Benstock, Shari, editor. *The Private Self: Theory and Practice of Women's Autobiographical Writings*. U of North Carolina P, 1988.

Benstock, Shari. *Women of the Left Bank*. U of Texas P, 1986.

Berg, James J. and Chris Freeman, editors. *The American Isherwood*. U of Minnesota P, 2015.

Berg, James J. and Chris Freeman, editors. *Conversations with Christopher Isherwood*. UP of Mississippi, 2001.

Berg, James J. and Chris Freeman, editors. *The Isherwood Century*. U of Wisconsin P, 2000.

Berlant, Lauren. Introduction. In *Intimacy*, edited by Berlant, U of Chicago P, 2000, pp. 1–8.

Berman, Jessica. *Modernist Commitments: Ethics, Politics, and Transnational Modernism*. Columbia UP, 2011.

Best, Stephen and Sharon Marcus. "Surface Reading: An Introduction." *Representations*, vol. 108, no. 1, 2009, pp. 1–21.

Booth, Alison. *How to Make It as a Woman: Collective Biographical History from Victoria to the Present*. U of Chicago P, 2004.

Braidotti, Rosi. "Joy, Ethics of." In *Posthuman Glossary*, edited by Rosi Braidotti and Maria Hlavajova, Bloomsbury Academic, 2018, pp. 221–24.

Braidotti, Rosi. *Transpositions*. Polity, 2006.

Brain, Tracy. "Dangerous Confessions: The Problem of Reading Sylvia Plath Biographically." In *Modern Confessional Writing: New Critical Essays*, edited by Jo Gill, Routledge, 2006, pp. 11–32.

Brain, Tracy. "Sylvia Plath's Letters and Journals." Gill, pp. 139–55.

Breger, Claudia. "Affects in Configuration: A New Approach to Narrative Worldmaking." *Narrative*, vol. 25, no. 2, 2017, pp. 227–51.

Breger, Claudia. "Critically Affirmative Reconfigurations." Warhol and Lanser, pp. 340–47.

Broughton, Trev. "The Froude-Carlyle Embroilment: Married Life as Literary Problem." *Victorian Studies*, vol. 38, no. 4, 1995, pp. 551–85.

Broughton, Trev. *Men of Letters, Writing Lives: Masculinity and Literary Auto/Biography in the Late Victorian Period*. Routledge, 1999.

Bruss, Elizabeth. *Autobiographical Acts*. Johns Hopkins UP, 1976.

Bucknell, Katherine. Introduction. In *The Animals* by Christopher Isherwood and Don Bachardy, Farrar, Straus and Giroux, 2013, pp. ix–xxxv.

Bucknell, Katherine. Introduction. In *Diaries: Volume 1: 1939–1960* by Christopher Isherwood, HarperCollins, 1997, pp. vii–il.

Bucknell, Katherine. Introduction. In *Diaries: Volume 2: The Sixties, 1960–1969* by Christopher Isherwood, HarperCollins, 2010, pp. xi–xxxvii.

Bucknell, Katherine. "Who Is Christopher Isherwood?" Berg and Freeman, *Century*, pp. 13–30.

Butler, Judith. *Giving an Account of Oneself*. Fordham UP, 2003.

Castle, Terry. *The Apparitional Lesbian: Female Homosexuality and Modern Culture*. Columbia UP, 1993.

Cecil, Hugh and Mirabel Cecil. *Clever Hearts: Desmond & Molly MacCarthy*. Gollancz, 1991.

Chadwick, Whitney and Isabelle de Courtivron, editors. *Significant Others: Creativity and Intimate Partnership*. Thames and Hudson, 1993.

Chatman, Seymour. *Story and Discourse: Narrative Structure in Fiction and Film*. Cornell UP, 1978.

Chion, Michel. *The Voice in Cinema*. Translated by Claudia Gorbman, Columbia UP, 1999.

Chinn, Sarah E. "Queer Feelings/Feeling Queer: A Conversation with Heather Love about Politics, Teaching, and the 'Dark, Tender Thrills' of Affect." *Transformations: The Journal of Inclusive Scholarship & Pedagogy*, vol. 22, no. 2, 2011/2012, pp. 124–31.

Chris and Don: A Love Story, directed by Guido Santi and Tina Mascara, performances by Christopher Isherwood, Don Bachardy, and Michael York, Zeitgeist Films, 2007.

Clark, Heather. *The Grief of Influence: Sylvia Plath and Ted Hughes*. Oxford UP, 2011.

Coffman, Chris. "Visual Economies of Queer Desire in Gertrude Stein's *The Autobiography of Alice B. Toklas*." *Arizona Quarterly*, vol. 70, no. 4, 2014, pp. 49–83.

"Comics Code Revision of 1971." *Comic Book Legal Defense Fund* (accessed August 19, 2018).

Cope, Karin. *Passionate Collaborations: Learning to Live with Gertrude Stein*. U of Victoria P, 2005.

Crowther, Gail and Peter K. Steinberg. *These Ghostly Archives: The Unearthing of Sylvia Plath*. Fonthill Media, 2017.

Cucullu, Lois. "*A Single Man* and the American *Maurice*." Berg and Freeman, *American*, pp. 5–23.

Cvetkovich, Ann. *An Archive of Feelings: Trauma, Sexuality, and Lesbian Public Cultures*. Duke UP, 2003.

Davies, Gill. "The Corners That Held Her: The Importance of Place in Sylvia Townsend Warner's Writing." In *Critical Essays on Sylvia Townsend Warner, English Novelist: 1893–1978*, edited by Gill Davies, David Malcolm, and John Simons, Edwin Mellen Press, 2006, pp. 1–10.

Deleuze, Gilles and Félix Guattari. "What Is a Minor Literature?" Translated by Dana Polan. In *Out There: Marginalization and Contemporary Culture*, edited by Russell Ferguson, Martha Gever, Trinh T. Minh-ha, Cornel West, and Lisa Phillips, MIT Press, 1992, pp. 59–69.

de Man, Paul. "Autobiography as De-Facement." *Modern Language Notes*, vol. 94, no. 5, 1979, pp. 919–30.

DeSalvo, Louise. "'Tinder-and-Flint': Virginia Woolf & Vita Sackville-West." Chadwick and de Courtivron, pp. 83–96.

Detloff, Madelyn and Brenda Helt. Introduction. In *Queer Bloomsbury*, edited by Detloff and Helt, Edinburgh UP, 2016, pp. 1–12.

DiBattista, Maria and Emily O. Wittman. "Modernism and Autobiography: Introduction." In *Modernism and Autobiography*, edited by DiBattista and Wittman, Cambridge UP, 2014. pp. xi–xix.

Didion, Joan. *The Year of Magical Thinking*. Vintage, 2006.

Dillon, Sarah. *The Palimpsest*. Continuum, 2000.

Dubino, Jeanne. "The Bispecies Environment, Coevolution, and *Flush*." In *Virginia Woolf: Twenty-First Century Approaches*, edited by Jeanne Dubino, Gill Lowe, Vara Neverow, and Kathryn Simpson, Edinburgh UP, 2015, pp. 131–47.

Dydo, Ulla. *Gertrude Stein: The Language That Rises*. Northwestern UP, 2003.

Dydo, Ulla, editor. *A Stein Reader*. Northwestern UP, 1993.

Eakin, Paul John. "Foreword." In *On Autobiography* by Philippe Lejeune, U of Minnesota P, 1989, pp. viii–xxviii.

Eakin, Paul John. *How Our Lives Become Stories: Making Selves*. Cornell UP, 1999.

Eakin, Paul John. *Living Autobiographically: How We Create Identity in Narrative*. Cornell UP, 2008.

Eberly, David. "Housebroken: The Domesticated Relations of *Flush*." In *Virginia Woolf: Texts and Contexts: Selected Papers from the Fifth Annual Conference on Virginia Woolf*, edited by Beth Rigel Daugherty and Eileen Barrett, Pace UP, 1996, pp. 21–25.

Edel, Leon. *Literary Biography*. Indiana UP, 1973.

Edelman, Lee. *No Future: Queer Theory and the Death Drive*. Duke UP, 2004.

Enniss, Stephen C. and Karen V. Kukil. *"No Other Appetite": Sylvia Plath, Ted Hughes, and the Blood Jet of Poetry*. The Grolier Club, 2005.

Enns, Diane. *Love in the Dark: Philosophy by Another Name*. Columbia UP, 2016.

Fordham, Finn. *I Do I Undo I Redo: The Textual Genesis of Modernist Selves*. Oxford UP, 2010.

Fraser, James Alexander. *Joyce and Betrayal*. Palgrave Macmillan, 2016.

Freeman, Elizabeth. *Time Binds: Queer Temporalities, Queer Histories*. Duke UP, 2010.

Friedman, Susan Stanford. "Women's Autobiographical Selves." Benstock, pp. 34–62.

Garland, Sarah. "'A Cook Book to be Read. What About It?': Alice Toklas, Gertrude Stein, and the Language of the Kitchen." *Comparative American Studies*, vol. 7, no. 1, 2009, pp. 34–56.

Gay, Peter. *The Education of the Senses*. Oxford UP, 1984.

Geherin, David. "An Interview with Christopher Isherwood." *Journal of Narrative Technique*, vol. 2, 1972, pp. 143–58. Reprinted in Berg and Freeman, *Conversations*, pp. 74–89.

Gelles, Edith. *Abigail and John: Portrait of a Marriage*. Harper Perennial, 2010.

Genette, Gérard. *Narrative Discourse: An Essay on Method*. Translated by Jane E. Lewin, Cornell UP, 1980.

Gifford, Terry, editor. *The Cambridge Companion to Ted Hughes*. Cambridge UP, 2011.

Gill, Jo. "Ted Hughes and Sylvia Plath." Gifford, 2011, pp. 53–66.

Gill, Jo, editor. *The Cambridge Companion to Sylvia Plath*. Cambridge UP, 2006.

Gilmore, Leigh. "A Signature of Lesbian Autobiography: 'Gertrice/Altrude.'" *Prose Studies*, vol. 14, no. 2, 1991, pp. 56–75.

Godwin, William and Mary Wollstonecraft. *Memoirs of the Author of "The Rights of Woman" with A Short Residence in Sweden*. Penguin, 1987.

Goodwin, Doris Kearns. *No Ordinary Time: Franklin & Eleanor Roosevelt*. Simon & Schuster, 1995.

Goodwin, Sarah and Elisabeth Bronfen. Introduction. In *Death and Representation*, edited by Goodwin and Bronfen, Johns Hopkins UP, 1993, pp. 3–26.

Goldie, Peter. *The Mess Inside: Narrative, Emotion, and the Mind*. Oxford UP, 2012.

Granne, Ailsa. "Fantasy, Writing and Relationship in the Texts of Valentine Ackland and Sylvia Townsend Warner." *Literature Compass*, vol. 11/12, 2014, pp. 776–85.

Granne, Ailsa. "The Silent Self: Valentine Ackland's Diaries after 1939." *The Journal of the Sylvia Townsend Warner Society*, 2012, pp. 31–49.

Hachtman, Tom. *Gertrude's Follies*. Now What Media, 2012.

Hamilton, Nigel. *Biography: A Brief History*. Harvard UP, 2010.

Harman, Claire. Introduction. In *Diaries of Sylvia Townsend Warner* by Sylvia Townsend Warner, edited by Harman, Virago, 1995, pp. ix–xvi.

Harman, Claire. Introduction. In *New Collected Poems* by Sylvia Townsend Warner, edited by Harman, Carcanet, 2008, pp. 1–30.

Harman, Claire. *Sylvia Townsend Warner: A Biography*. Chatto and Windus, 1989.

Heidt, Sarah J. "'The Materials for a "Life"': Collaboration, Publication, and the Carlyles' Afterlives." *Nineteenth-Century Contexts*, vol. 28, no. 1, 2006, pp. 21–33.

Hemingway, Ernest. *A Moveable Feast: The Restored Edition*. Scribner, 2009.

Herman, David. *Story Logic: Problems and Possibilities of Narrative*. U of Nebraska P, 2002.

Hill, Katherine C. "Virginia Woolf and Leslie Stephen: History and Literary Revolution." *PMLA*, vol. 96, no. 3, 1981, pp. 361–62.

Hemingway, Ernest. *A Moveable Feast: The Restored Edition*. Scribner, 2009.

Hoberman, Ruth. *Modernizing Lives: Experiments in English Biography, 1918–1939*. Southern Illinois UP, 1986.

Holden, Stephen. "A May-December Love For All Seasons." *New York Times*, June 13, 2008 (accessed August 30, 2018).

Holroyd, Michael. *Lytton Strachey: A Critical Biography*. 2 vols. Holt, Rinehart and Winston, 1967–1968.

Hovey, Jaime. *A Thousand Words: Portraiture, Style, and Queer Modernism*. Ohio State UP, 2006.

Hughes, Frieda. "Sylvia Plath's Letters from the Brink." *Daily Mail*, August 24, 2018 (accessed August 26, 2018).

Hughes, Gerald. *Ted & I: A Brother's Memoir*. Thomas Dunne, 2014.

Hughes, Ted. *Collected Poems*. Farrar, Straus and Giroux, 2003.

Hughes, Ted. *Letters of Ted Hughes*, edited by Christopher Reid, Farrar, Straus and Giroux, 2007.

Isherwood, Christopher. *Christopher and His Kind*. 1976. U of Minnesota P, 2001.

Isherwood, Christopher. *Diaries*: *Volume 1*: *1939–1960*, edited by Katherine Bucknell, HarperCollins, 1997.

Isherwood, Christopher. *Diaries*: *Volume 2*: *The Sixties, 1960–1969*, edited by Katherine Bucknell, HarperCollins, 2010.

Isherwood, Christopher. *Diaries*: *Volume 3*: *Liberation, 1970–1983*, edited by Katherine Bucknell, HarperCollins, 2012.

Isherwood, Christopher. *Kathleen and Frank*. Simon and Schuster, 1971.

Isherwood, Christopher and Don Bachardy. *The Animals: Love Letters between Christopher Isherwood and Don Bachardy*, edited by Katherine Bucknell, Farrar, Straus and Giroux, 2013.

Isherwood, Christopher and Don Bachardy. *October*. Twelvetrees Press, 1981.

Jardine, Alice. "Death Sentences: Writing Couples and Ideology." *Poetics Today*, vol. 6, no. 1/2, pp. 119–31.

Johnson, Jenny Olivia. *Glass Heart (Bells for Sylvia Plath)*. Moss and Kukil.

Johnston, Georgia. *The Formation of 20th-Century Queer Autobiography: Reading Vita Sackville-West, Virginia Woolf, Hilda Doolittle, and Gertrude Stein*. Palgrave Macmillan, 2007.

Judd, Peter Haring. *The Akeing Heart: Passionate Attachments and Their Aftermath: Sylvia Townsend Warner, Valentine Ackland, and Elizabeth Wade White*. Peter Haring Judd, 2013.

Kadar, Marlene. "Coming to Terms: Life Writing—From Genre to Critical Practice." In *Essays on Life Writing*, edited by Kadar, U of Toronto P, 1992, pp. 3–16.

Kamel, Rose. "'Unravelling One's Personal Myth': Christopher Isherwood's Autobiographical Strategies." *Biography*, vol. 5, no. 2, 1982, pp. 161–75.

Kaplan, Sydney Janet. *Circulating Genius: John Middleton Murry, Katherine Mansfield, and D. H. Lawrence*. Edinburgh UP, 2012.

Kelleter, Frank, editor. *Media of Serial Narrative*. Ohio State UP, 2017.

Kipnis, Laura. *Against Love*. Vintage, 2004.

Koren, Yehuda and Eilat Negev. *Lover of Unreason: Assia Wevill, Sylvia Plath's Rival and Ted Hughes' Doomed Love*. Da Capo Press, 2006.

Kukil, Karen V. "Reviving the Journals of Sylvia Plath." *Discovering Literature: 20th Century*, The British Library (accessed August 30, 2018).

Lee, John Alan. "Through the Looking Glass: Life after Isherwood—A Conversation with Don Bachardy." *Journal of Homosexuality*, vol. 20, 1990, pp. 33–63.

Lee, Sidney. *Principles of Biography*. 1911. Cambridge UP, 2014.

Lejeune, Philippe. *On Autobiography*. Translated by Katherine Leary, U of Minnesota P, 1989.

Lejeune, Philippe. *On Diary*, edited by Jeremy D. Popkin and Julie Rak, U of Hawai'i P, 2009.

Levinas, Emmanuel. *Time and the Other*. Translated by Richard Cohen, Duquesne UP, 1990.

Levinas, Emmanuel. *Totality and Infinity*. Translated by Alphonso Lingis, Duquesne UP, 1969.

Levine, Caroline. *Forms: Whole, Rhythm, Hierarchy, Network*. Princeton UP, 2015.

Lewis, Thomas S. W. "Combining 'the Advantages of Fact and Fiction': Virginia Woolf's Biographies of Vita Sackville-West, Flush, and Roger Fry." In *Virginia Woolf: Centennial Essays*, edited by Elaine K. Ginsberg and Laura Moss Gottlieb, Whitson, 1983, pp. 295–324.

Leyland, Winston. "Gay Sunshine Interviews." In *Gay Sunshine Press*, 1978, pp. 199–206. Reprinted in Berg and Freeman, *Conversations*, pp. 98–109.

Linzie, Anna. *The True Story of Alice B. Toklas: A Study of Three Autobiographies*. U of Iowa P, 2006.

Lorange, Astrid. *How Reading Is Written: A Brief Index to Gertrude Stein*. Wesleyan UP, 2014.

Love, Heather. *Feeling Backward: Loss and the Politics of Queer Theory*. Harvard UP, 2007.

Lovell, Mary S. *A Rage to Live: A Biography of Richard and Isabel Burton*. Norton, 2000.

Maddox, Brenda. *D. H. Lawrence: The Story of a Marriage*. Simon & Schuster, 1994.

Mager, Donald. "Deathwatch." In Berg and Freeman, *Century*, pp. 128–36.

Malcolm, Janet. *The Silent Woman: Sylvia Plath and Ted Hughes*. Vintage, 1993.

Malcolm, Janet. *Two Lives: Gertrude and Alice*. Yale UP, 2007.

Malcolm, Janet. "A Very Sadistic Man." Review of *Ted Hughes: The Unauthorised Life* by Jonathan Bate. *New York Review of Books*, February 11, 2016 (accessed August 28, 2018).

Marcus, Laura. *Auto/Biographical Discourses*. Manchester UP, 1994.

Marcus, Laura. "The Newness of 'The New Biography': Biographical Theory and Practice in the Early Twentieth Century." In *Mapping Lives: The Uses of Biography*, edited by Peter France and William St. Claire, Oxford UP, 2004, pp. 193–218.

Marshik, Celia. *British Modernism and Censorship*. Cambridge UP, 2009.

Marshik, Celia and Allison Pease. *Modernism, Sex, and Gender*. Bloomsbury Academic, 2018.

Mason, Mary. "The Other Voice: Autobiographies of Women Writers." *Autobiography: Essays Theoretical and Critical*, edited by James Olney, Princeton UP, 1980, pp. 207–305.

Matz, Jesse. "'No Future' vs. 'It Gets Better': Queer Prospects for Narrative Temporality." Warhol and Lanser, pp. 227–50.

Maupin, Armistead. "Don Bachardy: Drawings of the Male Nude." *The Advocate*, March 18, 1986, 48–49.

McDowell, Lesley. *Between the Sheets: The Literary Liaisons of Nine 20th-Century Women*. Duckworth, 2012.

McGann, Jerome. *The Textual Condition*. Princeton UP, 1991.

Mendez, Carlos. "Isherwood and Bachardy on Each Other: *The Diaries* Are Published; Don Bachardy Is Interviewed." *The Harvard Gay & Lesbian Review*, Spring 1997, pp. 7–9.

Merleau-Ponty, M. *Phenomenology of Perception*. Translated by Colin Smith, Routledge, 1962.

Michie, Helena. *Victorian Honeymoons: Journeys to the Conjugal*. Cambridge UP, 2014.

Micir, Melanie. "'Living in two tenses': The Intimate Archives of Sylvia Townsend Warner." *Journal of Modern Literature*, vol. 36, no. 1, 2012, pp. 119–31.

Middlebrook, Diane. *Her Husband: Ted Hughes & Sylvia Plath: A Marriage*. Penguin, 2003.

Middlebrook, Diane. "The Poetry of Sylvia Plath and Ted Hughes: Call and Response." Gill, pp. 156–71.

Minich, Julie Avril. "Writing Queer Lives: Autobiography and Memoir." In *Cambridge Companion to American Gay and Lesbian Literature*, edited by Scott Herring, Cambridge UP, 2015, pp. 59–72.

Miller, Nancy K. "Representing Others: Gender and the Subjects of Autobiography." *Differences: A Journal of Feminist Cultural Studies*, vol. 6, no. 1, 1994, pp. 1–27.

Mitchell, Jennifer. "*Flush*, Courtship, and Suffering." *Virginia Woolf Miscellany*, vol. 87, 2015, pp. 28–30.

Moffat, Wendy. "The Narrative Case for Queer Biography." Warhol and Lanser, pp. 210–26.

Montefiore, Janet. "Sylvia Townsend Warner, Authority, and the Biographer's 'Moral Sense.'" In *Imitating Art: Essays in Biography*, edited by David Ellis, Pluto, 1993, pp. 125–48.

Montefiore, Janet. "Sylvia Townsend Warner Scholarship 1978–2013: An Annotated Bibliography with Introduction." *Literature Compass*, vol. 11/12, 2014, pp. 786–811.

Morley, Rachel. "Fighting Feeling: Re-Thinking Biographical Praxis." *Life Writing*, vol. 9, no. 1, 2012, pp. 77–95.

Moss, Dorothy. "'Glass Heart (Bells for Sylvia Plath)' Activates *One Life: Sylvia Plath*." *National Portrait Gallery: Face to Face*, July 3, 2017 (accessed August 30, 2018).

Moss, Dorothy and Karen V. Kukil. *One Life: Sylvia Plath*. National Portrait Gallery, Smithsonian Institution, Washington, DC, June 30, 2017–May 20, 2018.

Moulin, Joanny. "The Problem of Biography." Gifford, 2011, pp. 14–26.

Mulford, Wendy. *This Narrow Place: Sylvia Townsend Warner and Valentine Ackland: Life, Letters, and Politics, 1930–1951*. Pandora, 1988.

Muñoz, José Esteban. *Cruising Utopia: The Then and There of Queer Futurity*. New York UP, 2009.

Murphy, Margueritte. "'Familiar Strangers': The Household Words of Gertrude Stein's *Tender Buttons*." *Contemporary Literature*, vol. 32, no. 3, 1991, pp. 383–402.

Murray, Noel. "*Chris & Don: A Love Story*." *The A. V. Club*, June 19, 2008 (accessed August 30, 2018).

Nadel, Ira. *Biography: Fiction, Fact and Form*. Macmillan, 1984.

Newton, Adam Zachary. *Narrative Ethics*. Harvard UP, 1995.

Nicolson, Harold. *The Development of English Biography*. Hogarth Press, 1927. Internet Archieve (accessed August 4, 2019).

Nicolson, Nigel. *Portrait of a Marriage: Vita Sackville-West and Harold Nicolson*. U of Chicago P, 1973.

Nozick, Robert. *The Examined Life*. Simon & Schuster, 1990.

Nunez, Sigrid. *The Friend*. Riverhead Books, 2018.

Oates, Joyce Carol. *A Widow's Story*. Ecco, 2012.

O'Brien, Maeve. "Sylvia Plath's Youthful Letters Rescue Her from the Bell Jar." *The Irish Times*, October 21, 2017 (accessed August 30, 2018).

Osborne, John. *Look Back in Anger*. 1956. Penguin, 1982.

Oser, Lee. *The Ethics of Modernism*. New York: Cambridge UP, 2007.

Palmer, Alan. *Fictional Minds*. U of Nebraska P, 2004.

Palmer, Alan. *Social Minds in the Novel*. Ohio State UP, 2010.

Parker, Peter. *Isherwood: A Life Revealed*. Random House, 2004.

Parsons, Trekkie Ritchie. Introduction. In *Flush* by Virginia Woolf, Harcourt, 1983.

Pease, Allison. *Modernism, Mass Culture, and the Aesthetics of Obscenity*. Cambridge UP, 2000.

Perloff, Marjorie. "The Two *Ariels*: The (Re)Making of the Sylvia Plath Canon." In *Poems in Their Place: The Intertextuality and Order of Poetic Collections*, edited by Neil Fraistat, U of North Carolina P, 1986, pp. 308–33.

Perry, Ruth and Martine Brownley, editors. *Mothering the Mind: Twelve Studies of Writers and their Silent Partners*. Holmes and Meier, 1984.

Phelan, James. *Living to Tell About It: A Rhetoric and Ethics of Character Narration*. Cornell UP, 2005.

Plath, Sylvia. *The Unabridged Journals of Sylvia Plath*, edited by Karen V. Kukil, Anchor, 2000.

Rabinowitz, Peter J. "Toward a Narratology of Cognitive Flavor." In *The Oxford Handbook of Cognitive Literary Studies*, edited by Lisa Zunshine, Oxford UP, 2015, pp. 85–103.

Raitt, Suzanne. *Vita and Virginia: The Work and Friendship of V. Sackville-West and Virginia Woolf*. Clarendon Press, 1993.

"Rare BBC Interview with Sylvia Plath and Ted Hughes." *Brainpickings* (accessed August 28, 2018).

Regan, Tom. *Bloomsbury's Prophet: G. E. Moore and the Development of His Moral Philosophy*. Wipf and Stock, 2012.

Regis, Amber K. "Competing Life Narratives: Portraits of Vita Sackville-West." *Life Writing*, vol. 8, no. 3, 2011, pp. 287–300.

Reiman, Jeffrey. "Privacy, Intimacy, and Personhood." In *Philosophical Dimensions of Privacy*, edited by Ferdinand Schoeman, Cambridge UP, 1984, pp. 300–16.

Roiphe, Katie. *Uncommon Arrangements: Seven Portraits of Married Life in London Literary Circles, 1910–1939*. Dial Press, 2007.

Roof, Judith. *Come As You Are: Sexuality and Narrative*. Columbia UP, 1996.

Rose, Jacqueline. *The Haunting of Sylvia Plath*. Harvard UP, 1993.

Rose, Phyllis. *Parallel Lives: Five Victorian Marriages*. Vintage, 1983.

Rosenbaum, S. P. *The Bloomsbury Group Memoir Club*. Palgrave Macmillan, 2014.

Rosenfeld, Natania. *Outsiders Together: Virginia and Leonard Woolf*. Princeton UP, 2000.

Rowley, Hazel. *Tête à Tête: The Tumultuous Lives & Loves of Simone de Beauvoir & Jean-Paul Sartre*. HarperCollins, 2009.

Ryan, Derek. *Virginia Woolf and the Materiality of Theory*. Edinburgh UP, 2013.

Ryan, Marie-Laure. *Possible Worlds, Artificial Intelligence, and Narrative Theory*. Indiana UP, 1991.

Sackville-West, Vita. *Challenge*. 1924. Avon, 1974.

Sackville-West, Vita and Harold Nicolson. *Vita and Harold: The Letters of Vita Sackville-West and Harold Nicolson*, edited by Nigel Nicolson, G. P. Putnam's Sons, 1992.

Santi, Guido and Tina Mascara. "Labor of Love: Making *Chris & Don*." In Berg and Freeman, *American*, pp. 26–36.

Saunders, Max. *Self Impression: Life-Writing, Autobiografiction, and the Forms of Modern Literature*. Oxford UP, 2010.

Sedgwick, Eve Kosofsky. *Touching Feeling: Affect, Pedagogy, Performativity*. Duke UP, 2002.

Seigworth, Gregory J. and Melissa Gregg. "An Inventory of Shimmers." In *The Affect Theory Reader*, edited by Seigworth and Gregg, Duke UP, 2010, pp. 1–25.

Shelden, Ashley T. *Unmaking Love: The Contemporary Novel and the Impossibility of Union*. Columbia UP, 2017.

Shillinglaw, Susan. *Carol and John Steinbeck: Portrait of a Marriage*. U of Nevada P, 2013.

Smith, Sidonie. "Performativity, Autobiographical Practice, Resistance." *a/b: Autobiographical Studies*, vol. 10, no. 1, 1995, pp. 17–33.

Smith, Sidonie and Julia Watson. *Reading Autobiography: A Guide for Interpreting Life Narratives*, 2nd ed. U of Minnesota P, 2010.

Smith, Sidonie and Julia Watson. "The Trouble with Autobiography: Cautionary Notes for Narrative Theorists." In *A Companion to Narrative Theory*, edited by James Phelan and Peter Rabinowitz, Blackwell, 2005, pp. 356–71.

Snaith, Anna. "Of Fanciers, Footnotes, and Fascism: Virginia Woolf's *Flush*." *Modern Fiction Studies*, vol. 48, no. 3, 2002, pp. 614–36.

Snediker, Michael D. *Queer Optimism*. U of Minnesota P, 2009.

Solomon, Robert C. *About Love*. Madison Books, 2001.

Souhami, Diana. *Gertrude and Alice*. Pandora, 1991.

Spater, George and Ian Parsons. *A Marriage of True Minds: An Intimate Portrait of Leonard and Virginia Woolf*. Harcourt Brace Jovanovich, 1977.

Spolsky, Ellen. *Gaps in Nature: Literary Interpretation and the Modular Mind*. SUNY Press, 1993.

Spraggs, Gilliam. "Exiled to Home: The Poetry of Sylvia Townsend Warner and Valentine Ackland." In *Lesbian and Gay Writing*, edited by Mark Lilly, Temple UP, 1990, pp. 109–25.

Sproles, Karyn Z. *Desiring Women: The Partnership of Virginia Woolf and Vita Sackville-West*. U of Toronto P, 2006.

Stanley, Liz. *The Auto/Biographical I: The Theory and Practice of Feminist Auto/Biography*. Manchester UP, 1992.

Stein, Gertrude. "Ada." In *A Stein Reader*, edited by Ulla Dydo, Northwestern UP, 1993, pp. 100–103.

Stein, Gertrude. *The Autobiography of Alice B. Toklas*. 1933. Vintage, 1990.

Stein, Gertrude. *A Book Concluding With As a Wife Has a Cow: A Love Story*. 1926. Something Else Press, 1973.

Stein, Gertrude. *How to Write*. Dover, 1974.

Stein, Gertrude. *Lifting Belly*, edited by Rebecca Mark, Naiad Press, 1989.

Stein, Gertrude. *Tender Buttons*. 1914, edited by Seth Perlow, City Lights Books, 2014.

Stein, Gertrude and Alice B. Toklas. *Baby Precious Always Shines*, edited by Kay Turner, St. Martin's Press, 1999.

Stephen, Leslie. *Sir Leslie Stephen's Mausoleum Book*. Clarendon Press, 1977.

Stevenson, Anne. *Bitter Fame: A Life of Sylvia Plath*. Houghton Mifflin, 1989.

Stimpson, Catharine R. "Gertrice/Altrude: Stein, Toklas, and the Paradox of the Happy Marriage." Perry and Brownley, pp. 122–39.

Stimpson, Catharine R. "The Somagrams of Gertrude Stein." *Poetics Today*, vol. 6, no. 1/2, 1985, pp. 67–80.

Stone, Marjorie and Judith Thompson, editors. *Literary Couplings: Writing Couples, Collaborators, and the Construction of Authorship*. U of Wisconsin P, 2007.

Strachey, Lytton. *Elizabeth and Essex*. 1928. Harcourt Brace Jovanovich, 1956.

Sullivan, Hannah. "Autobiography and the Problem of Finish." *Biography*, vol. 34, no. 2, 2011, pp. 298–325.

Thiselton-Dyer, T. F. *The Loves and Marriages of Some Eminent Persons*. Ward and Downey, 1890. Hathi Trust (accessed August 4, 2019).

Thomas, David P. "'Goodbye to Berlin': Refocusing Isherwood's Camera." *Contemporary Literature*, vol. 13, no. 1, 1972, pp. 44–52.

Toklas, Alice B. *The Alice B. Toklas Cook Book*. 1954. Harper Perennial, 1984.

Toklas, Alice B. *Staying on Alone: Letters of Alice B. Toklas*, edited by Edward Burns, Vintage, 1975.

Tomalin, Claire. *The Invisible Woman: The Story of Nelly Ternan and Charles Dickens*. Penguin, 2012.

Torres, Alissa and Sungyoon Choi. *American Widow*. Villard, 2008.

Trilling, Diana. *The Beginning of the Journey: The Marriage of Diana and Lionel Trilling*. Harcourt Brace, 1993.

Turner, Kay. "This 'Very Beautiful Form of Literature.'" Introduction. In *Baby Precious Always Shines: Selected Love Notes Between Gertrude Stein and Alice B. Toklas* by Gertrude Stein and Alice B. Toklas, St. Martin's Press, 1999, pp. 1–44.

Uroff, Margaret. *Sylvia Plath and Ted Hughes*. U of Illinois P, 1986.

Utell, Janine. *Engagements with Narrative*. Routledge, 2015.

Utell, Janine. *James Joyce and the Revolt of Love: Marriage, Adultery, Desire*. Palgrave Macmillan, 2010.

Utell, Janine. "Narrative Ethics." In *Oxford Handbook of Virginia Woolf*, edited by Anne Fernald, Oxford UP, forthcoming.

Van Dyne, Susan. "The Problem of Biography." Gill, pp. 3–20.

Van Dyne, Susan. *Revising Life: Sylvia Plath's* Ariel *Poems*. U of North Carolina P, 1994.

Van Dyne, Susan. "'Your Story. My Story': Having the Last Word in Sylvia Plath and Ted Hughes." In *Last Letters*, edited by Sylvie Criquand, Cambridge Scholars Press, 2008, pp. 85–97.

Vanita, Ruth. "'Love Unspeakable': The Uses of Allusion in *Flush*." In *Virginia Woolf: Themes and Variations: Selected Papers from the Second Annual Conference on Virginia Woolf*, edited by Vara Neverow and Mark Hussey, Pace UP, 1993, pp. 248–57.

Wagner, Erica. *Ariel's Gift: Ted Hughes, Sylvia Plath, and the Story of Birthday Letters*. Norton, 2002.

Warhol, Robyn and Susan Lanser. Introduction. Warhol and Lanser, pp. 1–20.

Warhol, Robyn and Susan Lanser, editors. *Narrative Theory Unbound: Queer and Feminist Interventions*. Ohio State UP, 2015.

Warner, Sylvia Townsend. *The Diaries of Sylvia Townsend Warner*, edited by Claire Harman, Virago, 1995.

Warner, Sylvia Townsend. *Letters*, edited by William Maxwell, Viking, 1982.

Warner, Sylvia Townsend. *New Collected Poems*, edited by Claire Harman, Carcanet, 2008.

Warner, Sylvia Townsend and Valentine Ackland. *I'll Stand By You: Selected Letters of Sylvia Townsend Warner and Valentine Ackland: with Narrative by Sylvia Townsend Warner*, edited by Susanna Pinney, Pimlico, 1998.

Warner, Sylvia Townsend and David Garnett. *Sylvia and David: The Townsend Warner/Garnett Letters*, edited by Richard Garnett, Sinclair-Stevenson, 1994.

Warner, Sylvia Townsend and William Maxwell. *The Element of Lavishness: Letters of Sylvia Townsend Warner and William Maxwell, 1938–1978*, edited by Michael Steinman, Counterpoint, 2001.

Watson, Julia. "Is Relationality a Genre?" *European Journal of Life Writing*, vol. 5, 2016 (accessed August 30, 2018).

Whelan, Richard. "Don Bachardy: Getting a Likeness." *Christopher Street*, July 1979, pp. 12–15.

Wilson, Aimee Armande. *Conceived in Modernism: The Aesthetics and Politics of Birth Control*. Bloomsbury Academic, 2016.

Wolfe, Jesse. *Bloomsbury, Modernism, and the Reinvention of Intimacy*. Cambridge UP, 2011.

Woolf, Leonard. *The Autobiography of Leonard Woolf*. 5 vols. Harcourt, 1975.

Woolf, Leonard. *The Wise Virgins*. 1914. Yale UP, 2007.

Woolf, Virginia. "The Art of Biography" 1939. In *Selected Essays*, Oxford UP, pp. 95–100.

Woolf, Virginia. *Flush*, 1933. Harcourt, 1983.

Woolf, Virginia. *Moments of Being*. Mariner, 1985.

Woolf, Virginia. "The New Biography." 1927. In *Selected Essays*, Oxford UP, pp. 116–24.

Zwerdling, Alex. *The Rise of Memoir*. Oxford UP, 2017.

Index

www.ingramcontent.com/pod-product-compliance
Lightning Source LLC
Chambersburg PA
CBHW071356100726
47908CB00004B/1007

* 9 7 8 1 3 5 0 2 3 4 4 1 3 *